# SAC & FOX - SHAWNEE
# GUARDIANSHIPS, PART 3
### (UNDER SAC & FOX AGENCY, OKLAHOMA)
# 1906-1914
# VOLUME XIV

I0222744

TRANSCRIBED BY
# JEFF BOWEN

NATIVE STUDY
**Gallipolis, Ohio**
USA

Originally published:
Santa Maria, California
2019


Reprinted by:

Native Study LLC
Gallipolis, OH
*www.nativestudy.com*


Library of Congress Control Number: 2022900261

ISBN: 978-1-64968-143-0

*Made in the United States of America.*

# Other Books and Series by Jeff Bowen

*Compilation of History of the Cherokee Indians and Early History of the Cherokees by Emmet Starr with Combined Full Name Index*
(Hardbound & Softbound)

*1901-1907 Native American Census   Seneca, Eastern Shawnee, Miami, Modoc, Ottawa, Peoria, Quapaw, and Wyandotte Indians  (Under Seneca School, Indian Territory)*

*1932 Census of The Standing Rock Sioux Reservation with Births And Deaths 1924-1932*

*Census of The Blackfeet, Montana, 1897- 1901  Expanded Edition*

*Eastern Cherokee by Blood, 1906-1910, Volumes I thru XIII*

*Choctaw of Mississippi Indian Census 1929-1932 with Births and Deaths 1924-1931     Volume I*
*Choctaw of Mississippi Indian Census 1933, 1934 & 1937, Supplemental Rolls to 1934 & 1935 with Births and Deaths 1932-1938, and Marriages 1936-1938 Volume II*

*Eastern Cherokee Census Cherokee, North Carolina 1930-1939*
*Census 1930-1931 with Births And Deaths 1924-1931 Taken By Agent L. W. Page Volume I*
*Eastern Cherokee Census Cherokee, North Carolina 1930-1939*
*Census 1932-1933 with Births And Deaths 1930-1932 Taken By Agent R. L. Spalsbury    Volume II*
*Eastern Cherokee Census Cherokee, North Carolina 1930-1939*
*Census 1934-1937 with Births and Deaths 1925-1938 and Marriages 1936 & 1938 Taken by Agents R. L. Spalsbury And Harold W. Foght Volume III*

*Seminole of Florida Indian Census, 1930-1940 with Birth and Death Records, 1930-1938*

*Texas Cherokees 1820-1839  A Document For Litigation 1921*

*Starr Roll 1894   (Cherokee Payment Rolls) Districts: Canadian, Cooweescoowee, and Delaware Volume One*
*Starr Roll 1894 (Cherokee Payment Rolls) Districts: Flint, Going Snake, and Illinois   Volume Two*
*Starr Roll 1894 (Cherokee Payment Rolls) Districts: Saline, Sequoyah, and Tahlequah; Including Orphan Roll   Volume Three*

*Cherokee Intruder Cases  Dockets of Hearings 1901-1909  Volumes I & II*

*Indian Wills, 1911-1921  Records of the Bureau of Indian Affairs*
*Books One thru Seven*

# Other Books and Series by Jeff Bowen

*Native American Wills & Probate Records 1911-1921*

*Turtle Mountain Reservation Chippewa Indians 1932 Census with Births & Deaths, 1924-1932*

*Chickasaw By Blood Enrollment Cards 1898-1914 Volume I thru V*

*Cherokee Descendants East An Index to the Guion Miller Applications Volume I*
*Cherokee Descendants West An Index to the Guion Miller Applications Volume II (A-M)*
*Cherokee Descendants West An Index to the Guion Miller Applications Volume III (N-Z)*

*Applications for Enrollment of Seminole Newborn Freedmen, Act of 1905*

*Eastern Cherokee Census, Cherokee, North Carolina, 1915-1922, Taken by Agent James E. Henderson*    *Volume I (1915-1916)*
    *Volume II (1917-1918)*
    *Volume III (1919-1920)*
    *Volume IV (1921-1922)*

*Complete Delaware Roll of 1898*

*Eastern Cherokee Census, Cherokee, North Carolina, 1923-1929, Taken by Agent James E. Henderson*    *Volume I (1923-1924)*
    *Volume II (1925-1926)*
    *Volume III (1927-1929)*

*Applications for Enrollment of Seminole Newborn Act of 1905 Volumes I & II*

*North Carolina Eastern Cherokee Indian Census 1898-1899, 1904, 1906, 1909-1912, 1914 Revised and Expanded Edition*

*1932 Hopi and Navajo Native American Census with Birth & Death Rolls (1925-1931) Volume 1 - Hopi*
*1932 Hopi and Navajo Native American Census with Birth & Death Rolls (1930-1932) Volume 2 - Navajo*

*Western Navajo Reservation Navajo, Hopi and Paiute 1933 Census with Birth & Death Rolls 1925-1933*

*Cherokee Citizenship Commission Dockets 1880-1884 and 1887-1889 Volumes I thru V*

*Applications for Enrollment of Chickasaw Newborn Act of 1905 Volumes I thru VII*

# Other Books and Series by Jeff Bowen

*Cherokee Intermarried White 1906 Volume I thru X*

*Applications for Enrollment of Creek Newborn Act of 1905*
*Volumes I thru XIV*

*Applications for Enrollment of Choctaw Newborn Act of 1905 Volumes I thru XX*

*Choctaw By Blood Enrollment Cards 1898-1914 Volumes I thru XX*

*Oglala Sioux Indians Pine Ridge Reservation 1932 Census Book I*
*Oglala Sioux Indians Pine Ridge Reservation Birth and Death Rolls 1924-1932*
*Book II*

*Census of the Sioux and Cheyenne Indians of Pine Ridge Agency*
*1896 - 1897 Book I*
*Census of the Sioux and Cheyenne Indians of Pine Ridge Agency*
*1898 - 1899 Book II*

*Northern Cheyenne Tongue River, Montana 1904 - 1932 Census*
*1904-1916 Volume I*

*Northern Cheyenne Tongue River, Montana 1904 - 1932 Census*
*1917-1926 Volume II*

*Identified Mississippi Choctaw Enrollment Cards 1902-1909 Volumes I, II & III*

*Sac & Fox - Shawnee Estates 1885-1910 (Under Sac & Fox Agency)*
*Volumes I-VIII*
*Sac & Fox - Shawnee Estates 1920-1924 (Under The Sac & Fox Agency,*
*Oklahoma) & Wills 1889-1924 Volume IX*
*Sac & Fox - Shawnee Deaths, Cemetery, Births, & Marriage Cards (Under The Sac*
*& Fox Agency, Oklahoma) 1853-1933 Volume X*
*Sac & Fox - Shawnee Marriages, Divorces, Estates Log Books Volumes 1 & 2, Log*
*Book Births & Deaths (Under Sac & Fox Agency, Oklahoma)1846-1924 Volume XI*
*Sac & Fox - Shawnee Guardianships Part 1 (Under Sac & Fox Agency, Oklahoma)*
*1892-1909 Volume XII*
*Sac & Fox - Shawnee Guardianships, Part 2 (Under The Sac & Fox Agency,*
*Oklahoma) 1902-1910 Volume XIII*

Portrait of Tecumseh from Lossing's
*The Pictorial Field-Book of the War of 1812*
is a pencil sketch drawn by Pierre Le Dru,
a young French trader at Vincennes, circa 1808.

This series is dedicated to
Tanner Tackett
the Constant Gardner
and Friend
and
In memory of
Raina Mae Fulks.

# Ab·sen·tee

noun: **absentee**; plural noun: **absentees**

1. a person who is expected or required to be present at a place or event but is not.

(According to Webster)

# Shawnee

noun, plural Shaw-nees, (especially collectively) Shaw-nee.

1. a member of an Algonquian-speaking tribe formerly in the east-central U.S., now in Oklahoma.

(According to Dictionary.com)

## Shawnee Teaching

*"Tagi nsi walr mvci-lutvwi mr-pvyaci-grlahkv, xvga mytv inv gi mvci-lutvwv, gi mvci-ludr-geiv. Walv uwas-panvsi inv, wa-ciganv-hi gi gol-utvwv u kvgesakv-namv manwi-lanvwawewa yasi golutv-mvni geyrgi.*

*"Tagi bemi-lutvwi walr segalami mr-pvyaci-grlahkv, xvga mvtv inv gi bemi-lutvwv, gi bemi-ludr-geiv gelv. Wakv vhqalami inv, xvga nahfrpi Moneto ut vhqalamrli nili yasi vhqalamahgi gelv!"*

Translation:

"Do not kill or injure your neighbor, for it is not him that you injure, you injure yourself. But do good to him, therefore add to his days of happiness as you add to your own.

"Do not wrong or hate your neighbor, for it is not him that you wrong, you wrong yourself. But love him, for Moneto loves him also as He loves you!"

Thomas Wildcat Alford
*circa 1936*

## Special Note

You will notice throughout these volumes the author has attempted to duplicate from the original documents places on the page that were destroyed due to water damage. Whole sections of a page could be missing or torn into multiple pieces. In order to duplicate the damage you will find various shapes with a white format to try to represent the damage and the loss of the ability to completely transcribe many of the pages.

# TABLE OF CONTENTS

# INTRODUCTION

The history of the Shawnee is fascinating. Naturally the most famous Shawnee known would be Tecumseh, born circa. 1768, after four other siblings before him. His father was Puckeshinwa, a Shawnee war chief from Ohio. Puckeshinwa crossed the Ohio close to what is now Gallipolis with his fourteen year son Chiksika by his side. As they followed the lead of Chief Cornstalk during the fall of 1774. Tecumseh's famous father was mortally wounded during the fight they would soon encounter. The Shawnees were unexpectedly discovered by a couple of early morning turkey hunters from the settlement called Point Pleasant. These hunters ran as fast as possible back to where the Ohio and Kanawha Rivers meet and sounded the alarm that the Shawnees were coming, the fight lasted most of the day but not without loss to both sides. The Shawnees were badly outnumbered. Pucheshinwa was carried back across the Ohio or as the Shawnees called it the *Spaylaywitheepi*, with the intention to take him back to his village. He must have known his time was short as he laid there telling Chiksika to make sure he devoted his time not only to Tecumseh's but also his younger brothers training in becoming warriors. Pucheshinwa succumbed to his wounds shortly after that request and was secretly buried deep in the forest that day. Chiksika saw his father mortally wounded while defending their home. He had a reverence for his father as a great warrior. He wanted to follow his father's path and not die an average death. In his heart, it had to be on the battlefield as a warrior. Tecumseh followed his brother's every step and planned to die defending his land as his father and brother had. There was no surrendering or giving in to the Americans.

There are several descriptions out there of Tecumseh from his contemporaries, but David Edmunds found one during his research that seems to be the most commanding of any found. "Captain John B. Glegg, Brock's aide-de-camp, who was present at the meetings between Brock and Tecumseh, recorded one of the most vivid descriptions of the Shawnee. According to Glegg, in August 1812 Tecumseh still was in the prime of his life, giving the impression of a man ten years younger. Tecumseh's appearance was very prepossessing; his figure light and finely proportioned; his age I imagined to be about five and thirty [he actually was forty four]; in height, five feet nine or ten inches; his complexion, light copper; countenance, oval, with bright hazle eyes, beaming cheerfulness, energy, and decision. Three small silver crowns, or coronets were suspended from the lower cartilage of his aquiline nose; and a large silver medallion of George the Third, which I believe his ancestor had received from Lord Dorchester, when governor-general of Canada, was attached to a mixed coloured wampum string, and hung around his neck. His dress consisted of a plain, neat uniform, tanned deer-skin jacket, with long trousers of the same material, the seams of both being covered with neatly cut fringe; and he had on his feet leather moccasins, much ornamented with work made from the dyed quills of the porcupine."[1]

There were approximately 39 years that passed between Tecumseh's and his father's deaths.

It is hard to believe that the Shawnee's history being as extensive as it was during the early stages of the United States that their descendants' records were so closely guarded under the care of a vegetable bind in an leaky attic. Not only the Shawnee's but also the Sac & Fox, the Pottawatomie and the Kickapoo. There are also many other tribal affiliates to be found in this series, not to mention someone like Jim Thorpe and his family members of the Sac and Fox tribe. Not only was he a gold metal Olympian and multiple sport competitor, but at the time one of America's favorite sons. Thank goodness someone was finally conscious of the situation. The description in the next paragraph explains the neglect of these important documents as given by the Oklahoma Historical Societies Microfilm Catalog.

"In 1933 a survey of Indian tribal records in Oklahoma revealed that the files of the Shawnee and the old Sac and Fox agencies had been sadly neglected, and the lack of space for storing them properly had resulted in much loss. Charles Eggers, Superintendent of the Shawnee Agency, reported that most of the non-current records of his agency were boxed in a storehouse. The papers of the old Sac and Fox Agency were in the loft of a warehouse which was also used for storing vegetables. The roof of the building leaked and the papers were in danger of destruction from moisture. Following the passage of the Congressional Act of March 27, 1934 (H.R. 5631 Public No. 133) which placed the tribal records in the custody of the Oklahoma Historical Society."

As described above the history of the Shawnee people isn't an ordinary history but an extraordinary time in all of our ancestors' lives. Reading Allen W. Eckert's extensive studies taken from what is known as the Draper Papers, a historical record meticulously documented beginning circa 1830. Though Draper covered an approximate time between the 1740's to the 1810's, his collection covered documents and transcriptions concerning Boone, Kenton, Rogers Clark and Joseph Brant, not to mention a considerable amount of Shawnee history from the entirety of the Ohio and Mississippi Valley's. Other authors such as Colin G. Calloway and R. David Edmunds provide an in depth study of the Shawnee people as well as Tecumseh and his life leaving no rock unturned in their research.

As you read different references you find diverse opinions on Tecumseh's mother as to what tribe she came from. Eckert through Draper's work says, "This was

---

[1] Tecumseh, R. David Edmunds Pg. 162-163, Para. 3-4

when Pucksinwah, then twenty-six, led the war party against the Cherokees that had resulted in the capture of Methotasa."[2] Indicating Tecumseh's mother might have been Cherokee. Yet, R. David Edmunds writes, "In 1768, while the Iroquois were selling Shawnee lands at the Treaty of Fort Stanwix, a Creek woman married to a Shawnee man gave birth to a son at Old Piqua, a Shawnee village on the Mad River in Western Ohio. The woman had a difficult labor before giving birth in the small lodge especially constructed for that purpose, some distance from the family's wigwam. The mother, Methoataske (Turtle Laying Its Eggs), had grown up among the Creek villages in Alabama and had met her husband when some of the Shawnee sought refuge among the Creeks during the 1750s. The father Puckeshinwa, remained with his wife's people until about 1760, when the family left Alabama and migrated to Ohio."[3]

You also will find different opinions on how they dressed back then or wore their hair. In Edmunds' book *Tecumseh*, his brother the Prophet Tenskwatawa states, "Warriors should again shave their heads and wear the scalp locks worn by their ancestors." And yet in Thomas Wildcat Alford's *Civilization,* he says, "We boys wore our hair short, very much as the girls of today wear their hair bobbed. This is the way Shawnee men always have worn their hair. Never did they braid it, as some other tribes do."

Alford's book *Civilization* out of the many resources read was likely one of the most informative and enjoyable references in the study. Thomas Wildcat Alford was born in 1860 and belonged to the Absentee Shawnee tribe. He states that he was a descendant of Tecumseh. He spoke about when his family slept under the stars each night and that he never had an English name until his father had him go to school at a Quaker mission. Mr. Alford also talks about two things with real clarity. Alford educates us about clans in the sixth chapter, expounding upon the active history of the Shawnees and the different responsibilities of each as well as divisions among the clans that created tribal changes. These dissensions were nothing new. Anyone that has read extensively about the Shawnee will realize that Alford understood his people and their history. When he wrote about tribal clashes or divisions during the early days, he managed to translate on paper their strength and character. He showed for generations they literally believed they were given an ability to make themselves self-reliant when it came to survival. They traveled far and wide following their own path while installing their own way of life that made them powerful adversaries whether it be against the British, the French or the Americans moving west. Other tribes found them to be awful enemies or potent allies. Then he compares their tribal government

---

[2]  A Sorrow in Our Heart, Allen W. Eckert Pg. 22, Para. 3

[3]  Tecumseh, R. David Edmunds, Pg. 17 Para. 1

and the clan leaders to being quite similar to the U.S. Presidency and the different government entities. Alford also brings up business committees for the tribe.

He starts with a concise description of the clans, "Originally there were five clans composing the Shawnee tribe, including the two principle clans, Tha-we-gi-la and Cha-lah-kaw-tha, from one of which came the national or principal chief. The remaining three, the Pec-ku-we, the Kis-pu-go, and the May-ku-jay, each had its own chief who was subordinate to the principal chief in national matters, but independent in matters pertaining to the duties of his clan. Each clan had a certain duty to perform for the whole tribe. For instance the Pec-ku-we clan, or its chief, had charge of the maintenance of order and looked after the celebration of things pertaining to religion or faith; the Kis-pu-go clan had charge of matters pertaining to war and the preparation and training of warriors; the May-ku-jay clan had charge of things relating to health and medicine and food for the whole tribe. But the two powerful clans, the Tha-we-gi-la and the Cha-lah-kaw-tha, had charge of political affairs and all matters that affected the tribe as a whole. Indeed, the tribal government may be likened to the government of the United States, in which each state (clan), with it governor (chief), is sovereign in local matters, but subordinate to the president of the United States (principal chief) in national matters. The difference is that the president of the United States must be elected, and may be changed with each election, while the principal chief came to his office by heritage and held it for life, or during good behavior.

At the time of which I write the Shawnee tribe had been divided for many years, and only the Tha-we-gi-la, the Pec-ku-we, and the Kis-pu-go clans were represented in the Absentee Shawnee band. These three clans always had been closely related, while the Cha-lah-kaw-tha and the May-ku-jay had always stood together, and were represented in the group that I have mentioned as living in Kansas at the time of the Civil War."[4]

As referenced earlier Thomas Wildcat Alford brought up their present Indian agent, Thomas, on September 13, 1893, wanting him to present a list of prominent men in their tribe to hold positions on a business committee. This presented a whole new world for the tribe with new pressures through white change so to speak. The government was instilling in their world the destruction of their heritage in tribal customs and culture all to control Indian land through allotment. When he was being told to help form this committee, he was actually being told, what we are doing is we are wiping out your way of life forever. The Congress of the United States was presenting the abolition of all tribal governments so the land could be manipulated through the Curtis Act of 1898. They said, we are splitting the land up. They were allotting so many acres to each tribal member. How much they got depended on

---

[4] Civilization, Alford; Pg. 44, Para. 1-2

whether they planned to farm or raise cattle. If they were building herds they were given double the land for grazing. Alford said, "It was on the thirteenth day of September, 1893 that Agent Thomas informed the Shawnees that he had been directed by the Commissioner of Indian Affairs to submit for approval the names of seven of the most prominent men of the tribe who would constitute a Business Committee to supersede the chiefs and councilors of the old tribal government. The Business Committee was to represent the Absentee Shawnees as a tribe in all dealings with the United States and to act in an advisory capacity to the individual members of the tribe. They were to certify to the identity of grantors of sales of land and to act for the tribe in other matters.[5]

During the study it was noticed that the Curtis Act being enacted on June 28, 1898 and Alford's mentioning its initiation during 1893 became a point of interest or at least premature. It was found that Congress had actually started working in this area of seizure approximately five years prior to the agent's notification, "In 1893 Congress began a special allotment process for the Five Tribes, enacting a number of laws that affect the governmental powers of the tribes. Some of these laws, like the 1889 and 1890 Acts, extended certain Arkansas laws over Indian Territory and expanded federal court jurisdiction; they are relevant today only insofar as they may indirectly affect tribal judicial powers."[6]

Their mention of these laws only being relevant today, though actually not spoken, plead plausible deniability while coinciding with the Indian Reorganization Act of 1934. The government was on a mission. Land and control. The allotment had to take place. They were wanting statehood. They were wanting the Native people to be under one umbrella with everyone else. Tribes were nations. Just like a foreign nation, they were their own government. Originally our constitution was modeled after the Iroquois model, had to start somewhere? So what we did was split up the land among the people that already owned it. Then we took what was left, approximately 90 million acres and sold it at a profit. Who got the money? Only the politicians at the time know? But years after taking the chiefs and councils away there was likely mass chaos like a town hall today. So the government likely was wanting out of the tribal control business. At least enough that they could just control it without being in the bullseye so to speak. Congress and the state had already achieved its goals. So this act was written with the statement that it was a model to make all think we do this for you. "The IRA was intended to provide a mechanism for the tribe as a governmental unit to interact with and adapt to a modern society, rather than to force the assimilation of individual Indians.

---

[5] Civilization, Alford; Pg. 161, Para. 2

[6] Federal Indian Law, Cohen; Pg. 781, Para. 3

The IRA was also an attempt to improve the economic situation of Indians. The Act was intended to stop the alienation of tribal land needed to support Indians, and to provide for acquisition of additional acreage for tribes. Tribes were encouraged to organize along the lines of modern business corporations; a system of financial credit was included to reach this economic objective."[7] Interestingly enough Cohen and Alford both mention this same organizational technique, only one as law and another as a tribal member.

It is disconcerting just in reading a reference from Senator Charles Curtis as he mentioned in his biography that by the time Congress finished rewriting the bill he had submitted he hardly recognized it. "Officially titled the "Act for the Protection of the People of Indian Territory", the Act is named for Charles Curtis, congressman from Kansas and its author. He was of mixed Native American and European descent: on his mother's side -Kansa, Osage, Potawatomi, and French; and on his father's - three ethnic lines of British Isles ancestry. Curtis was raised in part on the Kaw Reservation of his maternal grandparents, but also lived with his paternal grandparents and attended Topeka High School. He read law, became an attorney, and later was elected to the United States House of Representatives and Senate. He served as Vice-President under Herbert Hoover. In the usual fashion, by the time the bill HR 8581 had gone through five revisions in committees in both the House of Representatives and the Senate, there was little left of Curtis' original draft. In his hand-written autobiography, Curtis noted having been unhappy with the final version of the Curtis Act. He believed that the Five Civilized Tribes needed to make changes. He thought that the way ahead for Native Americans was through education and use of both their and the majority cultures, but he also had hoped to give more support to Native American transitions."[8]

The records within this series concern The Absentee Shawnee as well as many other people with different tribal affiliations. Also within these pages are closely related tribes that were under the same agency (The Sac & Fox Agency, Oklahoma) for many years like the Sac & Fox, the Pottawatomie and the Kickapoo. There are likely state recognized Shawnee tribes in the United States, but, "The Absentee Shawnee Tribe of Indians of Oklahoma (or Absentee Shawnee) is one of three federally recognized tribes of Shawnee people. Historically residing in the Eastern United States, the original Shawnee lived in the areas that are now Ohio, Indiana, Illinois, Kentucky, Tennessee, Pennsylvania, and other neighboring states. It is documented that they occupied and traveled through lands from Canada to Florida, from the Mississippi River to the eastern continental coast. In contemporary times, the Absentee Shawnee Tribe headquarters in Shawnee, Oklahoma; its tribal jurisdiction

---

[7] Federal Indian Law, Cohen; Pg. 147 Para. 1-2

[8] Curtis Act of 1898, Wikipedia

area includes land properties in Oklahoma in both Cleveland County and Pottawatomie County." [Today] "There are approximately 3,050 enrolled Absentee Shawnee tribal members, 2,315 of whom live in Oklahoma. Tribal membership follows blood quantum criteria, with applicants requiring a minimum of one eighth (1/8) documented Absentee-Shawnee blood to be placed on its membership rolls, as set forth by the tribal constitution. Though it is not a formal division, there is a social separation within its current tribal membership between the traditionalist Big Jim Band, which kept cultural traditions and ceremonies and has its primary populace in the Little Axe, Norman area, and the assimilationist White Turkey Band, which adopted European ways of the European majority, with many families based in the Shawnee area. Regardless of historical viewpoints, the bands cooperate for the future of the tribe."[9]

When this study was first pursued an old Xerox copy of a catalog that sat on the shelf for twenty five years was the first place searched for a viable source. It was titled, "Catalog of Microfilm Holdings in the Archives & Manuscripts Div. Oklahoma Historical Society 1976-1989". As mentioned in the description from this catalog's Introduction for the Sac and Fox Indian Agencies, it states, "In 1901 the Sac and Fox Agency was divided. The Sac and Fox Agency itself remained at the old site near Stroud with jurisdiction over the Sac and Fox and the Iowa. The Shawnee, Potawatomi and Kickapoo Agency (sometimes simply called the Shawnee Agency) was established about two miles south of Shawnee, Oklahoma. The agencies continued their separate existence until 1919 when they were merged becoming the Shawnee Agency.

Of course today in 2018, everything is digital and on the computer. You have to be thankful for having an old catalog and books on a shelf. There is nothing like the feel of holding a book in your hand. You can pick it up when you want and let your eyes travel to anywhere or any time in history. It has solid print that nobody can manipulate or change. It's just yours to wrap yourself up in without any glowing distractions as Native Americans call them, "Talking Leaves".

Jeff Bowen
Gallipolis, Ohio
*NativeStudy.com*

---

[9] Absentee-Shawnee Tribe of Indians Wikipedia

*Guthrie, Okla.,* _____ 11/26 _____ *190* 9

*M.* ___ Frank A. Thackery ___

IN ACCOUNT WITH
## J. B. BEADLES & SON.
BONDS, WARRANTS,
AND INVESTMENTS.

Mark Charlie
Little Charlie

Pd 9-23/10   534⁰⁰

JBBeadles & Son
LNB
By F.A. Thackery

$350

---

DEPARTMENT OF THE INTERIOR   **RECEIVED**

UNITED STATES INDIAN SERVICE        NOV 27 1909

SAC & FOX AGENCY,
311-12 Scott Thompson Bldg. OKLAHOMA.

Oklahoma City Okla. Nov. 26th.09.

W. C. Kohlenberg, Supt.

Sac and Fox Agency Okla.

Dear Sir:

Is it possible to get from your office a record of the Guardians and Administrators now acting for Sac and Fox and Iowa Indians? I presume you have a record of all cases in which you are acting; Have you a record of cases in which others are serving? If you can furnish me with any of this information advise me and I will send you a memoranda of what I want.

Very respectfully,

A W Dannagan
District Agent.

Ex-Judge Fifth Judicial District of Nebraska

TELEPHONE { OFFICE, No. 112 / RESIDENCE, No. 113

**ROBERT WHEELER,**
ATTORNEY AND COUNSELOR
TECUMSEH, OKLA.

Nov. 29/09.

Hon. Frank A. Thackery,

Shawnee, Okla.   **1465**

Dear Sir:-

In the matter of the guardianship of Mark Charley I am enclosing report of sale, which please execute and return to me. The appraisement and sale bond in this case have not been returned to me, and unless they have been maile[sic] direct from your office to judge[sic] Sharp, and the sale bond approved, it will be necessary for you to change the date of sale in the blank I am enclosing, as the sale cannot be made at a date prior to the date of the approval of the bond.

Yours very truly,
Robert Wheeler

---

No. _____

## DEPARTMENT OF THE INTERIOR

UNITED STATES INDIAN SERVICE.

Shawnee, Oklahoma

December 3rd, 1909.

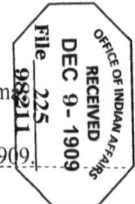

[stamp: File 98211 / DEC 9-1909 / RECEIVED / OFFICE OF INDIAN AFFAIRS / 225]

Commissioner of Indian Affairs,
Washington, D. C.

Sir:

I have the honor to recommend that I be authorized to approve the checks of _____ Minnie Foreman, _____

whose balance in bank is $ 178/93 _____, in the amounts and for the purposes specified below:

| | AMOUNT | EXPENDITURES. |
|---|---|---|

| | OF AUTHORITY. | DATE. | AMOUNT. |
|---|---|---|---|
| Court and guardianship expenses due former guardian - | 38|00 | | |

Frank A. Thackery
*Agent or Superintendent.*

Approved: ___ RG Valentine ___

*Commissioner.*

Date, _____ APR -9 1910

---

EX-JUDGE FIFTH JUDICIAL DISTRICT OF NEBRASKA

**ROBERT WHEELER,**
ATTORNEY AND COUNSELOR
TECUMSEH, OKLA.

TELEPHONE { OFFICE, No. 112
RESIDENCE, No. 113

Dec. 4/09.

Hon. Frank A. Thackery,

Shawnee, Okla.   **1468**

Dear Sir:-

In the matter of the guardianship of Pa-mi-kim-se, et als, I am enclosing report of sale, which please sign and have verified and returned to me.

You can also sign and return to report of sale in the Mark Charley matter, as the sale bonds have been approved in both of these cases.

Yours very truly,
Robert Wheeler

LULA M REGNIER, COURT STENOGRAPHER              P. D. MITCHELL, JUDGE              BERT CAULEY, CLERK

## County Court

Payne County

STILLWATER, OKLA.

RECEIVED
DEC 9 1909
SAC & FOX AGENCY,
OKLAHOMA.

December 7, 1909.

Hon. W. C. Kohlenberg,

Sac & Fox Agency, Oklahoma.

Dear Friend:-

I received your guardians[sic] report of Harrison Hunter, Gertrude Hunter, David Harris, Laura Ellis, and Esther Bigwalker, and filed them under date of the sixth. In examining the records I find them all of age.

There has been no costs paid in your guardianship and I find that there is due or will be when the discharges are issued, amounts as follows:

Harrison Hunter . . . . . . . . . . . . . . . . . .$6.35;

Gertrude Hunter . . . . . . . . . . . . . . . . . . 6.35;

David Harris . . . . . . . . . . . . . . . . . . . . 16.70:

Laura Ellis . . . . . . . . . . . . . . . . . . . . . 11.95;

Esther Bigwalker . . . . . . . . . . . . . . . . 18.45.

If you find it inconvenient to come up, you may send these amounts of costs and receipts from wards from their balance, where there is a balance and I will close the cases up and enter your discharge. If, however, you can get away, please write me and let me know about when you can be here and I will try to be in the office. If notice of final settlement is posted, the costs will be about $1.75 more in each estate. We seldom ever give any notice at all.

Very truly,

PDM-HFP                                   __P. D. Mitchell__

Sam Hooker, Judge
C. P. Offutt, Clerk
F. G. Offutt, Deputy
Inez Minshall, Reporter

M. C. Binion, Sheriff
G. D. Lockhart, Bailiff

# County Court

## OKLAHOMA COUNTY, OKLAHOMA

REGULAR TERMS BEGIN ON THE FIRST MONDAY
IN JANUARY, APRIL, JULY AND OCTOBER

OKLAHOMA CITY,

December 28, 1909

Frank Thackery,

Shawnee, Oklahoma.

Dear Sir.-    I write in regard to cases 687 and 688, Estates of Ah-che-ko
and Way-hah-bona-se and Tah-nah-ke and I-nesh-kin
<small>Way lah com se</small>

I would like to have a report from you as their guardian and would
like to know whether there has ever been any rent reported from these
allotments.

Yours truly,

Sam Hooker
Judge

---

Sam Hooker, Judge
E. M. Hurry, Clerk
Inez Minshall, Reporter

G. W. Garrison, Sheriff
C. P. Offutt, Bailiff

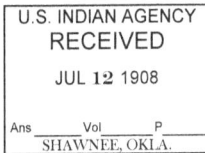

# County Court

## OKLAHOMA COUNTY, OKLAHOMA

OKLAHOMA CITY,

July 10, 1908

Frank A. Thackery,

Shawnee, Oklahoma.

Dear Sir.-    On January 30th, 1907, you qualified as the guardian of
two Mexican Kickapoo Indians, whose narmes[sic] are Pe-ah-che-that
and Ma-she-ka-pat.

I would like to have a report from you

Yours truly,

*Sam Hooker*

SAM HOOKER, JUDGE
C. P. OFFUTT, CLERK
F. G. OFFUTT, DEPUTY
INEZ MINSHALL, REPORTER

M. C. BINION, SHERIFF
G. D. LOCKHART, BAILIFF

# County Court

## OKLAHOMA COUNTY, OKLAHOMA

REGULAR TERMS BEGIN ON THE FIRST MONDAY
IN JANUARY, APRIL, JULY AND OCTOBER

OKLAHOMA CITY,

December 24, 1909

Frank Thackery,

Shawnee, Oklahoma.

Dear Sir.- Case #218 in re. Guardianship of Pe-ah-che-that and Nah-the-hah-pot. Would like to have a report from you in this case by January 3rd, 1910 or else I will deem it my duty to remove you for failing to make reports as the law requires.

Yours truly,

Sam Hooker.

---

REFER IN REPLY TO THE FOLLOWING:

ADDRESS ONLY THE
COMMISSIONER OF INDIAN AFFAIRS

Land-
Sales **DEPARTMENT OF THE INTERIOR,**
98210-11-1909
E K W        OFFICE OF INDIAN AFFAIRS,

WASHINGTON.

DEC 30 1909

Check approval,
Minnie and Thomas
Freeman.

F. A. Thackery, Esq.,

Superintendent Shawnee Indian School,

Shawnee, Oklahoma.

Sir:

The Office is in receipt of your requests of December 3, for authority to approve checks of Minnie and Thomas Freeman, for court and guardianship expenses due former guardian.

The information given in this case is too meagre to afford a basis for intelligent action by this Office. It should be shown clearly and definitely in what connection the guardianship proceedings were instituted in the first place; whether or not the court has accepted the resignation of the former guardian and whether or not the superintendent has been appointed in his place. An itemized bill and affidavit should be submitted by the former guardian setting forth the necessity for the guardianship proceedings, referring to the sale in which these proceedings played a part, stating definitely whether or not any amount had been paid to the attorney, and showing cash costs.

It is not understood from the itemized bill given in your letter why the "Deposit in County Court for costs $15.00" did not include "Court expenses, $8.00". Neither is it understood why Minnie Freeman's share of the guardianship expenses is represented as $38.00, while Thomas Freeman's is shown as $10.00, they being brother and sister and both minors.

In submitting requests for guardianship and probate expenses, greater care should be exercised to give all the data necessary to enable the Office to take intelligent action.

Very respectfully,

JMA-24
6814

John Francis, Jr
Acting Chief Land Division.

---

EX-JUDGE FIFTH JUDICIAL DISTRICT OF NEBRASKA

TELEPHONE { OFFICE, No. 112
RESIDENCE, No. 113

**ROBERT WHEELER,**
ATTORNEY AND COUNSELOR
TECUMSEH, OKLA.

Jan. 14/10.

Hon. Frank A. Thackery,

Shawnee, Okla.

Dear Sir:-

In the matter of the guardianship of Mark Charley, enclosed find Certified copy of order confirming sale, guardian's deed, and bill of costs from the county court.

The total costs in this care are as follows:

| | |
|---|---|
| Court costs, | $14.10. |
| Advertising, | 3.75. |
| Posting notices, | .50. |

| Recording order, | 1.25. |
| My fee, | 35.00 |
| Total, | $54.60. |

Of this sum Claud F. Banning advanced $45. to be repaid him out of the purchase mone[sic] whan[sic] the same is approved. After applying this there is still due my on my fees $5. and due the county court on costs $4.60.

Yours very truly,
Robert Wheeler

---

Ex-Judge Fifth Judicial District of Nebraska

**ROBERT WHEELER,**
ATTORNEY AND COUNSELOR
TECUMSEH, OKLA.

TELEPHONE { OFFICE, No. 112
RESIDENCE, No. 113

Jan. 14/10.

Hon. Frank A. Thackery,

Shawnee, Okla.

Dear Sir:-

In the matter of the guardianship of Pa-mi-kim-se, et als. I am enclosing certified copy of order confirming sale, guardian's deed, and bill of costs from the county court.

The costs in this case are as follows:

| Court costs, | $12.00. |
| Advertising, | 3.75. |
| Posting notices, | .75. |
| Recording order, | 1.25. |
| My fee, | 35.00. |
| Total, | $52.75. |

Of this sum, the purchaser[sic], W. R. McFerron, advanced $50. for costs, to be repaid to him when the sale is approved. After applying this there is still due the county court $2.75 in costs.

Yours very truly,
Robert Wheeler

[The letter below typed as given]

**ROSCOE C. ARRINGTON**
ATTORNEY AT LAW
ROOM 4, RAINS BUILDING.

TECUMSEH, OKLA.   Jan., 18th., 1910.

Hon. Frank A. Thackery,

Shawnee,

Okla.

Dear sir: In going over my records I find that I was appointed administrator of the estate of Mah-mah-to-meah in 1905.I also find that you are guardian of Peah-ah-puck-o-ke, a minor, and that I am your attorney in that matter.I find that I represent Mr. Ratzlaff in the administration of Tah-ah-kah-me.I do not want to be officious but I also want to keep from neglecting any of these matters if they need attention.I do nog know what policy you want persued in these matters.If there is any thing that I can do I will gladly do it.If it is your desire to not take any action at this time I will let the matter rest.  I thought that perhaps you might desire to dispose of the property or to partition or to have a decree of distribution or some other action.I thought best to call your attention to them.I had overlooked these matters for months and have done nothing with them and in fact did not know what was desired,if any thing.

Yours very truly,
Roscoe C. Arrington

---

## NOTICE TO ATTORNEYS.

No  575

In re Guardianship
Plaintiff

VS.

of Ethel Shawnee  a minor
Defendant

To ___ Frank A. Thackery ___ Attorney for ___ Guardian ___

___ Shawnee ___, Oklahoma.

You are hereby notified that the above entitled case has been set for ___ Hearing on ___

[illegible] Proceeding ___ on the __24__ day of __ January ___ 19 10

___ R. C. Green ___

Clerk Co. Court

By ___ Deputy.

Please Notify your attys.

No. ___

## DEPARTMENT OF THE INTERIOR

### UNITED STATES INDIAN SERVICE.

Shawnee Indian Agency,
Shawnee, Oklahoma, Feb. 3, 1910.

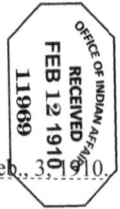

Commissioner of Indian Affairs,
Washington, D. C.

Sir:

I have the honor to recommend that I be authorized to approve the checks

of ___ OLIVER HUMBARGAR, Legal Guardian of May-thah-nah-kea, a minor

whose balance in bank is $ 238.28 ___, in the amounts and for the purposes

specified below:

| | AMOUNT OF AUTHORITY. | EXPENDITURES. | |
| --- | --- | --- | --- |
| | | DATE. | AMOUNT. |
| To pay to Stella Blanchard, mother of said minor, for his support, per month, ......... | 5\|00 | | |
| (The minor in this case is 5 years of age, and the mother needs the above amount to assist her in the proper support of her child.) | | | |

CTP

Frank A. Thackery
*Agent or Superintendent.*

Approved: _____FH Abbott_____

Assistant *Commissioner.*

Date. _____

FEB 16 1910

---

No. _____

## DEPARTMENT OF THE INTERIOR

### UNITED STATES INDIAN SERVICE.

OFFICE OF INDIAN AFFAIRS
FEB 12 1910
RECEIVED
11970

Shawnee Indian Agency,
Shawnee, Oklahoma, Feb., 3, 1910.

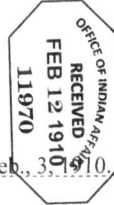

Commissioner of Indian Affairs,
Washington, D. C.

Sir:

I have the honor to recommend that I be authorized to approve the checks

of ___OLIVER HUMBARGAR, L. GUARDIAN of Hol-o-wahpea-se-ka_____

whose balance in bank is  $ 222.29_____, in the amounts and for the purposes
a minor.

specified below:

| | AMOUNT OF AUTHORITY. | EXPENDITURES. | |
| --- | --- | --- | --- |
| | | DATE. | AMOUNT. |
| To pay to Stella Blanchard, mother of said minor, for his support, per month, ......... | 5 | | |
| (The minor, in this case is six years of age, and the mother needs the above amount each month to assist her in the proper support of her child.) | | | |

CTP

11

Frank A. Thackery
*Agent or Superintendent.*

Approved:_____FH Abbott_____

Assistant *Commissioner.*

Date,_____FEB 16 1910_____

# DEPARTMENT OF THE INTERIOR

### UNITED STATES INDIAN SERVICE

SAc[sic] and Fox Agency, Okla.,

Feb. 4, 1910.

Mr. Hiram Holt,

Indiahoma, Okla.

Dear sir:

I write you asking you to file your resignation as the guardian of the Thorp heirs. You will remember that Mary and Jim are of age while Adaline and Edward are still minors. It is necessary to have a guardian in this case who will look after some court matters and as soon as you resign I will file my request for appointment. Whatever costs you have can be allowed to go over and I will arrange to pay them. The Department will not permit the advance of any funds to the guardians any more. Please attend to this at once. Send your resignation to the court so that they can take some action at once.

We dont[sic] want to take action to have you dismissed outright for this would not look good on your part.

Very respectfully,

W.C. Kohlenberg

WCK

Supt. & Spl. Disb. Agent.

Department of Justice.

———

Office of the United States Attorney.
District of Oklahoma.
Guthrie.

May 6th, 1910.

W. C. Kohlenberg,

Supt. & Spl. Disb. Agent,

Sac and Fox Agency, Oklahoma.

Dear Sir:

You will remember that when we were at Shawnee some applications were filed in the guardianships of some of your Indians asking that the guardians be required to file report. I will rely upon you to keep me advised as to when any of those reports are filed and set down for action by the court. It will be well for you to look up the matter occasionally when you are down at Shawnee and if the court has not cited the guardians to report he should be urged to issue such directions to them.

Very respectfully,

Isaac D. Taylor
Asst. U.S. Attorney.

Department of Justice.

———

Office of the United States Attorney.
District of Oklahoma.
Guthrie.

Feby. 11, 1910.

Frank A. Thackery,
Supt. & Spcl. Disb. Agent,
Shawnee, Okla.

Dear Sir:

I 'phoned to Judge Baker, at Wewoka, yesterday and he desires to take up the Ethel Shawnee guardianship case on Monday, February 14th, on which date it is set for hearing.

I will go over to Tecumseh as quickly as I can after the arrival of the M.K.&T. train from Oklahoma City Monday morning, and will desire that you be there, and if there are any witnesses in the case you should have them there, although I presume that our case is largely a matter of record and questions of law.

Very respectfully,

Isaac D. Taylor
Assistant U.S. Attorney.

---

*Law Offices Of*

## Burdick & Grubbs

Stillwater, Okla.

C. L. Burdick
J. M. Grubbs

May-17th-10.

Hon. W. C. Kohlenberg,

Sac & Fox Agency,

Oklahoma.

Dear sir and friend:-      As it has been some time since we had any correspondence, I thought I would ask you about an entirely new matter and see if you coulf[sic] not dig up for me my attorney fees in those guardianship matters. I under stand the costs have been paid and thought you had forgotten me. Wishing you well, I am,

Yours very truly,

C. L. Burdick

---

R. C. GREEN, CLERK                                          CALLIE E PENNEY, STENOGRAPHER
            REGULAR TERM BEGINS ON THE FIRST MONDAY IN JANUARY, APRIL, JULY AND OCTOBER

# 𝔓ottawatomie County Court

## E. D. REASOR, JUDGE

CONCURRENT JURISDICTION WITH THE DISTRICT COURT IN CIVIL MATTERS TO THE EXTENT OF $1,000 IN ALL CRIMINAL OTHER THAN CRIMES INFAMOUS

### TECUMSEH, OKLAHOMA

Hon. Frank A. Thackery,

      Shawnee, Okla.

Dear Sir:-

      I herewith return to you the copy of your final report, as Guardian. I return this copy for the purpose of having you get the Notary Public, to write the words, Notary Public, after his signature, wich[sic] will make it a correct and complete copy, of the origional[sic], final report, which is signed by him as it should be.

      I also hand you copy of my receipt for $15, costs paid by you in this matter. The original receipt is attached to your original report, together with all of the other receipts, and your final report has been filed and approved, and your application for discharge, has been filed and the order of final discharge, signed and recorded, and I will send you a certified copy of the final order of discharge, and when ~~you~~ I receive this copy of your report back, correct as I suggest, I will certify that it is a true copy of your original, final report, and return it to you.

      Hoping this will be satisfactory, I am,

                    Your Friend:

                      __E.D. Reasor__
                      County Judge.

EDR/NMC.
Feb., 18, 1910.

Ex-Judge Fifth Judicial District of Nebraska

Telephone { Office, No. 112
{ Residence, No. 113

**ROBERT WHEELER,**
ATTORNEY AND COUNSELOR
TECUMSEH, OKLA.

Mar. 10/10.

Hon. Frank A. Thackery,

Shawnee, Okla.

Dear Sir:-

In the matter of the guardianship of Ma-tahthka-ka et al. your favor of the 9, inst. is received, and I am enclosing a waiver of notice which you and the two adult heirs can sign, and owing to the age of the minors have them sign if at all convenient.

I will prepare the petition and have it ready to be executed as soon as the waiver is signed.

I have written the purchaser asking him to advance $50. to cover costs and attorneys[sic] fees, and referred him to you for any information he may want concerning the matter.

Yours very truly,
Robert Wheeler

**********

Ex-Judge Fifth Judicial District of Nebraska

Telephone { Office, No. 112
{ Residence, No. 113

**ROBERT WHEELER,**
ATTORNEY AND COUNSELOR
TECUMSEH, OKLA.

Apr. 4/10.

Hon. Frank A. Thackery,

Shawnee, Okla.

Dear Sir:-

I am enclosing the petition for sale of land in the matter of the guardianship of Nah-wah-tahth-ka-ka to be executed by you.

I also enclose the waivers in this matter and in the matter of the guardianship of Ma-tahthka-ka. Our law requires that where a person signs by mark the person writing the name shall also write his own name as a witness, and this applies to a thumb mark the same as to any other. Have the

person who wrote the names on the waivers sign each as a witness, and then
return them to me.

Yours very truly,
Robert Wheeler

**********

Ex-Judge Fifth Judicial District of Nebraska                    Telephone  { Office, No. 112
                                                                            { Residence, No. 113

**ROBERT WHEELER,**
Attorney and Counselor
Tecumseh, Okla.

Mar. 10/10.

Hon. Frank A. Thackery,

Shawnee, Okla.

Dear Sir:-

In the matter of the guardianship of Na-wah-tahth-ka-ka, your favor of the 9,
inst. is received, and I am enclosing a waiver of notice which you and the two adult
heirs can sign, and if convenient have the ninor[sic] sign also.

I will prepare the petition and have it ready to be executed as soon as the
waiver is signed.

In your letter you say that Jim Charley died in 1894. But in a former case
we had the record shows that he died July 10, 1898. Which is correct?

I have written the purchaser asking him to advance $50. to cover costs and
attorney's fees, and referred him to you for any information he may want concerning
the matter.

Thanking you for favoring me with this business, I am

Yours very truly,
Robert Wheeler

**********

Ex-Judge Fifth Judicial District of Nebraska                    Telephone  { Office, No. 112
                                                                            { Residence, No. 113

**ROBERT WHEELER,**
Attorney and Counselor
Tecumseh, Okla.

Mar. 10/10.

Hon. Frank A. Thackery,

Shawnee, Okla.

Dear Sir:-

In the matter of the guardianship of Na-wah-tahth-ka-ka, I note that you say that Jim Charley is not the same person as Fire Gibson, and I want to get this matter straight.

In a matter carried through the court some time ago in selling the minors interest in the allotment No. 417, of Co-tay-quah-pea-se, or Mrs. Gibson, the petition and the entire proceedings showed that she had had five children, viz: Eliza Panther, Fire Gibson, Tah-pea or Mary Mack, nee Gibson and Alex Gibson.

That Fire Gibson died July 10/98, leaving as his heirs, Thah-kah-che-wa-se, widow, Nah-wah-tahth-ka-ka, son, and Pah-mah-way-se, daughter.

If Jim Charley, allottee No. 497, is not the same person as Fire Gibson mentioned in the Mrs. Gibson estate matter, then I have been laboring under a mistake, but a very natural mistake as the named[sic] of the widow and children are the same.

Please let me know how it is, so that I can get the papers exactly right in the case I now have.

Yours very truly,
Robert Wheeler

---

REFER IN REPLY TO THE FOLLOWING:

Land-
Sales
8145-1910
C H I

Application of May-
thah-nah-kea.

ADDRESS ONLY THE
COMMISSIONER OF INDIAN AFFAIRS

**DEPARTMENT OF THE INTERIOR,**
OFFICE OF INDIAN AFFAIRS,
WASHINGTON.

APR -5 1910

F. A. Thackery, Esq.,

Superintendent Shawnee Indian School,

Shawnee, Oklahoma.

Sir:

The Office has received your letter dated January 26. 1910.

You are informed that authority to approve the check of Oliver Humbargar as legal guardian of May-thah-nah-kea, in the sum of $16.13, for the purpose of paying certain court costs was granted on October 11, 1909. In taking up the amount in your accounts you should refer to Office file No. 79369-1909 as your authority.

Very respectfully,

C.F. Hauke
Chief Clerk.

THP-2
9005

---

Ex-Judge Fifth Judicial District of Nebraska

TELEPHONE  { OFFICE, No. 112
{ RESIDENCE, No. 113

ROBERT WHEELER,
ATTORNEY AND COUNSELOR
TECUMSEH, OKLA.

Apr. 6/10.

Hon. Frank A. Thackery,

Shawnee, Okla.

Dear Sir:-

Referring to your favor of this date conserning[sic] the sale of the Alz[sic] Gibson allotment to Mr. Herminghousen, would say: I am perfectly satisfied to proceed with the sale of the minors interest and wait for my fees until the matter is closed up: but the court has always required a cash deposit to cover to cover[sic] court costs, and the printers demand their pay, or that I guarantee the bill. If Mr. Herminghousen will advance $15. to cover these costs there will not be anything in the way of proceeding with the case. Or if you have any money belonging to the minor that can be used for that purpose.

If it cannot be gotten from either source, then I will ask the judge and the printer to wait until the matter is closed up, and they may be willing to do this.

Yours very truly,
Robert Wheeler

---

In the District Court of Creek County Oklahoma.

Frank A. Thackery and
CL. Kilpatrick--- Plaintiffs.

vs          PETITION.

Wallace Doolin --- Defendant.

The plaintiffs Frank A Thackery and C L Kilpatrick show to the court that Frank A Thackery is the legal and acting guardian of David Williams or Shawnee a minor, and that said minor is the legal owner of the S E 1/4 of Section 31, Township 19 N Range 8 East in Creek County, Oklahoma. That the plaintiff Frank A Thackery, as the guardian of said minor made and executed a five year lease on said land belonging to said minor to the co-plaintiff C L Kilpatrick; that said lease was dated _____ October, 1909, to begin January 1st, 1910.

Plaintiffs further allege that the plaintiff C L Kilpatrick took possession of said land under said lease on February 1st, 1910, and has broken out fifteen or twenty acres of said ground, drilled a well, bought wire for fences and lumber for a house; that he has built a stable and corn-crib and preformed other work on said land proparatiry[sic] to putting in a crop for 1910.

Plaintiffs allege that the defendant, soon after the said C L Kilpatrick took possession of said land as a tenant under Frank A Thackery, guardian of David Williams, minor, bagan[sic] to harass the said C L Kilpatrick and threatened to remove him from said land and to prevent him from cultivating said land; that the defendant, Wallace Doolin, did on or about the 20th day of March, 1910, build a fence across said land east and wast[sic] leaving but 35 or 40 acres of said quarter section of land on the south side of said fence, and shutting the said plaintiff C L Kilpatrick out of all of said 160 acres of land except that part of said quarter section south of said fence so constructed by the defendant Wallace Doolin.

Plaintiffs further allege that said defendant Wallace Doolin is trespassing upon said land wrongfully and without right and is now preventing said plaintiff C L Kilpatrick from occupying said land under his said lease.

Plaintiffs further allege that they are entitled to the possession of said S E 1/4 of Section 31, Township 19, Range 8 East in Creek County, Oklahoma, and have been since the 1st day of January, 1910. That the acts of the defendant herein complained of has worked a great and irreparable injury to the plaintiffs, and that the plaintiffs have not an adequate remedy at law.   Therefore plaintiffs pray for a judgement against said defendant, and that he be perpetually enjoined and restrained from entering upon said S E 1/4 of Section 31, Township 19 N, R 8 E in Creek County, Oklahoma, and constructing fences upon or in any way using said land in violation of the rights of the plaintiffs herein, and for all and other proper and equitable relief and for costs.

_____

State of Oklahoma,

County of Creek          SS.

C. L. Kilpatrick, one of the plaintiffs herein, says that he has read the foregoing petition, and that the facts therein stated are true.

_____

Subscribed and sworn to before me this 9th day of April, 1910.

_____
                                        Notary Public.

My commission expires _____

\*\*\*\*\*\*\*\*\*\*

LEROY J. BURT.                    WARREN H. BROWN.
**BURT & BROWN.**
ATTORNEYS AND COUNSELORS AT LAW,
SAPULPA, OKLA.

4 / 9 / 1910.

Hon Frank A Thackery,

     Shawnee, Okla.

Dear Sir:   I have just made out petition for injunction against Wallace Doolin, a copy of which I enclose you, and I have sent out notice to Doolin that a hearing will be had at 9 oclock A M April 18th, or as soon thereafter as we can get a hearing before the court.

    You must be here then and bring with you certified copies of your letters of guardianship on David Williams or Shawnee: I do not fing[sic] your letters on file here, and your lease with Kilpatrick is not on file here.  Did you ever have this lease approved by the County Court of your County?  If you have not you better do so at once, and bring with you the allotment deed.

    There is a lease on David's land given by C O Potter, curator, of Grayson, Okla, to Wallace Doolin, Dated, May 1906, fo[sic] five years.  It seems that Doolin has never complied with the provisions of this lease.  I am told that Potter was appointed at Wetumka as the curation of these minors prior to statehood.  I wish you coud[sic] fing[sic] out and also if he has ever reported to any court his doings in the last three years.  This lease provided a yearly rent of $48.00.  Now has this been paid and has he ever filed any reports?  The taxes have not been paid on these minors[sic] lands here.  If he is guardian why hasent[sic] he done that?  I think you ought to see after the taxes as they have not been paid for two years and these lands are taxable under the law.
We must rout this fellow if possible and we must be prepared with all the necessary papers to make out our case,

    Under Doolin's lease he was to break out 30 acres each year for the first three years.  He has never turned a furrow nor done anything but to fence it and pasture it.  I would like to know if he ever paid any rent.  I will depend on you to get these facts if you can.

    Be sure to be here on the 18th.

                    Respectfully,
                    LJ Burt

EX-JUDGE FIFTH JUDICIAL DISTRICT OF NEBRASKA

TELEPHONE { OFFICE, No. 112
          { RESIDENCE, No. 113

**ROBERT WHEELER,**
ATTORNEY AND COUNSELOR
TECUMSEH, OKLA.

Apr. 12/10.

Received of Margaret Tierney by Frank A. Thackery the sum of $20.

in full for my sevices[sic] in the matter of the guardianship of Thomas C.

Tierney et als.

Robert Wheeler

---

FRED A. WAGONER.
JUDGE

GRACE WOLF,
CLERK

OFFICE OF

COUNTY COURT OF LINCOLN COUNTY

CHANDLER, OKLAHOMA

4-25-1910.

Mr. Frank Thackery,

Shawnee, Okla.

Dear Sir:

Find enclosed cards with statements of the costs in the

estate of the Guardianship of the named minors, due this County,

of which you are the Guardian.   Please remit the amounts by

check, draft or money order at once, and oblige.

Yours truly,

Fred A. Wagoner

DD.                                    County Judge.

**********

FRED A. WAGONER.
JUDGE

GRACE WOLF,
CLERK

OFFICE OF

COUNTY COURT OF LINCOLN COUNTY

CHANDLER, OKLAHOMA

4-25-1910.

Mr. W. C. Colenberg[sic],

Sac and Fox Agency, Okla.

Dear Sir:

Find enclosed a card with the statement of the costs due this office in the estate of which you are the Administrator. Please remit the same at once by check, draft or money order.

Yours truly,

Fred Wagoner

DD.                                                                County Judge.

**********

**Office of County Judge,**
Lincoln County, Oklahoma.                          Case No.   795

CHANDLER, OKLA.,           4 - 23           190 10

In the case of           Guardianship of William H Jefferson

The fees due in the above case, to this date, are as follows, which must be paid by the           First           day of           May           19 10

| | | | |
|---|---|---|---|
| Court - $  11.45 | | Witness - $ | |
| Sheriff - $ | | Jurors  - $ | |
| Printer - $  23.75 | | Total $  35.20 | |

FRED A. WAGONER, County Judge.

PLEASE BRING OR MAIL THIS CARD WHEN PAYMENT IS MADE.

W.C. Colenberg[sic]   S & F Agency

**********

FRED A. WAGONER.                                                   GRACE WOLF,
JUDGE                                                                    CLERK
                              OFFICE OF                      RECEIVED
              COUNTY COURT OF LINCOLN COUNTY        APR 28 1910
                      CHANDLER, OKLAHOMA                SAC & FOX AGENCY,
                                                              OKLAHOMA.

4-27-1910.

Mr. W. C. Kohelenberg[sic],

Sac and Fox Agency, Okla.

Dear Sir:

The law requires that all costs earned in the County Judges office shall be collected and paid to the County Treasurer, as we are now preparing our report to submit to the County Commisssioners[sic] we desire to collect all costs in all cases due this office to date, so that they same may be paid to the Treasurer at the time of the filing of the report. You will find enclosed a card which is a statment[sic] of the costs due in this matter. Please remit the same by return mail together with the card, either by check, draft or money order. A prompt reply will be greatly appreciated by us.

Yours truly,

DD                                                              County Judge.

**********

**Office of County Judge,**
Lincoln County, Oklahoma.                              Case No. ___943___

CHANDLER, OKLA., ___4 - 23___ 1901 0

In the case of _____ Guardianship of David Pennock _____.

The fees due in the above case, to this date, are as follows, which must be paid by the ___first___ day of _____ May _____ 191 0

| | | | |
|---|---|---|---|
| Court - 8 ___5.95___ | Witness - 8 _____ |
| Sheriff - 8 _____ | Jurors - 8 _____ |
| Printer - 8 _____ | Total 8 ___5.95___ |

FRED A. WAGONER, County Judge.

PLEASE BRING OR MAIL THIS CARD WHEN PAYMENT IS MADE.

W.C. Kolenberg[sic]   S & F Agency

**********

FRED A. WAGONER.
JUDGE

OFFICE OF

**COUNTY COURT OF LINCOLN COUNTY**

CHANDLER, OKLAHOMA

GRACE WOLF,
CLERK

RECEIVED

MAY 30 1910

SAC & FOX AGENCY
OKLAHOMA

5-23-1910.

Dear Sir:

You will find enclosed a card which shows the amount of costs due the Office of the County Judge in the Case herein named in which you are interested.

The law requires that all fees earned in the County Judge's office must be paid into the County Treasury, and it is therefore necessary that you give this matter your immediate attention by remitting the amount due by Check, Draft or P. O. Money Order together with the card herein enclosed, not later than June 10th, 1910.

It will be a great favor to us for you to comply with this irequest[sic] promptly so that we may include the collection in our next report to the County Commissioners. Thanking you in advance, we beg to remain

Yours truly,

Dolly Diamond
Clerk of the County Court.

**********

**Office of County Judge,**
Lincoln County, Oklahoma.                    Case No. ___799___

                              CHANDLER, OKLA., ___5 - 27___ 19010

In the case of _____ Guardianship of Harvey Madison _____

The fees due in the above case, to this date, are as follows, which must be paid by the _____ first _____ day of _____ June _____ 1910

| | | | |
|---|---|---|---|
| Court - $ | 1.90 | Witness - $ | |
| Sheriff - $ | | Jurors - $ | |
| Printer - $ | | Total $ | 1.90 |

FRED A. WAGONER, County Judge.

PLEASE BRING OR MAIL THIS CARD WHEN PAYMENT IS MADE.

W.C. Kohlenberg    Agency

**********

**Office of County Judge,**
Lincoln County, Oklahoma.                    Case No. ___806___

                              CHANDLER, OKLA., ___5 - 26___ 19010

In the case of _____ Guardianship of Thos Glover and _____
_____ Susan Morris _____

The fees due in the above case, to this date, are as follows, which must be paid by the _____ 10th _____ day of _____ June _____ 1910

| | | | |
|---|---|---|---|
| Court - $ | .40 | Witness - $ | |
| Sheriff - $ | | Jurors - $ | |
| Printer - $ | | Total $ | .40 |

FRED A. WAGONER, County Judge.

PLEASE BRING OR MAIL THIS CARD WHEN PAYMENT IS MADE.

W.C. Kohlenberg    Agency

**********

**Office of County Judge,**
Lincoln County, Oklahoma.                                   Case No. 939

CHANDLER, OKLA., 5 - 26 1901 0

In the case of  Guardianship of Albert and Ruth Moore

The fees due in the above case, to this date, are as follows, which must be paid by
the 10th day of June 1910

Court - $ 4.35              Witness - $
Sheriff - $                 Jurors - $
Printer - $                 Total $ 4.35

FRED A. WAGONER, County Judge.

PLEASE BRING OR MAIL THIS CARD WHEN PAYMENT IS MADE.
W.C. Kohlenberg

\*\*\*\*\*\*\*\*\*\*

**Office of County Judge,**
Lincoln County, Oklahoma.                                   Case No. 943

CHANDLER, OKLA., 5 - 26 1901 0

In the case of  Guardianship of David Pennock

The fees due in the above case, to this date, are as follows, which must be paid by
the 10th day of June 1910

Court - $ 5.95              Witness - $
Sheriff - $                 Jurors - $
Printer - $                 Total $ 5.95

FRED A. WAGONER, County Judge.

PLEASE BRING OR MAIL THIS CARD WHEN PAYMENT IS MADE.
W.C. Kohlenberg

\*\*\*\*\*\*\*\*\*\*

**Office of County Judge,**
Lincoln County, Oklahoma.                                   Case No. 958

CHANDLER, OKLA., 5 - 26 1901 0

In the case of  Guardianship of Elmer Manatowa et el

The fees due in the above case, to this date, are as follows, which must be paid by
the 10th day of June 1910

Court - $ 2.85              Witness - $
Sheriff - $                 Jurors - $
Printer - $                 Total $ 2.85

FRED A. WAGONER, County Judge.

PLEASE BRING OR MAIL THIS CARD WHEN PAYMENT IS MADE.
W.C. Kohlenberg

\*\*\*\*\*\*\*\*\*\*

**Office of County Judge,**
Lincoln County, Oklahoma.                          Case No. ___795___

CHANDLER, OKLA., ___5 - 26___ 190 10

In the case of _____ Guardianship of William H Jefferson _____

--------------------------------------------------------------------

The fees due in the above case, to this date, are as follows, which must be paid by

the ____10th____ day of _____June_____ 19 10

Court - $ __11.35__                    Witness - $ _____

Sheriff - $ _____               Jurors  - $ _____

Printer - $ __23.85__                     Total $ __35.30__

FRED A. WAGONER, County Judge.

PLEASE BRING OR MAIL THIS CARD WHEN PAYMENT IS MADE.

W.C. Kohlenberg        Agency

---

R. C. GREEN, CLERK                                      GEO. E. SMITH, STENOGRAPHER

REGULAR TERM BEGINS ON THE FIRST MONDAY IN JANUARY, APRIL, JULY AND OCTOBER

# Pottawatomie County Court

### E. D. REASOR, JUDGE

CONCURRENT JURISDICTION WITH THE DISTRICT COURT IN CIVIL MATTERS TO THE EXTENT OF $1,000 IN ALL CRIMINAL OTHER THAN CRIMES INFAMOUS

TECUMSEH, OKLAHOMA        June 6", 1910.

Mr. F. A. Thackery,

Shawnee, Okla.

Dear Sir & Friend:-

Find enclosed a list of costs in the cases in which you filed annual report as guardian.

I will send you a duplicate annual report in a day or so.

You will kindly remitt[sic] the costs in these cases at your earlist[sic] convenience.

Yours respectfully,

_____R. C. Green_____
CLERK COUNTY COURT.

**********

Mr. Frank A. Thackery,
        Shawnee, Okla.
Dear Sir and Friend:-
        The following is the amount of costs due and unpaid in the following
cases:

| | | |
|---|---|---|
| Py-a-tho | cost | $ 2.20 |
| Myrtle Shawnee | " | 2.70 |
| David Shawnee | " | 2.70 |
| Mah-ko-the-quah (Laura Sah ah peah) | " | 2.20 |
| Rosa Skah kah | " | 2.20 |
| Victor Sloan | " | 2.20 |
| Anna Sultuska | " | 2.66 |
| Harry Smith or Nesh a quot | " | 7.50 |
| Louise Sultuska | " | 2.66 |
| Jerome Sultuska | " | 2.66 |
| Hilda Sultuska | " | 2.66 |
| George A. Sultuska | " | 2.66 |
| Effie Douglas ( We sko peth o que) | " | 2.20 |
| Wah ko nah ka ka or Henry Bentley | " | 10.95 54¢ |
| Puck e skin no | " | 2.20 |
| Lafayette Shawnee | " | 2.70 |
| Ah ko the | " | 2.20 |
| Webster Alford | " | 2.20 |
| Bernadine Haas | " | 2.20 |
| Ethel Haas | " | 2.20 |
| Jesse Haas | " | 2.20 |
| Jesse Haas | " | 2.20 |
| Lucile Haas | " | 2.20 |
| Paul Merritt Haas | " | 2.20 |
| Reuben Haas | " | 2.20 |
| Nah she pe eth | " | 2.20 |
| Ne pah hah | " | 2.20 |
| Clarence Fox | " | 2.20 |
| Ke se to quah | " | 29.10 |
| Ethel Kirk | " | 2.20 |
| Mah teck que net nee | " | 2.20 |
| Pe can | " | 4.40 |
| | Total | 117.35 |

# COUNTY COURT

## CLEVELAND COUNTY

### N. E. SHARP, COUNTY JUDGE
AMY NOLAN, STENOGRAPHER AND CLERK

1559

NORMAN, OKLA.,___Nov 30th___19 09

Frank A. Thackery,
   Indian Agent,
      Shawnee, Okla.
Dear Sir:
     In compliance with your request of recent date, I give you full information desired regarding the estate of minors wherein you are guardian::
     No. of case. 164.
     Name, Indian_____ , American John A. Myres., Address_____
_____.

     Date of Appointment. July 16, 1906.
     Amount of Bond,
     Last report-- Final report of guardian filed Dec. 10th, 1908, report approved and guardian discharged.

. . . . . . . . . . . . . . . . . . . . . . . . . . .
     No. of case. 106.
     Name, Indian_____ , American, Lydia Ring. Address_____

     Amount of bond, $1500.00
     Date of appointment. Aug. 11, 1909.
     Names of Sureties, J. B. Beadles and L. N. Beadles.
     Last report filed_____

. . . . . . . . . . . . . . . . . . . . . . . . . . .

No. of case. 188.
     Nmae[sic], Indian_____ American, John, George, Alex, Allice Pambogo.
     Date of appointment, Jan. 17, 1908,
     Amount of bond, $100.00
     Names of Sureties, O. Hambargar and T. W. Alford.
     Last report filed, Dec. 14, 1908.

. . . . . . . . . . . . . . . . . . . . . . . . . . .

No. of case, 213.
     Name, Indian Te-wah-ney Mack, American, Tom Mack. Address____

     Date of appointment,  Dec 7, 1908.
     Amount of Bond,  $250.00
     Names of Sureties,  J. B. Beadles and L. N. Beadles.
     Last report filed,_____

. . . . . . . . . . . . . . . . . . . . . . . . . . .

No. of case. 223
Name, Indian_____ American, Mark Charley, Address____

---

Date of appointment. July 19/1909
Amount of Bond, $400.00
Name of Surety, L. N. Beadles,
Last report filed_____

Respectfully,
_____N.E. Sharp_____
County Judge.

NEW-AN

**********

State of Oklahoma   ()
                    () SS.
Cleveland County.   ()

I, Amy Nolan, County Stenographer and Clerk of the County
Court of said County, do hereby certify that the above and foregoing report
and statement of the conditions of the guardianship matters aforesaid, are
true and correct as shown by the records of the County Court of said
County.

_____Amy Nolan_____
Co. Sten. & Clerk of the Co. Court

---

## Department of Justice.

—

### Office of the United States Attorney.
### District of Oklahoma.
#### Guthrie.

June 11, 1910.

F. A. Thackery,
    Supt. & Spcl. Disb. Agent,
    Shawnee, Okla.

Dear Frank:

We have directions to investigate the guardianship of L.C.
Grimes as guardianship of Wah-pe-come, Mexican Kickapoo minor.
Please advise us in full.

Very respectfully,

John Embry
U. S. Attorney.

---

June 17, 1910.

RECEIVED
JUN 20 1910
SAC & FOX AGENCY,
OKLAHOMA.

Mr. R. C. Green,

Tecumseh, Oklahoma.

Dear Sir:

I have your letter under date of the 16th relative to the Etta Shaw matter, not what you say. Of course I have always been under the impression that I had my final discharge, as I made my report on May 20, 1908, but of course if I have not complied with the laws, why, I am perfectly willing to do so, without being sited in the case, therefore, you set a date and if necessary have the agent or his attorney meet me in Tecumseh, and I will make the necessary report and get my final discharge.

Upon the order of the court on May 20, 1908, I paid over to the minor all moneys in my hand.

Please let me hear from you by return mail what is necessary for me to do, and when I must come to Tecumseh; there is no use to have any costs in this matter whatever, as you know I am willing to do what is necessary, and the bond is absolutely good.

I am sending the Indian Agent a copy of this letter, and am writing him to-day.

Yours very truly,

_____
President.

Dict.

\*\*\*\*\*\*\*\*\*\*

L. T. SAMMONS, President.   R. W. YAKISH, Cashier.   I. A. DRAPER, Asst. Cashier.

7619

# American National Bank

OF HOLDENVILLE.

**Holdenville, Okla.**

June 17, 1910.

RECEIVED JUN 20 1910 SAC & FOX AGENCY, OKLAHOMA.

Mr. W. C. Kohlenberg,

Supt/[sic] & Special Agent.

Sac and Fox Agency, Okla.

Dear Sir:

Inclosed you will find a copy of a letter which I have just written to the Clerk of the County Court of Pottawatomie County. You will note what I say in the matter is, I thought I had my final discharge as I had settled with the ward by order of the court on May 20, 1908, and thought that was all there was to it, but however, I am perfectly willing without any costs whatever to any body to meet you or your attorney in Tecumseh if neseccary[sic], and adjust this matter according to law.

Awaiting a reply, I beg to remain

Yours very truly,

L. T. Sammons
President.

Dict.

\*\*\*\*\*\*\*\*\*\*

R. C. GREEN, Clerk   GEO. E. SMITH, Stenographer

REGULAR TERM BEGINS ON THE FIRST MONDAY IN JANUARY, APRIL, JULY AND OCTOBER

# Pottawatomie County Court

RECEIVED JUN 20 1910 SAC & FOX AGENCY, OKLAHOMA.

E. D. REASOR, Judge

CONCURRENT JURISDICTION WITH THE DISTRICT COURT IN CIVIL MATTERS TO THE EXTENT OF $1,000 IN ALL CRIMINAL CASES EXCEPT FELONIOUS

TECUMSEH, OKLAHOMA

June 18", 1910.

Mr. W. C. Kohlenberg,

Sac & Fox Agency, Okla.

Dear Sir:-

33

On receiving your application for an order citing L. T. Sammons, Guardian of Etta Shaw, Melton Bryan, Guardian of Bertha Pat ta que, and the Thurman Minor; Also Hiram Holt, guardian of another minor of which you have in charge, but I do not at this time remember the name.

I notified said parties instead of citing them to appear, however, telling them, in case they did not take notice, and abide by said notice, then it would be necessary for me to issue a citation for them

I have not, as yet, received answers to my letters, only but one, and that is from Mr. L. T. Sammons, Guardian of Etta Shaw[sic] Which he stated in his letter that he was of the impression that he had gotten his final discharge, May 20", 1908, and that he was willing to comply with all laws without being cited and requested a day to be set, and that you or your attorney be present, and he would make proper report.

He further states that he paid to said minor on said date, May 20", 1908, all money in his hands due said Minor, by order of the Court.

He also states that he has sent you a copy of this letter which I have received from him, and I would suggest that if it is convenient for you to meet Mr. Sammons here on Monday, June 27", 1910, and if not on that day, you may agree with him on some date that would be more convenient for both, but try to make the agreement to meet him on some Monday, and take this matter up and dispose of the same.

I have taken this method in notifying said guardians of the applications on file herein, so as to save as much cost as possible in these matters.

I will answer Mr. Sammons letter today telling him that he will receive a letter from you as to what date you can conveniently meet him here, as he seems to be willing at your convenience.

Hoping that you will approve the action I have taken in this matter, in notifying said guardians instead of citing them to appear, and avoiding any further costs.

The reason why I mentioned to you to try and meet here some Monday, during this campaign, the Judge will be in his Office on ever[sic] Monday, and thereby you will be sure and catch him here on some Monday.

Yours respectfully,

___R. C. Green___
Clerk County Court.

Hello. Mr. Kohlenberg; Tell all the people hello. How is Mrs. Kohlenberg's Chickens.[sic]

Yours,
Geo.

**********

R. C. GREEN, Clerk                                                    GEO. E. SMITH, Stenographer

REGULAR TERM BEGINS ON THE FIRST MONDAY IN JANUARY, APRIL, JULY AND OCTOBER

# Pottawatomie County Court

### E. D. REASOR, Judge

CONCURRENT JURISDICTION WITH THE DISTRICT COURT IN CIVIL MATTERS TO THE EXTENT OF $1,000 IN ALL CRIMINAL OTHER THAN CRIMES INFAMOUS

TECUMSEH, OKLAHOMA          June 18", 1910.

Mr. L. T. Sammons,

  Holdenville, Okla.

Dear Sir:-

  I am in receipt of yours of the 17", in regard to the gardianship[sic] of Etta Shaw, a Minor.

  I have this day wrote Mr. Kohlenberg, at the Sac & Fox Agency stating that I had received a letter from you, and that you were ready and willing, at his convenience, to meet him or his attorney here to take up this matter, and dispose of the same, and suggested that he write you what date, that it would be convenient for both of you to meet here, and dispose of said matter.

  I suggested to him, however, that if it would be convenient for you both, June 27" be set for hearing. However, in the mean time, he will consult you as to your convenience in the matter.

35

I merly[sic] suggested this date, for during the campaign the Judge will sure be in his office on ever[sic] Monday, at least, and so if it is impossible or inconvenient for either of you Gentlemen to be here on the 27" of June, I would suggest the[sic] you arrange to meet here on some Monday after that date.

I am very sorry, indeed, that there is a misunderstanding as to your final report, dated May 20", 1908. It was possible a clerical mistake of myself, and not of yours, and I will take pleasure in assisting you in any way possible to correct and dispose of this matter. As you well know that there is a great many Estate matters and things for me to look after, and that this mistake was accidentally, on my part, and not intentionally in any way.

Hoping that you and Mr. Kohlenberg will arrange this matter, and you possible can arrange the same so that you will not have to make the trip up here, after explaining as you did to Mr. Kohlenberg that you was under the impression that you had made your final report, and had gotten your discharge, which I am confident that you did, I failing to get said order, or misplaced the same, inasmuch as I failed to put the same on record.

Hoping that you can arrange this matter without the expense of making a trip up here, and I think that you can.

Yours respectfully,

R. C. Green
Clerk County Court.

---

REFER IN REPLY TO THE FOLLOWING:

Land-
Sales
C H I

Circular No. 413

**DEPARTMENT OF THE INTERIOR,**

**OFFICE OF INDIAN AFFAIRS,**

WASHINGTON,

JUL -5 1910

ADDRESS ONLY THE
COMMISSIONER OF INDIAN AFFAIRS

F. A. Thackery, Esq.,

Superintendent Shawnee Indian School,

Shawnee, Oklahoma.

Sir:

The Office has received your reports for the months of April and May of checks drawn by you under authority given in Circular No. 413.

You are informed that the authority given in the circular mentioned is not sufficient to cover guardianship costs.  Please submit request for authority therefor in the usual manner.

In this connection the Office wishes to call your attention to the fact that the reports mentioned are not submitted in accordance with the form outlined in Circular No. 413.  For the sake of uniformity and expediting the examination of your quarterly account the Office requests that you follow strictly the form outlined in the circular mentioned.

Very respectfully,

John Francis, Jr.
Acting Chief Land Division.

6-LK-30
11176

RECEIVED

JUL 16 1910

TREASURY DEPARTMENT

WASHINGTON   July 13, 1910.

SAC & FOX AGENCY.
OKLAHOMA.

Mr. W. H[sic]. Kohlenberg,

Sac & Fox Agency, Oklahoma.

Sir:

Referring to your answer, dated July 5, 1910, to the statement of differences sent you on settlement if your account for the third quarter, 1910, Certificate No. 2818, you are informed that the sum of $286.45 suspended on voucher 2, will be passed to your credit in the next Settlement, in view of the explanation submitted.

In the future all Indian checks should be signed by the person in whose name the account is carried.  Where, for sufficient reasons, this cannot be done and claimant's name is signed by the natural guardian, or other authorized person, both names should appear and the party signing should indicate the capacity in which he does so, as Robert Ray, by William Ray, natural guardian.

Respectfully,

J.B. Belk
Acting Auditor.

G.

---

## DEPARTMENT OF THE INTERIOR

### UNITED STATES INDIAN FIELD SERVICE

RECEIVED

AUG 31 1910

SAC & FOX AGENCY,
OKLAHOMA.

Otoe Agency, Otoe, Okla., July 15, 1910.

Maj. John Jensen,

Perry, Okla.

Dear Sir:-

At the instance of Supt. Kohlenberg of the Sac & Fox Agency, I am forwarding to you a deed for your signature as guardian of Vesting Grant.

After signing the same Mr. Kohlenberg desires that you return the same to his office.

Very respectfully,

Ralph P. Stanion
Supt. & S.D.A.

Here is this deed at last
[Illegible] just got authority from this County Judge to sign it.

Very resp

J Jensen

---

EX-JUDGE FIFTH JUDICIAL DISTRICT OF NEBRASKA

TELEPHONE { OFFICE, No. 112
RESIDENCE, No. 113

**ROBERT WHEELER,**
ATTORNEY AND COUNSELOR
TECUMSEH, OKLA.

Aug. 10/10.

Hon. Frank A. Thackery,

Shawnee, Okla.

Dear Sir:-

In the matter of the guardianship of Arther and Luther Rolette, I enclose a petition for the appointment of Mr. Odle as guardian, and a letter to Judge Sharp attached.  As the land is in Cleveland county I believe it better to proceed in that county, and if this meets with your approval finish filling the application and execute the same, and then mail it and my letter to Judge Sharp.  Notify me when you mail the application so that I can keep in touch with the matter.

Yours very truly,<br>Robert Wheeler

---

No. ....................

## DEPARTMENT OF THE INTERIOR

### UNITED STATES INDIAN SERVICE.

OFFICE OF INDIAN AFFAIRS
RECEIVED
AUG 22 1910.
685525

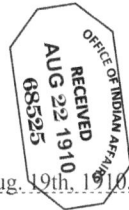

Shawnee, Oklahoma,  Aug. 19th, 1910.

Commissioner of Indian Affairs,
  Washington, D. C.

Sir:

I have the honor to recommend that I be authorized to approve the checks of ........ myself as the legal guardian of Minnie Foreman ............................ whose balance in bank is $ 114.16 .........., in the amounts and for the purposes specified below:

| | AMOUNT OF AUTHORITY. | EXPENDITURES. | |
| --- | --- | --- | --- |
| | | DATE. | AMOUNT. |
| Guardian costs -<br><br>(To cover my expenses in filing reports, signing papers, etc)<br><br>This request submitted in response to your letter: | 1 | | |

Land
Sales
C H I

Circular No. 413
\*\*\*\*\*\*\*\*\*\*\*\*\*\*\*

Frank A. Thackery
*Agent or Superintendent.*

Approved:___CF Hauke_____
*Second Assistant Commissioner.*

SEP -2 1910

Date,_____

No. _____

## DEPARTMENT OF THE INTERIOR

### UNITED STATES INDIAN SERVICE.

OFFICE OF INDIAN AFFAIRS
RECEIVED
AUG 22 1910
68601

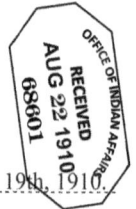

Shawnee, Okla., August 19th, 1910.

Commissioner of Indian Affairs,
    Washington, D. C.

Sir:

    I have the honor to recommend that I be authorized to approve the checks

of_____myself as the legal guardian of Frank Spybuck_____

whose balance in bank is $_123.37_____, in the amounts and for the purposes

specified below:

| | AMOUNT OF AUTHORITY. | EXPENDITURES. | |
| --- | --- | --- | --- |
| | | DATE. | AMOUNT. |
| Guardian costs - | 2 | | |
| (To cover my expenses in filing reports, signing papers, etc) | | | |
| This request submitted in response to your letter: | | | |

Land
Sales
C H I

Circular No. 413
＊＊＊＊＊＊＊＊＊＊＊＊＊＊

Frank A. Thackery
*Agent or Superintendent.*

Approved:___CF Hauke_____
*Second Assistant* **Commissioner.**

SEP -2 1910

Date._____

---

No. _____

## DEPARTMENT OF THE INTERIOR

### UNITED STATES INDIAN SERVICE.

RECEIVED AUG 22 1910 68584 OFFICE OF INDIAN AFFAIRS

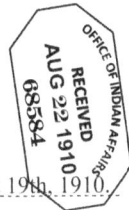

Shawnee, Okla., August 19th, 1910.

Commissioner of Indian Affairs,
            Washington, D. C.

Sir:

        I have the honor to recommend that I be authorized to approve the checks

of_____myself as the legal guardian of Lafayette Shawnee_____

whose balance in bank is $ 46.98_____, in the amounts and for the purposes

specified below:

| | AMOUNT OF AUTHORITY. | EXPENDITURES. | |
| --- | --- | --- | --- |
| | | DATE. | AMOUNT. |
| Guardian costs - | 5 38 | | |
| (To cover my expenses in filing reports, looking after his Creek allotment, etc) | | | |
| This request submitted in response to your letter: | | | |

41

Land
Sales
C H I

Circular No. 413
* * * * * * * * * * * * * *

Frank A. Thackery
*Agent or Superintendent.*

Approved: ___CF Hauke_____
*Second Assistant Commissioner.*                    SEP -2 1910

Date._____

No. _____

## DEPARTMENT OF THE INTERIOR

### UNITED STATES INDIAN SERVICE.

OFFICE OF INDIAN AFFAIRS
AUG 22 1910
RECEIVED
68522

__Shawnee, Okla., August 19th, 1910.__

Commissioner of Indian Affairs,
        Washington, D. C.

Sir:

        I have the honor to recommend that I be authorized to approve the checks

of _____myself as the legal guardian of Ke no che pe wa se_____

whose balance in bank is $ 13.40_____, in the amounts and for the purposes

specified below:

| | AMOUNT OF AUTHORITY. | EXPENDITURES. | |
|---|---|---|---|
| | | DATE. | AMOUNT. |
| Guardian costs - | 1.00 | | |
| (To cover my expenses in filing reports, signing papers, etc) | | | |
| This request submitted in response to your letter: | | | |

Land
Sales
C H I

Circular No. 413
* * * * * * * * * * * * * *

Frank A. Thackery
*Agent or Superintendent.*

Approved:___CF Hauke_____
*Second Assistant* **Commissioner.**

SEP -2 1910

Date,_____

---

No._____

**DEPARTMENT OF THE INTERIOR**

UNITED STATES INDIAN SERVICE.

*(stamp: OFFICE OF INDIAN AFFAIRS RECEIVED AUG 22 1910 68585)*

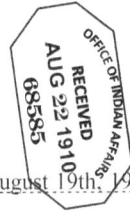

Shawnee, Oklahoma,  August 19th, 1910.

Commissioner of Indian Affairs,
            Washington, D. C.

Sir:

I have the honor to recommend that I be authorized to approve the checks

of_____myself, as the legal guardian of John Mesh que ken nock_____

whose balance in bank is  $ 1859.67_____ , in the amounts and for the purposes

specified below:

| | AMOUNT OF AUTHORITY. | EXPENDITURES. | |
| --- | --- | --- | --- |
| | | DATE. | AMOUNT. |
| Guardian costs - | 2 | | |
| (To cover my expenses in filing reports, signing papers, etc) | | | |
| This request submitted in response to your letter: | | | |

| Land<br>Sales<br>C H I<br><br>Circular No. 413<br>\*\*\*\*\*\*\*\*\*\*\*\*\*\*\* | | | | |
|---|---|---|---|---|

Frank A. Thackery
*Agent or Superintendent.*

Approved:___CF Hauke_____
         *Second Assistant Commissioner.*

Date,_____   SEP -2 1910

---

No. _____

## DEPARTMENT OF THE INTERIOR

### UNITED STATES INDIAN SERVICE.

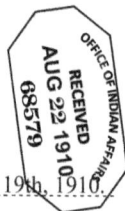

*[stamp: OFFICE OF INDIAN AFFAIRS RECEIVED AUG 22 1910 68579]*

Shawnee, Okla., August 19th, 1910.

Commissioner of Indian Affairs,
         Washington, D. C.

Sir:

        I have the honor to recommend that I be authorized to approve the checks
of_____myself as the legal guardian of Keah quah moke_____
whose balance in bank is $___5¢_____, in the amounts and for the purposes
specified below:

| | AMOUNT<br>OF AUTHORITY. | EXPENDITURES. | |
|---|---|---|---|
| | | DATE. | AMOUNT. |
| Guardian costs -<br><br>(To remove this small balance from the<br>books; and to apply on my expenses as<br>guardian)<br><br>This request submitted in response to your<br>letter: | 5¢ | | |

Land
Sales
C H I

Circular No. 413
\*\*\*\*\*\*\*\*\*\*\*\*\*\*

Frank A. Thackery
*Agent or Superintendent.*

Approved:___CF Hauke_____
          *Second Assistant Commissioner.*

SEP -2 1910

Date,_____

---

No. _____

## DEPARTMENT OF THE INTERIOR

### UNITED STATES INDIAN SERVICE.

RECEIVED
AUG 22 1910
68580
OFFICE OF INDIAN AFFAIRS

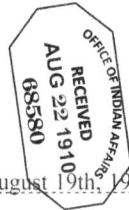

Shawnee, Oklahoma,  August 19th, 1910.

Commissioner of Indian Affairs,
          Washington, D. C.

Sir:

          I have the honor to recommend that I be authorized to approve the checks

of _____myself as the legal guardian of Louise Hardin_____

whose balance in bank is $_104.13_____, in the amounts and for the purposes

specified below:

| | AMOUNT OF AUTHORITY. | EXPENDITURES. | |
| | | DATE. | AMOUNT. |
| --- | --- | --- | --- |
| Guardian costs - | 1 | | |
| (To cover my expenses in filing reports, signing papers, etc) | | | |
| This request submitted in response to your letter: | | | |

Land
Sales
C H I

Circular No. 413
\*\*\*\*\*\*\*\*\*\*\*\*\*\*

Frank A. Thackery
*Agent or Superintendent.*

Approved:____CF Hauke_____
*Second Assistant Commissioner.*

SEP -2 1910

Date,_____

No. _____

## DEPARTMENT OF THE INTERIOR

### UNITED STATES INDIAN SERVICE.

RECEIVED
AUG 22 1910
68581
OFFICE OF INDIAN AFFAIRS

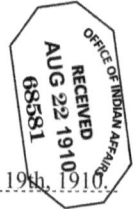

Shawnee, Okla., August 19th, 1910.

Commissioner of Indian Affairs,
    Washington, D. C.

Sir:

    I have the honor to recommend that I be authorized to approve the checks of _____myself as the legal guardian of Thomas Foreman_____ whose balance in bank is $ 1.00_____, in the amounts and for the purposes specified below:

| | AMOUNT OF AUTHORITY. | EXPENDITURES. | |
|---|---|---|---|
| | | DATE. | AMOUNT. |
| Guardian costs - | 1 | | |
| (To cover my expenses in filing reports, signing papers, etc) | | | |
| This request submitted in response to your letter: | | | |

Land
Sales
C H I

Circular No. 413
**************

Frank A. Thackery
*Agent or Superintendent.*

Approved:___CF Hauke_____
*Second Assistant **Commissioner.***

Date._____

SEP -2 1910

No. _____

## DEPARTMENT OF THE INTERIOR

### UNITED STATES INDIAN SERVICE.

RECEIVED
AUG 22 1910
68582
OFFICE OF INDIAN AFFAIRS

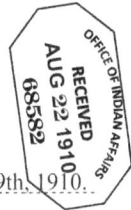

Shawnee, Okla., Aug. 19th, 1910.

Commissioner of Indian Affairs,
    Washington, D. C.

Sir:

I have the honor to recommend that I be authorized to approve the checks

of _____myself as the legal guardian of Peah puck o he_____

whose balance in bank is $ 333.88_____, in the amounts and for the purposes

specified below:

| | AMOUNT OF AUTHORITY. | EXPENDITURES. | |
|---|---|---|---|
| | | DATE. | AMOUNT. |
| Guardian costs - | 2 | | |
| (To cover my expenses in filing reports, signing papers, etc) | | | |
| This request submitted in response to your letter: | | | |

Land
Sales
C H I

Circular No. 413
***************

Frank A. Thackery
*Agent or Superintendent.*

Approved:___CF Hauke_____
*Second Assistant Commissioner.*

Date,_____

SEP -2 1910

No. _____

## DEPARTMENT OF THE INTERIOR

### UNITED STATES INDIAN SERVICE.

RECEIVED AUG 22 1910 OFFICE OF INDIAN AFFAIRS 68583

Shawnee, Okla., August 19th, 1910.

Commissioner of Indian Affairs,
        Washington, D. C.

Sir:

        I have the honor to recommend that I be authorized to approve the checks

of_____myself as the legal guardian of James Rock_____

whose balance in bank is $ 22.10_____, in the amounts and for the purposes

specified below:

| | AMOUNT OF AUTHORITY. | EXPENDITURES. | |
|---|---|---|---|
| | | DATE. | AMOUNT. |
| Guardian costs - | 1 | | |
| (To cover my expenses in filing reports, signing papers, etc) | | | |
| This request submitted in response to your letter: | | | |

Land
Sales
C H I

Circular No. 413
***************

Frank A. Thackery
*Agent or Superintendent.*

Approved: ___CF Hauke_____
*Second Assistant Commissioner.*

SEP -2 1910

Date,_____

No. _____

## DEPARTMENT OF THE INTERIOR

### UNITED STATES INDIAN SERVICE.

RECEIVED AUG 22 1910 68602 OFFICE OF INDIAN AFFAIRS

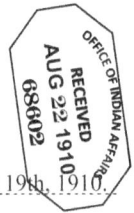

Shawnee, Okla., August 19th, 1910.

Commissioner of Indian Affairs,
Washington, D. C.

Sir:

I have the honor to recommend that I be authorized to approve the checks

of _____ myself as the legal guardian of Fredonia Shawnee _____

whose balance in bank is $ 1.24 _____, in the amounts and for the purposes

specified below:

| | AMOUNT OF AUTHORITY. | EXPENDITURES. | |
| --- | --- | --- | --- |
| | | DATE. | AMOUNT. |
| Guardian costs - | 1 24 | | |
| (To cover my expenses in filing reports, looking after her Creek allotment, etc) | | | |
| This request submitted in response to your letter: | | | |

| Land Sales C H I  Circular No. 413 ************** | | | |
|---|---|---|---|

Frank A. Thackery
*Agent or Superintendent.*

Approved:___CF Hauke_____
        *Second Assistant Commissioner.*

SEP -2 1910

Date._____

HENRY G PENNIMAN PRESIDENT

ROBERT A DOBBIN JR SECRETARY

HOME OFFICE.   BALTIMORE.MD.

PLATE GLASS, PERSONAL ACCIDENT & HEALTH

BEADLES & LAUX,
GENERAL AGENTS.
LEE BUILDING.

Aug. 23rd. 1910

OKLAHOMA CITY, OKLAHOMA,

Hon. Frank Thackery,

    Shawnee, Okla.

Dear sir:-

    As a member of the firm of J. B. Beadles & Son of Guthrie I executed a great many guardian bonds for you.  The firm mentioned was dissolved some months ago and I have taken over the surety end of the business with offices at 315 Lee Building, Oklahoma City, Okla.

    There are a large number of renewal and other premiums due from your office and I wish you would kindly look them up and remit to me at the address above or if you would rather I will run over to Shawnee and look them up with you.

            Very respectfully,

                L. N. Beadles

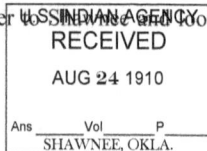

J. R. SCOTT

LAW OFFICE OF

L. L. COWLEY

# SCOTT & COWLEY

NORTH SIDE OF SQUARE
TELEPHONE 180
PERRY ∴ OKLAHOMA

Perry, Okla. Sept. 10  1910

Supt. & Spl. Disb. Agent,
 Sac & Fox Agency, Okla.
   In re Vestina Grant, Minor.

 Dear Sir:

  Enclosed find certified copies of the Letters of Guardianship granted to John Jensen, Petition of Guardian to sell land, and Order for Guardian tos ell real estate. The Confirmation of the sale will be sent to you together with the deed when the same is made by this Court here. The sale under the Oklahoma law will take place the 26th of Sept. 1910, then the report of the sale will have to be made and the matter set down for hearing by the Court. Just as soon as the Confirmation can be had I will see that you receive a certified copy of the same. Yours truly,

      L L Cowley

---

[Copy of Original]

No.

O. S. F. X.

In the matter of the
guardinship of Victor Sloan.

Journal Entry of Judgment.

Filed
Sept 3" 1910
R. C. Green
clerk

U. M. Newell & W J Jackson,
Attorneys for said Ward.

\*\*\*\*\*\*\*\*\*\*

[The Order below typed as given]

C O P Y

State of Oklahoma
_Pottowatomie County,_

_In the County Court thereof._

In the matter of the guardianship
of Victor Sloan.
_____Frank A. Thackery, Guardian._

_Journal Entry of Judgment._

It being shown that on the _____ day of _____ , 19 _ , Frank A. Thackery was by this court appointed guardian of the person and estate of Victor Sloan, then a minor; and a petition having been filed in said court alleging that said Victor Sloan is now over the age of twenty-one years and competent to transact his own business affairs,capable of careing for himself and maniging his own property; and praying the judgment of this court,declaring and finding him to be over the age of twenty-one years and,ordering his said guardian,Frank A.Thackery to file in said court his final account in the matter of said guardianship,and mike final settlement with his said ward,Victor Sloan,and that said guardian be discharged from said trust; and said matter having been submitted to said court by agreement of counsel for said guardian and his said ward upon affidavits filed in this court in said action; the court after reading all affidavcits filed in said matter and being fully advised in the premises,finds from the evidence that said Victor Sloan was born on Little River,in what is now Cleveland County,Oklahoma,in the fall of the year 1888,and is now over the age of 21 years,and that his petition filed herein should be,and the same is hereby sustained.

It is therefore hereby ordered,adjudged and decreed by this court, that said guardianFrank A.Thackery file in this court within _10_ days herefrom his final account in said guardinship matter and pay and deliver into this court for the use and benefit of his said ward,Victor Sloan all money and personal now in his hands or under his control as such guardian belonging to his said ward,Victor Sloan,and that thereupon he be discharged as such guardian and his bondsmen released.

Seal                                    E.D. Reasor
                                                Judge.

## DEPARTMENT OF THE INTERIOR

UNITED STATES INDIAN SERVICE

Otoe Agency, Otoe, Okla., Sept. 12, 1910.

W. C. Kohlenberg, Supt. & S.D.A.

Sac & Fox Agency, Okla.

Dear Sir:-

Replying to your inquiry of the 7th relative to the appointment of a legal guardian for Frank, Roy and Mark Burgess, I have to state for the purposes mentioned I would have no objections to acting as such guardian if it would further their interests, but I believe with you that Wm. Burgess is fully competent to act in such capacity.

Very respectfully,

Ralph P. Stanion
Supt. & S.D.A.

EX-JUDGE FIFTH JUDICIAL DISTRICT OF NEBRASKA          TELEPHONE { OFFICE, NO. 112 / RESIDENCE, NO. 113

**ROBERT WHEELER,**
ATTORNEY AND COUNSELOR
TECUMSEH, OKLA.

Sept. 13/10.

Hon. Frank A. Thackery,

Shawnee, Okla.

Dear Sir:-

On Apr. 11, last the County Court issued orders of sale in the cases of Nah-wah-that-ka-ka, and of Ma-tahth-ka-ka et al. and on Apr. 16, I mailed you a blank bond and appraisement blank in each case, and advised you that the court had appointed Oliver Humbargar, P. P. Ratzlaff and T. W. Alford as appraisers in each case, and fixed the amount of the bond at double the amount of the appraisement in each case.  Some time after you wrote me not to have these men appointed in any future cases, as they were no longer connected with the agency.  But I hope you can get two of them to make the appraisements in these cases, as it will delay the matters and be expensive to get other orders of sale.

I now enclose bond and appraisement blank in each case, and hope the bonds can be filled and the appraisements made, and all returned to me by or before Oct. I, for unless I can have this done, and have your reports of sales executed so as to file all before Oct. 11, I will have to apply for a new order of sale in each case, as an order of sale is only good for six months.  And I trust you will get it in on the present order of sale if possible.

Yours very truly,

Robert Wheeler

9-16-1910

[Illegible]:

Please make special trip soon as possible in this case as it will be the last one.

Thackery

---

[The letter below typed as given]

| J. M. HEATH | L. W. BAXTER | L. V. FORD |
|---|---|---|
| PRESIDENT | VICE-PRESIDENT | CASHIER |

## State Bank of Meridian

DEPOSITS GUARANTEED BY THE DEPOSITORS
GUARANTY FUND OF THE STATE
OF OKLAHOMA

Meridian, Oklahoma          9/14/10

W. C. Kohlenberg,
    Spl & Dis Agt,
        Sac & Fox Agency, Okla.

Dear Sir:-

I am in receipt of a letter from Scott & Cowle y[sic], of Pyerry Perry Okla,for the Guardian of Vestina Grant a miner, in the land of which I bought of you last, fall July to this effect:.

They want me to sign up that I will give to this Vestina Grant $1120.0 0 for the 1/2 undivided interest she holds in this said land,

Now Mr Kohlenberg,I must know where I am at in this deal, I will not pay any more money for this land,as My bid was accepted,& Pease take this matter up with these Attys,& adjust this matter, as I certainly have nothing more to do in the matter, only to pay over the bal due them , when you furnish me an abstract & deed that is perfecting the title, that any one would want.Kindly let me hear from you in this matter at once.

Yours Truly
Robert C Ball

---

EX-JUDGE FIFTH JUDICIAL DISTRICT OF NEBRASKA

TELEPHONE { OFFICE, No. 112
RESIDENCE, No. 113

**ROBERT WHEELER,**
ATTORNEY AND COUNSELOR
TECUMSEH, OKLA.

Sept. 17/10.

Hon. Frank A. Thackery,

Shawnee, Okla.

Dear Sir:-

me
On Aug. 9, ult. you wrote to take steps to have James H. Odle appointed guardian of Arthur and Luther Rolette, and then to proceed to sell through the county court a small interest they had in certain land.  And on the 10, I prepared a petition for his appointment, and mailed it and a letter for Judge Sharp to you, requesting that you sign the petition and mail it and the letter to the judge.  I have not heard from it since.  And as you were absent about that time, I thought the matter may have been overlooked.  If so, please sign the petition and return it to me, and I will write Judge Sharp another letter and then mail it to him.

Yours very truly,
Robert Wheeler

---

Terms of Court Begin on First Monday in
January, April, July and October

**OFFICE OF**
**H. E. ST. CLAIR,**
COUNTY JUDGE
Noble County
PERRY, OKLAHOMA

R E C E I V E D
Clerk of County Court
SEP 24 1910

SAC & FOX AGENCY,
OKLAHOMA.

September 22nd, 1910.

Mr. W.C. Kohlenberg, Supt.

Sac & Fox Agency, Okla.

Dear Sir:

Application has been made and the Guardian has been appointed for Fred and Lucy Vetter; F. G. Moore of this City having been appointed Guardian. I understand they desire to sell some land under the jurisdiction of your Agency. I will be pleased to have you let me know if this is a fact, and if so, send a description of the land and also the interests each minor has in the land.

Respectfully yours,

H.E. St Clair
County Judge.

## DEPARTMENT OF THE INTERIOR

### UNITED STATES INDIAN SERVICE

Shawnee, Oklahoma,

September 23rd, 1910.

Received of Frank A. Thackery, Supt. & Spcl. Disbg. Agent,

Twenty two & 25/100 ($22.25) Dollars, in payment of renewal bonds on the following cases:

Pea maw ske & Wah pah naw pe quah  - $2.00
Pem ma ho ko quah  -                   2.00
Ta pa she & Pah mah ka quah           2.00
Ah ske pah kah the ah                 8.50
Charles Barone                        1.75
Steve Pensoneau  -                    6.00
                                     $22.25.

            J.B. Beadles & Son

                [Illegible](Laux)

56

Ex-Judge Fifth Judicial District of Nebraska

TELEPHONE { OFFICE, No. 112
{ RESIDENCE, No. 113

**ROBERT WHEELER,**
ATTORNEY AND COUNSELOR
TECUMSEH, OKLA.

Sept. 28/10.

Hon. Frank A. Thackery,

Shawnee, Okla.

Dear Sir:-

In the guardianship matters of Ma-tahth-ka-ka et al. and Nah-wah-tahth-ka-ka, I am enclosing reports of sale. Please sign and swear to the same and then return them to me by early mail, together with the appraisements, if they have not been sent me.

I hope you will also be able to send me the sale bonds within a very few days, as I would like to have then when I file the report of sale.

Yours very truly,
Robert Wheeler

---

## DEPARTMENT OF THE INTERIOR

### UNITED STATES INDIAN SERVICE

U.S. Indian Agency,
Shawnee, Oklahoma,
September 29th, 1910.

Mr. Robert Wheeler,

Tecumseh, Okla.

Dear Sir:

I hand you herewith my check as the legal guardian of Te wah ney Mack, for $4.70, to cover the sheriff's costs in the John Taylor land sale through the probate court. I have already paid the outstanding court costs.

Thanking you for turning this check over to the proper parties, I am

Yours respectfully,
Frank A Thackery
Supt. & Spcl. Disbg. Agent.

57

Enclosed find duplicate receipt for the above, properly signed.

Yours very truly,
Robert Wheeler

---

HENRY G PENNIMAN PRESIDENT

ROBERT A DOBBIN.JR SECRETARY.

RECEIVED
SEP 30 1910
FOX AGENCY
OKLAHOMA

**United Surety Company**

HOME OFFICE.   BALTIMORE.MD.

PLATE GLASS, PERSONAL ACCIDENT & HEALTH

BEADLES & LAUX.
GENERAL AGENTS.
LEE BUILDING.

OKLAHOMA CITY, OKLAHOMA.

Sept. 28" 1910.

Hon. W. C. Kohlenberg,

Sac & Fox Agency, Okla.

Dear Sir:-

RE:-  Indian Guardian Bonds.

The premiums on the above bonds, executed in your behalf, will soon be due. I therefore desire that you send me a list of all bonds under which my liability as surety still exists.

The firm of J. B. Beadles & Son has dissolved, and the business of said firm will hereafter be conducted through this office.

Kindly send any matter relative to these bonds to;

L. N. Beadles,

Room 315--Lee Bldg.

Oklahoma City.

Yours very truly,

L.N. Beadles

---

Ex-Judge Fifth Judicial District of Nebraska          Telephone { OFFICE, No. 112
                                                                  { RESIDENCE, No. 113

**Robert Wheeler,**
Attorney and Counselor
Tecumseh, Okla.

Oct. 1/10.

Hon. Frank A. Thackery,

Shawnee, Okla.

Dear Sir:-

In the matter of the guardianship of George Anderson et als. your favor of the 30, ult. received. And I enclose an application for the appointment of Mrs. Sophia Anderson as guardian. Have Mrs. Anderson execute this and return to me the application, and if convenient she might send me $45. which will probably cover all expense, especially if I can induce the judge to allow notice of application for the appointment of a guardian to be made by posting. The law provides that such notice shall be given as the court may order, and it has been judge Reasor's invariable rule to requre[sic] the notice to be given by publication. But I am in hopes I can get him to make an order avoiding that unnecessary expense in this case.

I prepared papers in this case for John Anderson jr.[sic] a short time before his death, and the matter was then dropped for some reason. As I recollect it now, some of the heirs objected at that time.

----

Please send me to[sic] reports of sale, appraisements and bonds in the Ma-tahth-ka-ka and Nah-wah-tahth-ka-ka cases. If these are not filed by the 11, ist. we will have to go to the expense of getting another order of sale.

Yours very truly,
Robert Wheeler

HENRY G PENNIMAN PRESIDENT

ROBERT A DOBBIN JR SECRETARY

## United Surety Company

HOME OFFICE.   BALTIMORE.MD.

PLATE GLASS, PERSONAL ACCIDENT & HEALTH

BEADLES & LAUX.
GENERAL AGENTS.
LEE BUILDING.

OKLAHOMA CITY, OKLAHOMA,   Oct.3rd.1910.

Hon. Frank A. Thackery, Supt.

Shawnee, Okla.

Dear Sir:-

Enclosed please find guardian's sale bonds, as follows;

Ma-tahth-ka-ka and Ke-no-che-pea-wa-se. $625.00
Nah-wah-tahth-ka-ka--------------------------$100.00

Premiums $3.50 and $2.00 respectively.

Thanking you, we beg to remain,

Yours very truly,

K/L                                    Beadles & Laux

**********
[Copy of Original]

OKLAHOMA CITY. OKLA.

BEADLES & LAUX
GENERAL INSURANCE
SURETY BONDS
TITLE GUARANTEED

LEE BUILDING                                    PHONE 4658

\*\*\*\*\*\*\*\*\*\*

Ex-Judge Fifth Judicial District of Nebraska

TELEPHONE { OFFICE, No. 112
             RESIDENCE, No. 113

**ROBERT WHEELER,**
ATTORNEY AND COUNSELOR
TECUMSEH, OKLA.

Oct. 4/10.

Hon. Frank A. Thackery,

Shawnee, Okla.

Dear Sir:-

Your favor of the 3, inst. received, enclosing report of sale and appraisement in cases of Ma-tahth-ka-ka and Nah wah-tahth-ka-ka.

The bonds ought to be filed with the reports, and I will hold the papers until next Monday, the 10, if necessary, in hopes that the bonds will reach me before filing. However, if they do not reach me in time I will file what papers I have, and then file the bonds before the matters come up for confirmation.

I hope you will hurry the execution of the bonds if you can.

Yours very truly,
Robert Wheeler

---

Ex-Judge Fifth Judicial District of Nebraska

TELEPHONE { OFFICE, No. 112
             RESIDENCE, No. 113

**ROBERT WHEELER,**
ATTORNEY AND COUNSELOR
TECUMSEH, OKLA.

Oct. 6/10.

Hon. Frank A. Thackery,

Shawnee, Okla.

Dear Sir:-

In the matter of the guardianship of Arthur Rolette et al. the court made an order on the 3, inst. that on Mr. Odle filings a bond in the sum of $100. and taking the oath of office letters of guardianship issue to him. And I am enclosing blank bond and letters of guardianship. Have him fill the bond and take the oath he will find filled out on the letters, and then return the papers to me.

Yours very truly,
Robert Wheeler

**********

Ex-Judge Fifth Judicial District of Nebraska

ROBERT WHEELER,
ATTORNEY AND COUNSELOR
TECUMSEH, OKLA.

TELEPHONE { OFFICE, No. 112
RESIDENCE, No. 113

Oct. 8/10.

Hon. Frank A. Thackery,

Shawnee, Okla.

Dear Sir:-

The oath of office and bond of James H. Odle as guardian of Arthur Rolette et al. received, and as soon as the letters issue I will fordarf[sic] you a petition for the sale of the minors interests.

In the matter of the guardianship of Grace Anderson et als. I mailed you a petition some days ago for the appointment of Sopha[sic] Anderson as guardian, but it has not been returned to me. Of course the sooner we get this started the sooner we will get it through the court.

In the Nah-wah-tahth-ka-ka and Na-tahth-ka-ka cases the sale bonds have been approved, and the cases set for hearing on confirmation for the 19, inst. at 9 A.M.

Yours very truly,
Robert Wheeler

---

HENRY G. PENNIMAN PRESIDENT

ROBERT A DOBBIN JR SECRETARY

**United Surety Company**

HOME OFFICE. BALTIMORE, MD.

PLATE GLASS, PERSONAL ACCIDENT & HEALTH

BEADLES & LAUX,
GENERAL AGENTS.
LEE BUILDING.

OKLAHOMA CITY, OKLAHOMA, Oct. 10 1910.

Hon. Frank A. Thackery,

Sup't Indian Agency,

Shawnee, Okla.

Dear Sir:-

Re:- Guardians Bond Henry Starr, et al.

We beg to enclose you the above bond, together with our bill for same.

Trusting that you will find the same satisfactory, we beg to remain, yours very truly,

Beadles & Laux

**********
[Copy of Original]

EX-JUDGE FIFTH JUDICIAL DISTRICT OF NEBRASKA

**ROBERT WHEELER,**
ATTORNEY AND COUNSELOR
TECUMSEH, OKLA.

TELEPHONE { OFFICE, No. 112 / RESIDENCE, No. 113

Oct. 15/10.

Hon. Frank A. Thackery,

Shawnee, Okla.

Dear Sir:-

Your favor of this date received, enclosing application for the appoinment[sic] of Sophia Anderson as guardian of George, Lizzie, Benjamin and John B. Anderson. But the application does not give the approximate value of the personal property of these minors or the approximate value of the annual income from real estate. If you will give me these items I will insert them before filing the petition.

Mrs. Anderson has not advanced any money to cover costs, and the court will require a deposit. The costs will not be less than $15. and may be as much as $20. depending somewhat on the number of notices the court requires to be published. Aside from this, if it is convenient, Mrs. Anderson might advance my fees and it will be appreciated.

Yours very truly,
Robert Wheeler

---

[The letter below typed as given]

Cushing Okla
Oct 17 1910
Mr Agent
Sac and fox agency
Dear Sir
is the North East 1/4 of Sec 13-T-18-R-5-E for Lease.
and what Rental is wanted and what is the Indians
Name that owns the Land
let me hear from you
yours truly
P S
Your honor if the Rental is Not to high
I want to Lease it
J W Hemmer
Box 42 Cushing, okla

[The letter below typed as given]

> Tecumseh Okla
> R # 2, Box 103
>           Nov 7, 1910.
> My Dear Guardian
>      Please send me $15.00 in money, And want to
> buy little wagon for this little baby.  I want to get me
> shoes, and any thing for my winter use.  I would like
> to get me somethings for this baby too.
>                Yours Truly
>                   Mary Mack

No. .....................

## DEPARTMENT OF THE INTERIOR

### UNITED STATES INDIAN SERVICE.

OFFICE OF INDIAN AFFAIRS
RECEIVED
NOV 12 1910
900035

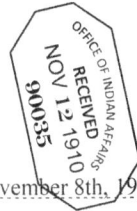

Shawnee, Oklahoma, November 8th, 1910.

Commissioner of Indian Affairs,
          Washington, D. C.

Sir:

          I have the honor to recommend that I be authorized to approve the checks
of.......myself as Supt.&Spcl.Disbg.Agent, for Viola Whipple........................
whose balance in bank is  $ 481.34..........., in the amounts and for the purposes
specified below:

| | AMOUNT OF AUTHORITY. | EXPENDITURES. | |
| --- | --- | --- | --- |
| | | DATE. | AMOUNT. |
| To turn same over to Arthur F. Schofield, legal guardian of this minor  - | 481 34 | | |

Frank A. Thackery
*Agent or Superintendent.*

Approved:___CF Hauke_____
*Second Assistant* **Commissioner.**

DEC 28 1910

Date,_____

\*\*\*\*\*\*\*\*\*\*

Land-
  Sales.
90035-1910
C H I

Supt. Shawnee.                    NOV 23 1910

Returned with the information that this Office would not be justified in turning over at one time to Mr. Schofield the entire amount to the credit of Viola Whipple. However, in view of the facts presented in his affidavit, the Office would be willing to turn over a reasonable amount per month for her support. Please re-submit the papers with your further recommendation, in accordance with the above suggestion.

Wm R Layne
Acting Chief Land Division.

DIRECTORS:

JACOB PUCKETT, President.        JACOB PUCKETT.        L. B. HAY.
C. W. CARPENTER, Vice-President.   C. W. CARPENTER.      J. B. CHARLES.
JOHN FOSTER, Cashier.             JOHN FOSTER.          E. L. CONKLIN.
                                  P. S. HOFFMAN

FIRST NATIONAL BANK
OF CUSHING.
CAPITAL STOCK, $25,000.00
CUSHING, OKLA. Nov. 10, 1910,      190___.

W. C. Kohlenberg,

    Sac & Fox Agency, Okla.

Dear Sir;

Enclosed find letter which explains itself. We do not know this man or the property described. You can answer the letter better than we can.

Respectfully,

John Foster
Cashier

\*\*\*\*\*\*\*\*\*\*

Chicago, Nov. 6, 1910.

Messrs. Puckett & Foster,
　　Cushing, Okla.

**RECEIVED**

NOV 12 1910

SAC & FOX AGENCY,
OKLAHOMA.

Gentlemen,
　　I wrote a letter to Mr. Wm. De DePue, regarding some land in Oklahoma, which, I was informed belonged to Mr. Geo. W. Kennedy who died here on July 2, 1909, and whose estate I have been trying to locate.

Mr. DePue informed me that you might know regarding his holding the property & the description of it. Mr. DePue says that Mr. Kennedy was the successful bidder on a quarter section of land, seven miles southeast of Cushing in the Indian Allottments[sic], but does not give any further description.

If you have any information as to the quality of the land and as to whether or not Mr. Kennedy still owns it, I will be pleased to hear from you.

Also, if you can give me the name of the town in Oklahoma in which W. C. Kohlenberg, Indian Agency, at Sac & Fox Agency, is located, I would be pleased to have you do so.

Very truly yours,
Ida M Kennedy
6122 Princeton Ave.
Chicago, Ill.

By Fleta Kennedy

REFER IN REPLY TO THE FOLLOWING:

Finance.

**DEPARTMENT OF THE INTERIOR,**
**OFFICE OF INDIAN AFFAIRS,**
WASHINGTON.

Claim No. 206062

RECEIVED
Nov 24 1910
SAC & FOX AGENCY
OKLAHOMA.

November 17, 1910.

The Auditor for the Interior Department,

Sir:

The accompanying account of        W. C. Kohlenberg

for      reimbursement of traveling expenses incurred during the 4th quarter 1910 in attending to guardianship matters at Tecumseh, Oklahoma, amounting to $_2.20_      has received administrative examination in this Office and is transmitted to you for settlement. The items allowed are in accordance with contract or have been authorized or approved as required by the Indian Office Regulations.

Payment should be made to        Claimant

Sac & Fox Agency, Oklahoma,

and the expense charged to appropriation

" Contingencies, Indian Department, 1910,"

Very respectfully,

*(Signed) C. F. Hauke*

Copy for information
of Claimant.

Second Assistant Commissioner.

Examiner. HFE.

---

Ex-Judge Fifth Judicial District of Nebraska

**ROBERT WHEELER,**
ATTORNEY AND COUNSELOR
TECUMSEH, OKLA.

In re.
Nah-wah-tahth-ka-ka, case.

TELEPHONE { OFFICE, No. 112
{ RESIDENCE, No. 113

Nov. 19/10.

Hon. Frank A. Thackery,

Shawnee, Okla.

Dear Sir:-

In the matter of the guardianship of Nah-wah-tahth-ka-ka, I am enclosing certified copy of the order confirming sale, and guardian's deed, for your signature and approval.

The total costs in this case were as follows:

| | | |
|---|---|---|
| Court costs, | | $11.00. |
| Advertising sale, | | 4.00. |
| Recording order confirming sale, | | 1.00. |
| My fee, | | 35.00. |
| | Total. | $51.00. |

Mr. John W. Wilson, the purchaser advanced $50. to cover expenses in this case, and out of that I have paid all court costs, advertising and recording, and am satisfied to let the remainder of $34. be in full of my fees.

Yours very truly,
Robert Wheeler

---

Ex-Judge Fifth Judicial District of Nebraska

Telephone { Office, No. 112
Residence, No. 113

ROBERT WHEELER,
Attorney and Counselor
Tecumseh, Okla.
In re.
Guardianship of
Webster W. Alford.          Nov. 22/10.

Hon. Frank A. Thackery,

Shawnee, Okla.

Dear Sir:-

In the matter of the guardianship of Webster W. Alford, the court has issued an order of sale, and I have advertised the sale for Dec. 12, Odle, Edmister & Seymour were appointed appraisers, and I am enclosing an appraisement blank and bond. The bond should be in double the amount of the appraisement, whatever that is.

If you can get these papers back to me before Dec. 12, we can soon have this matter closed up.

Yours very truly,
Robert Wheeler

---

[The letter below typed as given] **R E C E I V E D**

**NOV 30 1910**

Cushing Okla    SAC & FOX AGENCY,
NOKL29HOMA

honor Mr Cohlenberg[sic]

Dear friend

I got a letter from Wm Gray Eyes the other day he wants to Lease me the land that I asked you about some time ago.  will give him $200 two hundred Dollars for the North East 1/4 Sec 13 & 18 & 5 & E and the South East 1/4 Sec 13 & 18 & 5 & E. for the two quarter Sections as the East half of Sec. 13.& 18. 5. E  320 acres  $200

as for the North East 1/4 Sec 13 & 18 & 5 160 acres $150. one hundred and fifty Dollars, for a 3 year Lease. I want a 3 year Lease. I do not want to Build a house. an the land I want it first as it is.

P S   that is all it is worth $200 for the half section, if you want to let me have it for that fix up Lease Papers and send them to me or let me know about it, if I will get Lease or not.

P S  I think the Indian wants $300 but that is to much I want to Pay for what I get and I dont want to give to much so I cant make it

                    Yours truly
              J W Hemmer
      Box 42        Cushing
                    Okla

---

Ex-Judge Fifth Judicial District of Nebraska

**Robert Wheeler,**
Attorney and Counselor
Tecumseh, Okla.

Telephone { Office, No. 112 / Residence, No. 113

                In re.
        Ketch-che-quah.

                          Dec. 2/10.

Hon. Frank A. Thackery,

    Shawnee, Okla.

Dear Sir:-

In the matter of the guardianship of Ketch-che-quah, the court made an order today for your appointment as guardian, and fixed the bond at $250.

I am enclosin[sic] a bond, and as soon as the same is executed and returned to me I will prepare a petition for the sale of the minor's interest in the land.

Yours very truly,
Robert Wheeler

\*\*\*\*\*\*\*\*\*\*

EX-JUDGE FIFTH JUDICIAL DISTRICT OF NEBRASKA                    TELEPHONE     { OFFICE, No. 112
                                                                             { RESIDENCE, No. 113

**ROBERT WHEELER,**
ATTORNEY AND COUNSELOR
TECUMSEH, OKLA.
          In re.
     Ketch-che-quah.
       matter.                          Dec. 16/10.

Hon. Frank A. Thackery,

Shawnee, Okla.

Dear Sir:-

In the matter of the guardianship of Ketch-che-quah, your bond as guardian was approved on the 14, inst. and letter of guardianship issued.  I now enclose a petition for the sale of the minor's interest in the land and two copies of a waiver.

As soon as these papers can be completed and returned to me I will get an order of sale, and have the appraisers appointed.

Yours very truly,
Robert Wheeler

\*\*\*\*\*\*\*\*\*\*

EX-JUDGE FIFTH JUDICIAL DISTRICT OF NEBRASKA                    TELEPHONE     { OFFICE, No. 112
                                                                             { RESIDENCE, No. 113

**ROBERT WHEELER,**
ATTORNEY AND COUNSELOR
TECUMSEH, OKLA.
          In re.
     Ketch-che-quah.
       matter.                          Dec. 19/10.

Hon. Frank A. Thackery,

Shawnee, Okla.

Dear Sir:-

Your favor of the 17 inst, received, enclosing petition in the guardianship matter of Ketch-che-quah, and two copies of a waiver, with the suggestion that I sign the waiver for the other heirs if I can do so legally. But as neither you or I can legally sign the waiver for the other heirs without a written power of attorney, I am returning the same.

If the other heirs, Wah-pah-ho-ho, Qua-to-quah, Tah-pah-hah, Ko-nah-pah-pi-uk and Mah-tush-qua live in the same settlement it will only be necessary to send one copy of the waiver. If they sign by mark have two witnesses sign who can write. I would also like for the minor to sign the waiver, if it is convenient.

If it is going to be very difficult to get the signatures to the waiver I can get service by publication, which will cost about $5.

Yours very truly,<br>
Robert Wheeler

**********

EX-JUDGE FIFTH JUDICIAL DISTRICT OF NEBRASKA          TELEPHONE          { OFFICE, NO. 112
                                                                         { RESIDENCE, NO. 113

**ROBERT WHEELER,**
ATTORNEY AND COUNSELOR
TECUMSEH, OKLA.

Nov. 9/10.

Hon. Frank A. Thackery,

    Shawnee, Okla.

Dear Sir:-

In the matter of the guardianship of Ketch-che-quah, your letter of the 8, inst. received, enclosing a written request by the minor for your appointment as guardian. But as the request does not fully comply with the law, I am enclosing an application for you to sign. Full in the blanks as to property and rents, and then execute and return the same to me, and I will then file it and the written request of the minor.

This will be more expeditious than to wait for the minor to sign the proper petition for your appointment.

Yours very truly,<br>
Robert Wheeler

\*\*\*\*\*\*\*\*\*\*

HENRY G PENNIMAN PRESIDENT

ROBERT A DOBBIN JR SECRETARY

United Surety Company

HOME OFFICE. BALTIMORE.MD.

PLATE GLASS, PERSONAL ACCIDENT & HEALTH

BEADLES & LAUX,
GENERAL AGENTS.
LEE BUILDING

OKLAHOMA CITY, OKLAHOMA,   Dec 6th 1910.

Frank A. Thackery, Indian Agent,

Shawnee, Okla.

Dear Sir:-

Re:- Bond--$250.00 Ketch-che-quah.

Enclosed the above bond duly executed as per your request of the 5th inst.,

Yours very truly,

Beadles & Laux

---

BEADLES & LAUX

GENERAL  INSURANCE
SURETY BONDS
TITLES GUARANTEED

OKLAHOMA CITY ____ Dec. 14th, ____ 191 0.

Mr. Frank A. Thackery,

U. S. Indian Agent,

Shawnee, Okla.

Dear Sir:-

RE BONDS -

We beg to acknowledge receipt of your check covering the following bonds: -

$100,   Sale bond   Nah-Wah-Tahta-Ka-Ka   -   $2.00
625,     "     "     Ke-No-Che-Peh-Wah-Se  -    3.50
2400,   Guardians Bond, Henry, Annie& Gertrude Star -   $8.00

We also enclose you original and duplicate receipts to cover the above.

Yours truly,

Beadles & Laux

L-T                                                         General Agents.

---

REFER IN REPLY TO THE FOLLOWING:                            ADDRESS ONLY THE
Finance                                                     COMMISSIONER OF INDIAN AFFAIRS
97975/1910          **DEPARTMENT OF THE INTERIOR,**
A.W.C.                   **OFFICE OF INDIAN AFFAIRS,**
                              WASHINGTON,
Handling funds                                DEC 20 1910
of minors.

Mr. F. A. Thackery, Superintendent,

Indian School, Shawnee, Oklahoma.

Sir:

In reply to your letter of the 9th instant, with reference to the manner of handling funds of certain minors which you have in charge in the capacity of guardian, you are advised that these funds may be taken up in your account and held in trust by you as Superintendent and Special Disbursing Agent, provided the Indians are willing for you to do so, and provided, further, that the court under whose jurisdiction the matter comes is willing to discharge you from all responsibility as guardian upon your taking up the funds and becoming responsible for them in your official capacity as Superintendent and Special Disbursing Agent.

When this money was paid to you as guardian for the minor Indians, the Government was relieved of its trust in the matter, and upon your retirement as guardian you must make settlement with the Indian, to his satisfaction, and to the satisfaction of the court having jurisdiction.

Very respectfully,

CF Hauke
Second Assistant Commissioner.

Wx - 17.

---

BEADLES & LAUX

GENERAL  INSURANCE
SURETY  BONDS
TITLES GUARANTEED

OKLAHOMA CITY   Dec. 21st,         191 0.

Mr. Frank A. Thackery,
     Indian Agent,
          Shawnee, Okla.

Dear Sir:-

        We beg to advise you that the premium for the ensuing year is due on the following bonds and, as per your statement to our Mr. Laux while at the agency checking up the accounts that future payments would be made without delay, and desiring to close our books for the year, we will appreciate very much receiving your check for the following bonds, which are now due.:

| | |
|---|---|
| Pea-Manski, et al | $2.00 |
| Met-E-Nak, et al | 2.00 |
| Ah-Kah-Tah-She, et al | 3.50 |
| Pem-Ma-Ha-Ka-Quah | 2.00 |
| Ta-Pa-She | 2.00 |
| Ah-She-Pah-Kah-The-Ah | 8.50 |
| Albert Deere, et al | 6.00 |
| Chas. Baron | 1.75 |
| Laura Sah-Ah-Peah | 8.00 |
| Louis Bouschair, et al | 2.13 |
| Jesse & Ethel Haas | 3.50 |
| Bessie Hale, et al | 6.00 |
| Chas. Whipple, et al | 2.00 |
| Peah-Puck-Oh-He | 1.00 |
| Jno. Neah-Que-Ke-Nock | 1.00 |
| Betsy Little Captain, et al | 2.00 |
| Joseph Nona | 7.00 |
| Pe-Ah-Puck-She | 2.00 |
| Jno. Mosh-Que-Ka-Nock | 2.00 |
| TOTAL Dec. Premiums - | $64.38 |

The following premiums are past due, as follows:

| | | |
|---|---|---|
| Mark Charles, et al | (November) | $3.50 |
| Pe-Mi-Min-Se, et al | (October) | 2.00 |
| Nellie Ford,   et al | (November) | 3.50 |
| Stephen Pensoneau | (October) | 6.00 |
| | | 15.00 |

Kindly verify the above with your books and send us check, as requested.

Yours very truly,

Beadles & Laux

General Agents.

L-T

**********

BEADLES & LAUX

GENERAL   INSURANCE
SURETY   BONDS
TITLES GUARANTEED

RECEIVED
DEC 23 1910
SAC & FOX AGENCY,
OKLAHOMA.

OKLAHOMA CITY,   Dec. 21st,   191 0.

Mr. W. C. Kohlenberg,

Indian Agt. Sac & Fox Agency,

Oklahoma.

Dear Sir:-

Owing to the fact that we desire to close our books by the first of January, we again request you to send us your check for all unpaid Indian Guardian and sale bonds executed for you by Mr. L. N. Beadles.

We will appreciate your giving this your prompt attention.

Yours truly,

Beadles & Laux

L-T

General Agents.

**********

L. H. BEADLES

FRANK LAUX

## BEADLES & LAUX

GENERAL  INSURANCE
S U R E T Y  B O N D S
TITLES GUARANTEED

BOOK GIVEN BUILDING
PHONE 4075

OKLAHOMA CITY,  Dec. 24th,  191 0.

Mr. Frank A. Thackery,

      Indian Agent,

           Shawnee, Okla.

Dear Sir:-

      We herewith enclose you[sic] check submitted by you to us in payment for bond of Nah-Nah-That-Ka-Ka, amount $2.00.

      This check was returned by the First National Bank, Tecumseh for the reason that the same was not approved by the Disbursing officer.  Kindly approve check and return to us.

             Yours truly,

             Beadles & Laux

L-T

             General Agents.

---

Cushing Okla

      Dec. 26, 1910

Mr. W. C. Kohlenberg

      Sac-Fox Agency.

Dear Sir

RECEIVED DEC 28 1910 SAC & FOX AGENCY OKLAHOMA

      Inclosed you will find a Draft for Amount of One Hundred Dollars to pay my Leas Payment on the Jerome Wolf.

Place the N.E. 1/4 - Sec 4, Tw 17, R. 6

& Also a Draft Amount of $17 1/2 Seventeen Dollars & half to pay my lease payment on the Ada Stubble Lease  S.E. qr of Sec 4-Tw 17-R. 6

      H.O. Hetherington

          Cushing

R.R. 4, Box 32          Okla.

Tecumseh, Okla.
R. #2,  Box 103,        Jan. 18, 1910.
Mr. F.A. Thackery
Shawnee, Okla.

Mr Guardian:

In my letter I will say again that "I would like for you to send me $25.00," as I have'nt had any money which I have in your office since March 12th 1910. And I have'nt got time to come up there.

I am clearing here for Annie Pecan and am too busy to come. You are to be able to send me this much any how. Will not ask you again for long time. please

Your Friend
Victor Sloan

---

EX-JUDGE FIFTH JUDICIAL DISTRICT OF NEBRASKA                    TELEPHONE        { OFFICE, No. 112
                                                                                { RESIDENCE, No. 113

**ROBERT WHEELER,**
**ATTORNEY AND COUNSELOR**
**TECUMSEH, OKLA.**        In Alford case.

Jan. 21/11.

Hon. Frank A. Thackery,

Shawnee, Okla.

Dear Sir:

In the matter of the guardianship of Webster W. Alford, I am enclosing a certified copy of the order confirming sale and the guardian's deed, for your signature.

Yours very truly,
Robert Wheeler

**********

EX-JUDGE FIFTH JUDICIAL DISTRICT OF NEBRASKA                    TELEPHONE        { OFFICE, No. 112
                                                                                { RESIDENCE, No. 113

**ROBERT WHEELER,**
**ATTORNEY AND COUNSELOR**
**TECUMSEH, OKLA.**        In re. Webster W. Alford
                          matter.
                                                Dec. 12/10.

Hon. Frank A. Thackery,

Shawnee, Okla.

Dear Sir:-

In the matter of the guardianship of Webster W. Alford, I am enclosing bid and report of sale. As soon as the same is executed by you and returned to me I will get an order of court fixing the date for hearing on confirmation.

Yours very truly
Robert Wheeler

**********

Ex-Judge Fifth Judicial District of Nebraska                    TELEPHONE          { OFFICE, No. 112
                                                                                   { RESIDENCE, No. 113

ROBERT WHEELER,
ATTORNEY AND COUNSELOR
TECUMSEH, OKLA.

Sept. 16/10.

Hon. Frank A. Thackery,

Shawnee, Okla.

Dear Sir:-

In the matter of the guardianship of Webster W. Alford, I am enclosing a petition for the sale of the one acre for school house site, and a waiver of notice.

If you will sign the waiver and have the boy's father and mother, if living, sign it, and such adult, near king as it is convenient to get, and then return it and the petition you me, I will proceed to get the district a title to the land. Mr. Hyde says the district will pay all expense.

Yours very truly,
Robert Wheeler

Ex-Judge Fifth Judicial District of Nebraska                    TELEPHONE          { OFFICE, No. 112
                                                                                   { RESIDENCE, No. 113

ROBERT WHEELER,
ATTORNEY AND COUNSELOR
TECUMSEH, OKLA.     In Ketch-che-quah case.

Jan. 30/11.

Hon. Frank A. Thackery,

Shawnee, Okla.

Dear Sir:-

In the matter of the guardianship of Ketch-che-quah, your favor of the 28, inst. received, enclosing waiver of notice. I filed the same today, together with the petition, and the court issued the order of sale, fixed the bond at double the amount of appraisement, whatever that may be, and appointed James H. Odle, Charles W. Edmister and W. H. Seymour as appraisers.

I am enclosing blanks for appraisement and bond.

Yours very truly,
Robert Wheeler

---

**DEPARTMENT OF THE INTERIOR**   RECEIVED
FEB 27 1911

UNITED STATES INDIAN FIELD SERVICE   SAC & FOX AGENCY,

Sac and Fox Indian Agency, OKLAHOMA.

RFD 2, Stroud, Okla., Feb. 1, 1911.

Hon. P. D. Mitchell,

Stillwater, Okla.

Dear sir,-

Referring to the administration in the guardianship case of Harvey Madison, regarding which we spoke a short time ago, will you kindly look the matter up and inform me what is necessary to be done? I should like to settle this matter, as well as the case of Silas Hawk, as soon as possible. I inclose herewith a claim by Bettie Groinhorn for $600.00. I have not signed or approved this, as I am doubtful as to the justice of such an amount.

Thanking you for your attention, I am,

Very respectfully,

W.C. Kohlenberg
WCK/RS                         Supt. & Spl. Disb. Agt.


Above letter just reached me, am unable to tell just what is necessary from records -
When in Stillwater next call on me

W.H. Wilcox  Co J.

Ex-Judge Fifth Judicial District of Nebraska          TELEPHONE          { OFFICE, No. 112
                                                                         { RESIDENCE, No. 113

**ROBERT WHEELER,**
ATTORNEY AND COUNSELOR
TECUMSEH, OKLA.     In Nah-wah-tahth-ka-ka.

Febr. 13/11.

Hon. Frank A. Thackery,

Shawnee, Okla.

Dear Sir:-

In the matter of the guardianship of Nah-wah-tahth-ka-ka, I mailed you a letter today in answer to your letter of the 11, inst. and wish to say, that so far as my fees are concerned in the case I will be satisfied with whatever you suggest, and in no event will I accept any fees if to do so will in any way embarrass you.

As you will see by my letter, I am clearly of the opinion that Willie Gibson is an heir, and that our proceeding in the matter were right and proper.

Yours very truly.
Robert Wheeler

\* \* \* \* \* \* \* \* \* \*

Ex-Judge Fifth Judicial District of Nebraska          TELEPHONE          { OFFICE, No. 112
                                                                         { RESIDENCE, No. 113

**ROBERT WHEELER,**
ATTORNEY AND COUNSELOR
TECUMSEH, OKLA.     In  guardianship of
        Nah-wah-tahth-ka-ka.      Febr. 13/11.

Hon. Frank A. Thackery,

Shawnee, Okla.

Dear Sir:-

Your favor of the 11, inst. received, also a copy of the letter of Hon. C. F. Hauke, Second Assistant Commissioner under date of the 4, inst. concerning the sale of the Jim Charley, Absentee Shawnee, allottee No. 497.

Replying to the same would say, the Honorable Commissioners letter raises an interesting question.  Interesting for the reason that it is very difficult, if not impossible to know just what the legislature meant by the statute quoted. However the section is not correctly quoted in the letter.  It reads "unless the inheritance come to the intestate &c", not "came".

This section was considered by the court April 11, 1910, the time the order of sale was issued finding that Willie Gibson or Nah-wah-tahth-ka-ka was an heir of his half brother, Samuel Charley. And the court was clearly of the opinion that he was such heir, and made and entered an order accordingly: which order has not been appealed from, and I do not know of any proceedure[sic] by which the same can be set aside and vacated at this late day.

Aside from this I am clearly of the opinion that Willie Gibson is entitled to the interest found in his favor by the court. By the law of descent, the moment Jim Charley died in 1894 his property vested in and became the property of his widow and two children as absolutely as if the same had been conveyed to them by deed. And if it had been personal property, commingled with other property of the heirs, or had been converted into cas/[sic], I think no question could have been raised on the death of Samuel Charley as to the right of Willie Gibson to a part of his property. Just what the legislature meant, it is difficult for us to gather from the statute, and equally difficult to fit the statute into a supposed case where it will seem reasonable and consistent. The statute says "inheritance come to the intestate", and in this way have it fit with reasonable certainty into the general law of inheritance.

But as to the case being considered, there is uncertainty as to whether Willie Gibson is entitled to share in the property or not. Our Supreme Court has not construed the section quoted, And for us to say that he is not an heir, and sell the land without conveying his interest, if he has any, will be to place a cloud on the title and lessen the market value of the land for more than ten years to come. In my opinion it would be very difficult to sell the land without conveying the boy's interest, or supposed interest.

Aside from all this, the other heirs are of adult age: they knew if the court proceedings, and the claim that Willie Gibson was entitled to a 1/9 interest in the proceeds, amounting to $36.12, and they did not object or appeal from the decision of the court within the time when an appeal could have been taken, and in fact acquiessed[sic] in the whole proceeding, and I believe, are at this time perfectly satisfied.

If with this explanation of the situation the Hon. Commissioner is not willing to approve the sale, please let me know what steps he suggests, and I will be glad to do anything in my power to place the matter in a shape that will meet the approval of the Department.

Yours very truly,
Robert Wheeler

---

American Surety Company
of New York.

H. G. Lyman,
President.

LOCAL BOARD
JOHN THREADGILL, REG. VICE PRES.
D. W. HOGAN                    J. L. WILKIN
BD. L. DUNN
WM. F. WILSON, ATTORNEY
ADDRESS COMMUNICATIONS TO
HERMAN J. ROLEKE, MANAGER

BRANCH OFFICE FOR THE STATE OF OKLAHOMA
401-2-3-4 MAJESTIC BUILDING
TELEPHONE 1791

Home Office Building

HJR-B        OKLAHOMA CITY. OKLA.     Feb. 15, 1911.

Mr. Frank A. Thackery,
    Superintendent & Special Disbursing Agent,
        U. S. Indian Agency,
            Shawnee, Oklahoma.
Dear Sir:--

If I remember rightly, you are acting as guardian for quite a number of Indian minors under the regulations of the Department. In this connection you are filing bonds with the County Courts that appointed you. Will you be good enough and advise me what premium you are paying on these bonds? I presume you have a surety company acting as your surety. I should like to know what the rate is pre thousand per annum, whether there is an annual minimum for small bonds, and whether any reduction is allowed on second and subsequent years' premiums.

I assure you that your reply will be much appreciated.

Very truly yours,
Herman J Roleke
Manager.

---

Thos. M. Walker, *President*

Wm. T. Kemper, *Treasurer*

James Van Buren, *Vice President*   H. P. Jones, *Ass't Secretary*
John R. Mulvane, *Vice President*   Jo Luch Miller, III, *Ass't Secretary*
J. L. Miller, Jr., *Vice President*   E. Sanford Miller, *Ass't Secretary*

**Globe Surety Company**
*of Kansas City, Missouri*
*Capital $500,000.00*
*Surplus $100,000.00*

**BEADLES & LAUX**
SUITE 236 LEE BUILDING
GENERAL AGENTS
HIGHLEY & MILLS, ATTORNEYS
A. J. McCARTHY, ASSOCIATE ATTY.
H, M. SCALES, RES. VICE PRES.
CHAS. M. BOSWORTH, RES VICE PRES.

OKLAHOMA CITY, OKLAHOMA
Feb. 21st, 1911.

Hon. Frank A. Thackery,

Indian Agent,

Shawnee, Okla.

Dear Sir:-

We herewith enclose you Guardian's Sale Bond executed in behalf of Sophia Anderson, in favor of Ross F. Lockridge in the sum of $1616.16. The premium on this bond is $6.00.

Yours truly,
Beadles & Laux
L-T                                    General Agents.

---

COURT TERMS.
———
GUTHRIE-First Monday in January.
OKLAHOMA CITY-First Monday in March.
WOODARD-First Monday in May and
    second Monday in November.
ENID-First Monday in June.
LAWTON-First Monday in October.

**Department of Justice.**
———

**Office of the United States Attorney.**
Western District of Oklahoma.
Guthrie.

February 22, 1911.

Frank A. Thackery,
        Supt. & Spl. Disb. Agent,
            Shawnee, Oklahoma.

Dear Sir:

Herewith we enclose a letter from Bonds & Howard, lawyers, Claremore, Oklahoma, relative to the guardianship of Charley and Nathan Whipple, whose father was given an allotment by Kickapoo

84

Indians, and who has since died and the land sold through your agency; H. C. French being the guardian of said children.

You can give the letter such consideration and reply as you consider proper. I am advising them that the letter has been referred to you.

Very respectfully,

Isaac D. Taylor
Assistant U. S. Attorney.

Enclosure.
JRP.

---

COURT TERMS.

GUTHRIE-First Monday in January.
OKLAHOMA CITY-First Monday in March.
WOODARD-First Monday in May and
    second Monday in November.
ENID-First Monday in June.
LAWTON-First Monday in October.

**Department of Justice.**

**Office of the United States Attorney.**
Western District of Oklahoma.
Guthrie.

March 1, 1911.

Frank A. Thackery,
    Supt. & Spcl. Disb. Agent,
        Shawnee, Oklahoma.

Dear Sir:

Herewith I enclose exceptions in the guardianship matter of Wa-pe-co-me, L. C. Grimes, guardian, directed at his accounts filed therein.

Please sign the same and file at once with the County Judge at Tecumseh, and notify me of the date set for the hearing on said final report of the guardian and these exceptions.

I am sending a copy to Mr. Roleke, State agent for the American Surety Company.

Please suggest to the Judge that we would like for the matter to come up as soon as possible, but, of course, after the notice has been given, which the law requires, to all persons interested.

Kindly keep me advised in regard to this matter. I also enclose copy for your use.

I enclose the files in this case, which please return to the County Judge when you file the exceptions, and please see that my receipt for these files given the last time I was at your agency, is cancelled.

Very respectfully,

Enclosures
AB

Isaac D. Taylor<br>Assistant U.S. Attorney.

**********

Guthrie OK.  Mar 9-11

Frank A. Thackery, Supt.
    Shawnee, OK.
Dear Sir:-

Did the County Court set a date for hearing on final report of L. C. Grimes, gdn. of Wa-pe-come.[sic]  If so, please let me know the date, if not, please urge the Court to set the matter for some date.

Yours truly<br>Isaac D. Taylor<br>Asst. U.S. Atty.

---

[Copy of Original]

OKLAHOMA CITY, OKLA.

IN ACCOUNT WITH

## BEADLES & LAUX
GENERAL INSURANCE
SURETY BONDS
TITLE GUARANTEED

LEE BUILDING        PHONE 4658

| DATE | POLICY NO. | COMPANY | PROPERTY | TERM | RATE | AMOUNT | PREMIUM |
|------|-----------|---------|----------|------|------|--------|---------|
| | | | | | | | |

Ex-Judge Fifth Judicial District of Nebraska

TELEPHONE { OFFICE, No. 112
RESIDENCE, No. 113

**ROBERT WHEELER,**
ATTORNEY AND COUNSELOR
TECUMSEH, OKLA.

Ketch-che-quah case.

Mar. 23/11.

Hon. Frank A. Thackery,

Shawnee, Okla.

Dear Sir:-

In the matter of the guardianship of Ketch-che-quah, I am enclosing report of sale to be executed by you, and as soon as returend[sic] to me I will have the matter set for hearing on confirmation

Yours very truly,
Robert Wheeler

---

Ex-Judge Fifth Judicial District of Nebraska

TELEPHONE { OFFICE, No. 112
RESIDENCE, No. 113

**ROBERT WHEELER,**
ATTORNEY AND COUNSELOR
TECUMSEH, OKLA.

Thomas Brown et als.

Mar. 23/11.

Hon. W. C. Kohlenberg,

Sac and Fox, Okla.

Dear Sir:-

Your favor of the 17, inst received in due time, enclosing your application for appointment as guardian of the Brown children. As soon after as I could get the court's attention, which was this morning, I presented the matter and the order was made for your appointment, and you bond fixed at $2000.

As soon as the bond which I enclose is filled and returned to me I will file the same and have letters of guardianship issue to you.

I wish you would send me the dates when Thomas and Agnes Long died, and a complete list of the heirs left be[sic] each, and their relationship, as I want the petition, when I prepare it to show a complete chain of title to the property. I consider this important, especially if there has not been any administration of the estate.

The judge did not say anything about a deposit for costs, but his custom is to ask for a deposit of $10. And if it is convenient you might send me that amount when you return the bond.

Yours very truly,<br>
Robert Wheeler

---

Ex-Judge Fifth Judicial District of Nebraska

**ROBERT WHEELER,**
ATTORNEY AND COUNSELOR
TECUMSEH, OKLA.

TELEPHONE { OFFICE, No. 112 / RESIDENCE, No. 113

Mar. 24/11.

Hon. Frank A. Thackery,

Shawnee, Okla.

Dear Sir:-

Your favor of the 23, inst. received, directing me to proceed to sell the interest of the minors in the allotments of John Gibson and Tay-lah-mah. And in order for me to draw the petition, it will be necessary for you to give me the date of the death of John Gibson as nearly as possible, and the name of parents, if living at the time of his death, and the names of all brothers and sisters living at that time.

Also the names of all brothers and sisters and their husbands or wives who died either prior or subsequent to John Gibson, and left children, and the names of the children of each, so that I can show by my petition the exact line of descent to each heir. It is not enough to give a name and allege that such a one is a nephew or niece, and especially is this true where the heirship of each has not been fixed by a decree of court in an administration of the estate.

Also give me the date of the death of Tay-lah-mah, and advise me whether she died without leaving a husband or issue.

Yours very truly,<br>
Robert Wheeler

---

Ex-Judge Fifth Judicial District of Nebraska

TELEPHONE { OFFICE, No. 112
RESIDENCE, No. 113

**ROBERT WHEELER,**
ATTORNEY AND COUNSELOR
TECUMSEH, OKLA.

Nah-wah-tahth-ka-ka et al.                Mar. 29/11.

Hon. Frank A. Thackery,

Shawnee, Okla.

Dear Sir:-

In the matter of the guardianship of Nah-wah-tahth-ka-ka and Ma-tahth-ka-ka, I am enclosing you a petition for them as heirs of John Gibson, and a petition for them as heirs of Tay-la-mah, and three copies of a waiver in each case, to be signed by yourself and the heirs. I have made the extra copies so as to facilitate matters if they are living in widely separated localities.

I thought at first that I would only prepare one petition for the sale of both allotments, but I decided that that was not advisble[sic]; that as they were separate allotments, to proceed in that way, the record in each allotment would always confuse and encumber the record in the other, and then some circumstance might arise as to one allotment that would defeat the sale and confirmation of both. One thing is, the department may decide that Lizzie and Mary Coffee pot are not heirs in the John Gibson allotment. I am clearly of the opinion that they are heirs but there is room for difference of opinion as to them.

If you do not think the way I have proceeded advisable, write me.

Yours very truly,
Robert Wheeler

**********

Ex-Judge Fifth Judicial District of Nebraska

TELEPHONE { OFFICE, No. 112
RESIDENCE, No. 113

**ROBERT WHEELER,**
ATTORNEY AND COUNSELOR
TECUMSEH, OKLA.

Nah-wah-tahth-ka-ka et al.                Apr. 1/11.

Hon. Frank A. Thackery,

Shawnee, Okla.

Dear Sir:-

Your letter 31, ult. received, enclosing petitions in the Nah-wah-tahth-ka-ka et al matter, for correction.  In preparing a genealogical table of the family from the data given in your letter of the 25, ult. I made the mistake of writing 1890 instead of 1900, as you gave it, as the date of the death of Ke-so-wah-lay-mah.

I have rewritten a part of each petition, and believe I now have them right, and I am enclosing them for your signature.

Yours very truly,
Robert Wheeler

********

EX-JUDGE FIFTH JUDICIAL DISTRICT OF NEBRASKA

TELEPHONE { OFFICE, No. 112
RESIDENCE, No. 113

**ROBERT WHEELER,**
ATTORNEY AND COUNSELOR
TECUMSEH, OKLA.

Nah-wah-tahth-ka-ka et al.

Apr. 5/11.

Hon. Frank A. Thackery,

Shawnee, Okla.

Dear Sir:-

In the matter of the guardianship of Nah-wah-tahth-ka-ka et al. I am enclosing two petition[sic] for the sale of real estate, that I believe are absolutely correct.  Sorry I put you to the treouble of returning them to me.

Yours very truly,
Robert Wheeler

---

COURT TERMS.

GUTHRIE-First Monday in January.
OKLAHOMA CITY-First Monday in March.
WOODARD-First Monday in May and
    second Monday in November.
ENID-First Monday in June.
LAWTON-First Monday in October.

**Department of Justice.**
—
**Office of the United States Attorney.**
**Western District of Oklahoma.**
Guthrie.

April 5, 1911.

W. C. Kohlenberg,
        Supt. & Spcl. Disb. Agent,
                Stroud, Okla.

Dear Sir:

A few days ago I stopped at Chandler and talked with Col. Roy Hoffman in regard to the Moore guardianship cases.  He informed me that they had settled with Albert Moore and had his release, and that he was perfectly satisfied with the settlement.

I inquired of him whether his clients would be willing to pay any balance due in the Ruth Moore case provided you were able to procure authority to apply the funds of Samuel Moore, the guardian, upon the amount due Ruth Moore, his ward. I told him I did'nt[sic] know whether this could be done or not, but that I would take the matter up with you and that I thought that if Samuel Moore's funds could be used there would not be a very large balance for the defendant bondsman to pay.

Will you kindly advise me what amount you think might be used from the funds of Samuel Moore for this purpose, and also advise me whether you can procure such authority.

Of course if Samuel Moore has funds that can be used, we believe it proper that they should be used, as he is liable in the case.

Col. Hoffman stated that he thought the matter could be settled if this could be done and the balance was not too large.

Very respectfully,

AB

Isaac D. Taylor
Assistant U.S. Attorney.

---

U.S. INDIAN AGENCY
RECEIVED
APR 16 1908

Ans_____ Vol_____ P_____
SHAWNEE, OKLA.

LAW OFFICES
OF
NORVELL & LEAGUE

TULSA, OKLA.     April 11,     1908

Hon. Frank Thackery,
    U.S. Indian Agent,
    Shawnee, Okla.

Dear Sir:-

I send herein certified copy of guardianship papers showing my appointment as guardian of Beatrice Tiblow, according to direction by yuo[sic] and ask that you foward[sic] to me the amount of money remaining unpaid.

Very respectfully,

Sam Charley

---

COURT TERMS.

Guthrie-First Monday in January.
Oklahoma City-First Monday in March.
Woodard-First Monday in May and
    second Monday in November.
Enid-First Monday in June.
Lawton-First Monday in October.

Department of Justice RECEIVED

APR 15 1911

Office of the United States Attorney
Western District of Oklahoma.
Guthrie.

SAC & FOX AGENCY, OKLAHOMA

April 14, 1911.

W. C. Kohlenberg,
    Supt. & Spcl. Disb. Agent,
        Stroud, Okla.

Dear Sir:

Yours of the 10th instant relative to the Moore guardianship cases received and contents noted.

Relative to the guardianship of Ruth Moore, I believe that you will be able to effect settlement in the manner suggested, and I believe it would be well for you to go to Chandler as soon as possible and take up the matter with Mr. Hoffman and the sureties and see if you cannot get an agreement out of them. The amount that they have on hand in the Ruth Moore case, together with the amount of $200. which you think could be appropriated from the funds of Samuel Moore, would leave a balance which I think they would be willing to pay to dispose of the case.

Please let me know whether you will take the matter up with them at once, and, if so, the result of such action.

Very respectfully,

AB

Isaac D. Taylor
Assistant U.S. Attorney.

---

Ex-Judge Fifth Judicial District of Nebraska          TELEPHONE { OFFICE, No. 112
                                                                  RESIDENCE, No. 113

ROBERT WHEELER,
ATTORNEY AND COUNSELOR
TECUMSEH, OKLA.

Arthur Rolette et al.                              Apr. 19/11.

Hon. Frank A. Thackery,

　　　Shawnee, Okla.

Dear Sir:-

　　　Replying to your favor of the 18, inst. concerning the guardianship case in the Jim Holden attotment[sic] matter, would say:  that on Nov. 19/10 I wrote James H. Odle, guardians, as follows:

　　　"In the matter of the guardianship of Arthur Rolette et al. I am enclosing a waiver of notice.  Please sign the same as guardian, and have Hattie Rolette, William Bolden, Che-tah-wah-pea-se sign the same, and then return to me."

　　　The waiver has not been signed and returned to me, but as soon as it is I will forward the petition for Mr. Odles[sic] signature, and proceed at once with the sale of the minor's interests.

　　　I am enclosing you a copy of the waiver, and if the other has not been signed, you can have this signed and return to me.

　　　　　　　　　Yours very truly,
　　　　　　　　　Robert Wheeler

---

W. H. WILCOX, COUNTY JUDGE.                    DATUS E. SATER, COURT STENOGRAPHER.

## STATE OF OKLAHOMA, PAYNE COUNTY

OFFICE OF COUNTY JUDGE

STILLWATER, OKLAHOMA.

April 20, 1911

Mr. W. C. Kohlenberg,

Dear Sir:

　　　On making an investigation of our Guardian's records in this office, I discovered that you have failed to make any report since your applintment[sic] as Guardian of Rachael Hall.  Kindly file your report at any early day as I am trying to put our Guardian's rec0rds[sic] in better shape.

Respectfully,

WHW/WHS                              W. H. Wilcox

---

W. H. WILCOX, COUNTY JUDGE.                                    DATE EASATER, COURT STENOGRAPHER.

## STATE OF OKLAHOMA, PAYNE COUNTY
### OFFICE OF COUNTY JUDGE
STILLWATER, OKLAHOMA.

RECEIVED
APR 21  1911
SAC & FOX AGENCY,
OKLAHOMA.

April 20, 1911

Mr. W. C. Kohlenberg,

Dear Sir:

I beg to call your attention to the fact that the guardian's record in this office fails to show any report from you as the guardian of Maude Kakaque since your appointment in 1909.

Kindly give this matter your early attention.  I enclose form for your services.

Respectfully,

WHW/WHS                              W. H. Wilcox

---

EX-JUDGE FIFTH JUDICIAL DISTRICT OF NEBRASKA            TELEPHONE {  OFFICE, NO. 112
                                                                      RESIDENCE, NO. 113

### ROBERT WHEELER,
ATTORNEY AND COUNSELOR
TECUMSEH, OKLA.
                    Ketch-che-quah case.                    Apr. 22/11.

Hon. Frank A. Thackery,

Shawnee, Okla.

Dear Sir:-

In the matter of the guardianship of Kerch-che-quah[sic], I am enclosing certified and recorded copy of the order confirming sale and a guardian's to be executed by you.

The costs in this case are as follows:

| | |
|---|---|
| Court costs, | $17.25. |
| Pd. Co. Democrat, Advertising, | 4.00. |
| Pd. Register of Deeds, Recording, | 1.00 |
| My fee, | 35.00 |
| Total, | $57.25. |
| Advanced by Samuel M. Truss, purchaser, | 50.00. |
| Bal. due on Court Costs, | $7.25. |

Yours very truly,
Robert Wheeler

---

Ex-Judge Fifth Judicial District of Nebraska

ROBERT WHEELER,
ATTORNEY AND COUNSELOR
TECUMSEH, OKLA.

TELEPHONE    { OFFICE, No. 112
{ RESIDENCE, No. 113

In re.  Ah-che-tha-quah.                    Sept. 13/11.

Hon. J. A. Buntin,

Shawnee, Okla.

Dear Sir:

In the matter of the guardianship of Ah-che-tha-quah, et al. I am enclosing certified copy of the order confirming sale, and a guardian's deed to be executed by James H. Odle, the guardian.

The costs in this case are as follows:

| | |
|---|---|
| Court costs, | $10.95. |
| Advertising, | 4.00. |
| Recording, | 1.00. |
| My fee, | 35.00. |
| Total, | $50.95. |

Mr. Henry Baade the purchaser, advanced $50. to cover costs and expenses in this case, the same to be repaid to him out of the purchase money when the sale is approved. At the time he advanced this money I deposited $10. with the clerk of the county court to cover court costs, but this was not quite enough, and there is still .95¢ due on court costs.

Yours very truly,
Robert Wheeler

---

Ex-Judge Fifth Judicial District of Nebraska                    Telephone { Office, No. 112
                                                                            Residence, No. 113

ROBERT WHEELER,
ATTORNEY AND COUNSELOR
TECUMSEH, OKLA.
In re. Ketch-che-quah &
Ah-che-tha-quah.

May 15/12/[sic]

Hon. J. A. Buntin,

Shawnee, Okla.

Dear Sir:-

Your favor of the 14, inst. received, with enclosures as state, in payment of balance due in the following cases.

In sale of allotment of Mah-tah-wah; probate proceedings in behalf of Ketch-che-quah, minor heir.                                  $7.25.

In I-nesh-kin land sale, Ah-che-tha-quahet al, minors,        .95.

Total,                     $8.20.

Yours very truly,
Robert Wheeler

---

W. H. WILCOX, COUNTY JUDGE.                                    DATUS E. SATER, COURT STENOGRAPHER.

## STATE OF OKLAHOMA, PAYNE COUNTY

OFFICE OF COUNTY JUDGE

STILLWATER, OKLAHOMA.

April 20, 1911

Mr. W. C. Kohlenberg,

Dear Sir:

I beg to call your attention to the fact that the guardian's record in this office fails to show any report from you as the guardian of Lee Bass and Ione C. Bass, since your appointment in 1909.

Kindly give this matter your early attention. I enclose form for your services.

Respectfully,

WHW/WHS                                          W. H. Wilcox

---

**H. E. St CLAIR**
LAWYER
Perry, - Oklahoma

A GENERAL PRACTICE IN ALL COURTS
ESTATE AND GUARDIANSHIP CASES
WILL RECEIVE CAREFUL ATTENTION

RECEIVED
APR 24 1911
SAC & FOX AGENCY,
OKLAHOMA.

Perry, Okla., April 22nd, 1911.

Mr. W.C. Kohlenberg, Supt.,

Sac and Fox, Oklahoma.

Dear Sir:-

A few days ago Devereux & Hildreth, Attorneys at Guthrie, requested the execution of Guardian's deed to certain land, belonging to Vestina Grant, and located in Logan County, Oklahoma, for which proceedings had been had and completed; and I have the same executed, and herewith enclose you the same. I sent this deed to you, not knowing whether or not the purchaser had completed the payment for the land, in order that you might protect any of the rights of the minor, as I believe you have charge of the land. Please communicate with the above names Attorneys, and if full settlement has been made for the land, forward them the deed.

I hope you will also look after the collection of the Court costs, and Attorney and Guardian's fees in this matter, for which I understand the Clerk of the County Court has sent you statement.

Respectfully yours,

Enc. 1                                            H.E. StClair
HES/WMH.

Ex-Judge Fifth Judicial District of Nebraska

TELEPHONE { OFFICE, No. 112
RESIDENCE, No. 113

**ROBERT WHEELER,**
ATTORNEY AND COUNSELOR
TECUMSEH, OKLA.    Thomas Brow[sic] et als.

Apr. 27/11.

W. C. Kohlenber[sic],

Sac and Fox, Okla.

Dear Sir:-

In the matter of the guardianship of Thomas Brown et als. you[sic] letter of the 24, inst. received, enclosing bond as guardian. I have filed the bond, and the same was approved as of this date and letters of guardianship issued.to[sic] you.

The court has a rule requiring a deposit for costs, but I did not say anything to him about costs, and I feel sure that nothing will be saud about costs until we get reday[sic] to pay them.

Yours very truly,
Robert Wheeler

**COURT TERMS.**

GUTHRIE-First Monday in January.
OKLAHOMA CITY-First Monday in March.
WOODARD-First Monday in May and
second Monday in November.
ENID-First Monday in June.
LAWTON-First Monday in October.

𝔇epartment of 𝔍ustice. RECEIVED

MAY 4 1911

𝔒ffice of the 𝔘nited 𝔖tates 𝔄ttorney X AGENCY,
𝔚estern 𝔇istrict of 𝔒klahoma. OKLAHOMA.
𝔊uthrie.

May 2, 1911.

W. C. Kohlenberg,
Supt. & Spl. Disb. Agt.,
R. F. D. #2,
Stroud, Oklahoma.

Dear Sir:

Yours of April 24th relative to the Moore guardianships, received. I note that you state that the probate decree calls for $706.72 in the Ruth Moore case, and that there is $451.49 in the bank in that guardianship which the parties representing the guardian and sureties are willing to turn over and apply upon the decree, and that you think that you can get authority to apply $255.23 from the funds of Samuel Moore, the guardian, to satisfy the balance due the ward.

We believe that this would be a proper settlement as the guardian is of course, the one primarily liable, and that the matter should be closed up as speedily as possible.   There are some matters of proceedure[sic] pertaining to the final settlement and appeal in this Ruth Moore case which look quite serious from our point of view, and as out[sic] object is to procure for the ward what is due her from Samuel Moore and the sureties, the settlement seems to accomplish this.  Please advise us when you get the matter closed up.

Relative to the other guardianships mentioned in your letter, I will be pleased to meet you in Shawnee on May 8th, A. M. if that date suits your, and I will spend what time is necessary for us to work them into shape for final disposition; I have a case set down there upon the 10th.  Please advise me if this is satisfactory.

Very respectfully,

Isaac D. Taylor
Assistant U. S. Attorney.

JRP.

---

Ex-Judge Fifth Judicial District of Nebraska

TELEPHONE { OFFICE, No. 112
RESIDENCE, No. 113

ROBERT WHEELER,
ATTORNEY AND COUNSELOR
TECUMSEH, OKLA.

Ke-so-way-la-mah        May 2/11.

Hon. Frank A. Thackery,

Shawnee, Okla.

Dear Sir:-

In the matter of the allotmant[sic] of Ke-so-way-la-mah, your latter[sic] of the 1, inst. received.  I will prepare the papers in this matter and mail them to you within a day or two.

Please tell me the amount Thomas J. Hillman is paying for the land so that I may know how to prepare the bids for the minors interests when we reach that stage in the procedure.

Yours very truly,
Robert Wheeler

---

Ex-Judge Fifth Judicial District of Nebraska          Telephone { Office, No. 112 / Residence, No. 113

**ROBERT WHEELER,**
Attorney and Counselor
Tecumseh, Okla.

Elizabeth Anderson.          May 2/11.

Hon. Frank A. Thackery,

Shawnee, Okla.

Dear Sir:-

In your favor of the 1, isnt. you say that Mrs Sophia Anderson wishes to purchase the NE/4 of SW/4 27-10-3 of John B. Anderson for her son George Anderson.

Is it her intention to purchase only the interest of John B. Anderson, or is she buying the interest of all of the other heirs, including the interest of her other children Elizabeth and Benjamin? If the latter, then what is the whole consideration?

Yours very truly,
Robert Wheeler

---

Ex-Judge Fifth Judicial District of Nebraska          Telephone { Office, No. 112 / Residence, No. 113

**ROBERT WHEELER,**
Attorney and Counselor
Tecumseh, Okla.

May 2/11.

Hon. Frank A. Thackery,

Shawnee, Okla.

Dear Sir:-

I am returning herewith the two petitions in the guardianship matter of Nah-wah-tahth-ka-ka et[sic] for your signature to the affidavis[sic], which you overlooked.

Yours very truly,
Robert Wheeler

---

Ex-Judge Fifth Judicial District of Nebraska

**ROBERT WHEELER,**
Attorney and Counselor
Tecumseh, Okla.

Telephone { Office, No. 112
Residence, No. 113

In re.  Ke-so-way-lay-ma.

May 3- 1911.

Hon. Frank A. Thackery,

Shawnee, Okla.

Dear Sir:

In the matter of the sale of the allotment of Ke-so-way-lay-ma, I am enclosing a petition for the sale of the interest of the two minors, and waiver of notice to be signed by the party as in the former cases.

Our statute provides for two witnesses who can write when a party signs by marks, and one of the witnesses to be the person who writes the name. I am of the opinion that so far as the signing of the waiver is concerned the two you sent me some days ago are sufficient, but the judge may possibly object to them when I fill the papers, for the reason that the signatures have not been witnessed. I do not know that he will do this, but in the present case and in all future waivers it will be well for the person who writes the name of the indian[sic] to sgn[sic] his name as a witness to mark, and have one other witness to mark where it is at all convenient to do so. This will save any question as to the legality of the waiver.

Yours very truly,
Robert Wheeler

Ex-Judge Fifth Judicial District of Nebraska                    TELEPHONE { OFFICE, No. 112 / RESIDENCE, No. 113

**ROBERT WHEELER,**
ATTORNEY AND COUNSELOR
TECUMSEH, OKLA.

In re.  George Anderson.          May 5/11.

Hon. Frank A. Thackery,

     Shawnee, Okla.

Dear Sir:-

     In the matter of the guardianship of George Anderson et als. I mailed a copy of the order conforming sale and a guardian's deed to Mrs. Anderson on Apr. 10, ult. And concerning the costs I wrote her:

     "The entire costs in the case are as follows:

| | |
|---|---|
| Court costs, | $18.35. |
| Pd. Co. Democrat, Pub. notice, | 4.00. |
| Pd. Register of Deeds, Recording, | 1.00. |
| My fee, | 35.00. |
| Total, | 58.35. |
| Pd. by Mrs. Anderson Guar. | 15.00. |
| Bal. Due, | $43.35. |

Concerning my fee, would say:  that prior to the death of your husband, John Anderson, jr.[sic] I prepared the papers for him for a settlement of this estate, but he decided for some reason not to go ahead with the matter, and said he would pay me $10. for the work I had done.  But he died soon after without sending me the money, and I have included that in my fee at this time.  I think Mr. Thackery can explain the matter fully to you.

     Please send me a check for the balance, $43.35, and I will then pay the balance due on court costs and receipt you in full."

     I have not had any reply to that letter, and thought that possibly it was not convenient for Mrs. Anderson to remit at this time:  if so I do not want to urge the immediate payment of my fee, but the balance of $8.35 due on court costs ought to be paid.

               Yours very truly,
               Robert Wheeler

Ex-Judge Fifth Judicial District of Nebraska

TELEPHONE  { OFFICE, No. 112
{ RESIDENCE, No. 113

**ROBERT WHEELER,**
ATTORNEY AND COUNSELOR
TECUMSEH, OKLA.

In re. Ah-che-tha-quah et al.

May 6/11.

Hon. Frank A. Thackery,
　　Shawnee, Okla.

Dear Sir:

　　Replying to your favor of this date, concerning the appointment of a guardian and the sale of lands of Ah-che-tha-quah et al, would say: A married woman cannot act as guardian or administrator in this state.

　　I enclose a petition for guardian to be signed by Mack Johnson, the father, which will obviate delay and notice. I also enclose an extra blank to be used if you need it.

　　　　　　　　　　Yours very truly,

　　　　　　　　　　　　Robert Wheeler

Ex-Judge Fifth Judicial District of Nebraska

TELEPHONE  { OFFICE, No. 112
{ RESIDENCE, No. 113

**ROBERT WHEELER,**
ATTORNEY AND COUNSELOR
TECUMSEH, OKLA.

In re. John Gibson, est.

May 12/11.

Hon. Frank A. Thackery,
　　Shawnee, Okla.

Dear Sir:-

　　In the guardianship of Nah-wah-tahth-ka-ka et al. as heirs of John Gibson, the court made the order for the sale of the minors[sic] interest and appointed Odle, Edmister & Seymour as appraisers.

　　I enclose blank for appraisement and blank sale bond. The bond must be in double the amount of the appraisement, and the sureties must qualify for double the amount of the bond. I have set the date of sale for the 29, inst.

　　　　　　　　　　Yours very truly,
　　　　　　　　　　　　Robert Wheeler

STATE OF OKLAHOMA, } ss.
Cleveland County

**IN THE COUNTY COURT.**

No. 172

......Guardianship...... of

......Victor Sloan......

**NOTICE**

......minor......

Norman, Okla., ...May 13...... 191 1

To ...... Frank A Thackery......

...... Shawnee, Okla.......

You are hereby notified that a report, duly sworn to, is due from you as the

......Guardian...... in the above entitled cause;

and two weeks from date of this notice is the time fixed by the Judge in which to

prepare and file such report in the County Court.

By Order of the Court.

...... R. E. Corbett......
Clerk County Court.

\*\*\*\*\*\*\*\*\*\*

STATE OF OKLAHOMA, } ss.
Cleveland County

**IN THE COUNTY COURT.**

No. 213

...Guardianship... of

...Tom Mack and To-...

...Wahn-neh- Mack...

incompetent

**NOTICE**

Norman, Okla., ...May 13...... 191 1

To ...... Frank A Thackery......

...... Shawnee, Okla.......

You are hereby notified that a report, duly sworn to, is due from you as the

......Guardian...... in the above entitled cause;

and two weeks from date of this notice is the time fixed by the Judge in which to

prepare and file such report in the County Court.

By Order of the Court.

...... R. E. Corbett......
Clerk County Court.

[The letter below typed as given]

H. M. JARRETT
Judge

GEO. F. CLARK
Clerk

OFFICE OF

**RECEIVED**

COUNTY COURT OF LINCOLN COUNTY

MAY 15 1911

CHANDLER, OKLAHOMA

SAC & FOX AGENCY,
OKLAHOMA.

Chandler Okla.
May 13th 1911.

W. C. Kohlenberg,

Dear Sir  :  Received petition for letters of guardianship on estate of Lorena Manatowa,minor.Your favor came while I was at Prague,hence the delay. I have fixed the hearing for May 29th and required notice by mailing and posting.Have posted the notices here.You can mail copies of the notice to Laura Carter and Elmer and Bertha Manatowa,and I believe I would mail one to the Haskell Institute at Lawrence Kansas.I suppose of course she is only temporarily there,otherwise you could not be appointed guardian of her person.Under the circumstances of the case and the wording of the Statute,I think to save any question,that notice should be given as above indicated,even though mother and ward have consented.I am sending blank affidavit which after you have mailed notices you can fill in and return to me.It will fix the bond at $500.00.$250.00 would do at this time but as I understand it you make surety bond and $500.00 does not come any higher.

Very truly,

HM Jarrett

Notices to be mailed postage prepaid at least 120 days before hearing

\*\*\*\*\*\*\*\*\*\*

Notice of Hearing Petition for Letters of Guardianship.          News Print, Chandler

# NOTICE.

**State of Oklahoma, County of Lincoln, ss.**

IN THE COUNTY COURT OF SAID COUNTY.

Notice is hereby given that on the 12th day of May 190 11 that W.C. Kohlenberg filed in the County Court of Lincoln County, State of Oklahoma, a petition praying for Letters of Guardianship to be issued to _____ him _____ upon the person and estate of____

_____ Lorena Manatowa _____

--------------------------------------------------------------

--------------------------------------------------------------

--------------------------------------------------------------

minor child ___ of ___ George Manatowa ___ deceased.

And pursuant to an order of said court the 29th day of May 190 11 at the hour of 9 o'clock A. M., of said day at the County Court room in Chandler in said County and State, has been appointed as the time and place for hearing said petition, when and where any person interested may appear and show cause, if any they can, why such appointment should not be made.

Witness my hand and seal of said Court, at my office in said Lincoln County, State of Oklahoma, this 12th day of May 1911 190

_____ H M Jarrett

County Judge.

HENRY OURSLER
ATTORNEY-AT-LAW
STILLWATER, OKLAHOMA.

RECEIVED
MAY 24 1911
SAC & FOX AGENCY,
OKLAHOMA.

May 18, 1911.

Hon. W. C. Kohlenberg,

Sac and Fox Agency, Okla.

Dear sir:-

Mr. Robert Small was in to see me in regard to being appointed guardian for his daughter, and said you had written him a letter in which was stated that he should pay a lawyer only $15.00. I told him I could not do the work for that amount of money, and insisted on his looking elsewhere, but he seemed to want me, and requested that I take the matter up with you. My charges for this work will be $50.00, and if you will authorize a contract for this amount, I will proceed in the matter.

Yours very truly,

J.M. Springer

---

COURT TERMS.

GUTHRIE-First Monday in January.
OKLAHOMA CITY-First Monday in March.
WOODARD-First Monday in May and
    second Monday in November.
ENID-First Monday in June.
LAWTON-First Monday in October.

Department of Justice.

Office of the United States Attorney.
Western District of Oklahoma.
Guthrie.

May 22nd, 1911.

Frank A. Thackery,
    Superintendent,
        Shawnee, Oklahoma.

Dear Sir:

Yours of the 18th instant, relative to the guardianship by George L. Rose over two or three Indian minors, received. You call special attention to the guardianship of Cooper Wilson, an insane Indian now confined in the State Insane Asylum. We would like to have some further information in regard to this case as follows:

What is the ae of Cooper Wilson? In what court is the guardianship pending? When did Mr. Rose make his last report in the case? We should also have copies of the reports already made.

Also please state whether Mr. Rose was appointed guardian on account of the minority of the ward or on account of mental incompetency.

If the ward is insane a guardian will be required and we might not be able to remove Mr. Rose unless we could show improper administration of the guardianship. Upon receiving this information we will take the matter up further. In replying refer to Miscellaneous No. 468.

Very respectfully,

Isaac D. Taylor
Assistant U.S. Attorney.

CCF.

---

A.C. CUMMINGS, Clerk

**County Court of Pottawatomie County**
ROSS F. LOCKRIDGE, Judge

JUVENILE
PROBATE
MISDEMEANOR
CIVIL

Tecumseh, Okla.,   May, 23rd, 1911.

Mr. Frank A. Thackery

Shawnee, Okla.

Dear Sir;

I received your final reports and filed them of to day, they will be filed and published for final settlement in the next term of court which will be in July, I cant tell you what the costs will be until they are settled up, the 3rd day of July is set for final settlement of all guardian and administrator filnal[sic] settlements.

Respectively yours,

A.C. Cummings
Clerk of the County Court

**********

| | |
|---|---|
| Anna Hale, | $3.37 |
| Ah-ko-the, | "3.20 |
| Henry Bentley, | "6.08 |
| Wah-ne-ma-quah, | 3.20 |
| Men-ah-pe, | 2.20 |
| Nah-she-pe-eth, | "3.20 |
| Laura Sah-ah-peah, | "3.20 |
| Effie Duglass[sic], | "4.40 |
| Millie Stevens, | |
| Peah-puck-o-he, | "7.95 |
| Quen-ne-po-thot, | "3.20 |
| Peah-twyh-tuck, | "9.50 |
| | $49.50 |

Final Reports.

| Henry Murdock, | $[sic] | |
|---|---|---|
| Roy Kickapoo, | "xxxxxxx | $ 6.20 |
| Mack Down, | xxxxxxx | " 7.60 |
| Mah-mah-to-me-ah, | | " 5.20 |
| Wah-sha-ko-skuck, | | " 6.20 |
| Mah-she-nah, | | " 5.20 |
| Much-e-ne-ne | | " 7.20 |
| Oscar Wilde, | | " 7.20 |
| George Kish-ke-ton, | | "3. 20[sic] |
| Joseph Murdock, | | " 6.20 |
| Mut-twa-ah-quah, | | " 6.20 |
| Ah-mah-tho-the, | | " 6.20 |
| Wah-pe-pah, | | " 5.20 |
| Ah-no-thah-huck, | | "6. 20.[sic] |

$78.20

Received, this 8th., day of December, 1908, the sum of $127.50 to be applied on the court cost in the above named guardianship matter.

R. C. Green
Clerk of the County Court.

**********

| Emma Kickapoo | 7.40 |
|---|---|
| She pah tho quah | 6.20 |
| Meck ke the quah | 5.20 |
| Shah kah tah | 5.20 |
| Pah ke she make | 6.20 |
| Shoe e nah quah | 5.20 |
| Achsa Lunt, or | |
| Pem ma ko ke | 5.20 |
| Pe ke ton o quah | 6.20 |
| Me na mesh | 6.20 |
| | $53.00 |

R. C. Green
Clerk.

COURT TERMS.

GUTHRIE-First Monday in January.
OKLAHOMA CITY-First Monday in March.
WOODARD-First Monday in May and
    second Monday in November.
ENID-First Monday in June.
LAWTON-First Monday in October.

**Department of Justice.**

**Office of the United States Attorney.**
Western District of Oklahoma.
Guthrie.

May 27th, 1911.

Frank A. Thackery,
Superintendent,
Shawnee, Oklahoma.

Dear Sir:

Yours of the 11th instant, with enclosure relative to the guardianship by C.M. Tedford of Rose and Samuel Charley in Cleveland County, received. We note that the guardian has filed receipt for final settlement a long time ago to-wit, in the year 1902. We have no way of telling from the face of the report enclosed whether the items charged were necessary or not. We wish you would investigate the items in the account and if you think there are items improper and excessive in such an amount that we would be justified in incurring the expense to have the account re-opened, we will take the matter up. Considering the lapse of time and the fact that the total expenditure only aggregate $155.65 I doubt whether there would be much chance of gaining anything for the wards, over and above expenses incurred. I assume that the guardian was discharged about the time the first settlement appears to have been made, that is, in 1902. We will do what we can however in this guardianship if you think action should be taken and indicate the excess charges.

P.S. We herewith return
        enclosure-
CCF.

Very respectfully,
Isaac D. Taylor
Assistant U.S. Attorney.

**********

R. E. CORBETT, CLERK.
R. A. ISOM, DEPUTY.

**County Court of Cleveland County**
F. B. SWANK, JUDGE

COURT TOWNS:
NORMAN.
LEXINGTON.

NORMAN, OKLA.,
May 8, 1911.

Mr. Frank A. Thackery,
        Shawnee, Okla.

Dear Sir:

In reply to your letter of inquiry as to the distribution of the funds in the guardianship of Rose and Samuel Charley, represented in your letter as $706.67, I am enclosing a copy of the Report of C. M. Tedford, Guardian, which indicates that the same was amended before settlement, the amount due the wards being $631.01, as shown by the report which is entered as a record in this Court.

I am also enclosing copies of receipts filed herein, which represent $615. or $615.65 of the above amount. The records are not very full regarding the settlement of this matter.

Trusting this will give some light on the subject, I am

Very truly,

R. E. Corbett
Clerk of the County Court

\*\*\*\*\*\*\*\*\*\*

(Copy)

IN THE PROBATE COURT, CLEVELAND COUNTY, OKLAHOMA TERRITORY.

In the matter of the Guardianship    )
of Rose and Samuel Charley, minors. )

Report of Guardian.

Comes now C. M. Tedford, guardian of the above named minors and files his report as follows, to-wit:

I am charged with the following amount, being the proceeds of the sale of the real estate of said minors, ----                            786.66

I am credited with the follwing[sic] amounts paid out as expenses incurred in the execution of my trust, to-wit:

| | |
|---|---|
| Probate Court costs------------------------------------------------------------ | 23.00 |
| Printing notices---------------------------------------------------------------- | 7.00 |
| Appraisers fee, in Probate Court-------------- ------------------------------ | 4.00 |
| Appraisers fee at Shawnee----------------------------------------------------- | 5.00 |
| Indian Business Committee at Shawnee------------------------------------- | 5.00 |

Interpreter fee in the Court proceedings----------------------------------- 25.00
Compensation of Guardian                                            $ 25.00
Expenses of guardian to Shawnee----------------------------------------- 6.00
   Attorney fee                                                  $ 50.00

     Total amount received------------------------------------------ 786.66 $155.65

     Total amount paid out------------------------------------------ ~~80.00~~

     Balance due-------------------------------------------------- ~~706.66~~ 631.01

That one of the minors herein named has reached her age of majority, as is shown by affidavits hereto attached; that the said guardian is ready to make final settlement with the said Rose Charley and to be discharged as her guardian.

Wherefore the said guardian prays that the said report be received and made a final report as to Rose Charley and that he be discharged as her guardian.

                                C. M. Tedford

                                  Guardian

**********

(Copy)

65                Norman, Okla., June 30th. 1902
$315.00

Received of C. M. Tedord[sic], guardian of Rose and Samuel Charley, minor heris[sic] of the late Jim Charley, deceased, the sum of Three Hundred Fifteen Dollars in full settlement of all my interest and share in the estate of the said Jim Charley deceased.

                          her
                    Rose x Charley
Witness.                 mark
  J. B. Dudley
  James W. Clark.         (Filed June 16, 1902)

(Copy)

              Norman, Okla., Oct. 4th. 1902.

$150.00.

Received of C. M. Tedford, guardian of Samuel who is now dead, the sum of One Hundred, Fifty & No/100 Dollars in full settlement of my share of the money now in the hands of said guardian belonging to said minor.

                     her
             Mrs. Jim x Charley
                 mark

Witness to mark.

J. B. Dudley                                    (Filed Oct 4, 1902)
Fred Carder.

(Copy)

$150.00                                    Norman, Okla., Oct. 4th/ 1902.

Received of C. M. Tedford, guardin[sic] of Samuel Charley, minor the sum of
One Hundred, fifty & No/100 Dollars in full settlement of my share of the money said
guardian holds as the money belonging to Samuel Charley, who is now dead.

                                               her
                                    Rose  x  Charley
                                              mark

Witness to mark.

J. B. Dudley
Fred Carder                                    (Filed Oct 4th, 1902)

**********

COURT TERMS.

GUTHRIE-First Monday in January.
OKLAHOMA CITY-First Monday in March.
WOODARD-First Monday in May and
      second Monday in November.
ENID-First Monday in June.
LAWTON-First Monday in October.

Department of Justice.
___

Office of the United States Attorney.
Western District of Oklahoma.
Guthrie.

April 3, 1911.

Frank A. Thackery,
      Supt. & Spcl. Dosb[sic]. Agent,
      Shawnee, Okla.

Dear Sir:

      Yours of the 21st ultimo relative to the guardianship of Rose and
                                                     Norman
Samuel Charley, C.M. Tedford, guardian, in Cleveland County, Oklahoma,
received.

      We will be glad to take this matter up as soon as we can reach it,
but may not be able to do so at once as we are very busy preparing for an
approaching term of court.

      It would assist us greatly if you were able to make an examination
of the files and see if there is anything you desire to charge as being irregular,
also advising us of the ages of the Indians, and any other pertinent matters.

113

Very respectfully,

Isaac D. Taylor
Assistant U.S. Attorney.

---

Washington, Conn.
May 31, 1911.

Mr. F. A. Thackery
Indian Agent
Shawnee, Okla.

Dear sir:

I have just received the "Final receipt of ward to guardian" with letter enclosed asking me to sign it so that you may make your final report.

I beg to say, which is in keeping with the contents of this document, that I have just received for signment[sic], that I have not received all papers of importance entrusted in your care.

I sent you, in the fall of 1909, papers sent me by Sullins, and in this envelope containing these papers was the note for ($500$^{00}$/$_{100}$) five hundred dollars which will come due in June 1912. Now if you will kindly look through the letters I have sent, you will be quite certain to find these papers and note.

Very respectfully,
Lafayette Shawnee

---

F.G. MOORE, President.

R E C E I V E D

H. W. McCall[?] BESS, Cashier

MAY 31 1911

**EXCHANGE BANK OF PERRY**

SAC & FOX AGENCY,

Capital Stock **$15,000**$^{00}$

OKLAHOMA.

*Perry, Oklahoma.*   May 29th 1911

W.C. Kohlenberg
Supt & SDAgt
Stroud Ok

Dr Sir:-

Here in please find application in dup. signed as guardian
requested in yours of 26th inst.

Truly yours

F.G. Moore

---

[The letter below typed as given]

H. M. JARRETT
Judge

GEO. F. CLARK
Clerk

OFFICE OF

R E C E I V E D

COUNTY COURT OF LINCOLN COUNTY   JUN 1 1911

CHANDLER, OKLAHOMA

SAC & FOX AGENCY,
OKLAHOMA.

Chandler May 29th 1911.

W. C. Kohlenberg,

Dear Sir :I herewith hand you letters of guardianship,with oath of
guardian attached.Kindly sign oath and return letters to me together with
bond which I have fixed in the sum of $500.00.

Very truly,

HM Jarrett

---

Ex-Judge Fifth Judicial District of Nebraska

TELEPHONE  { OFFICE, No. 112
           { RESIDENCE, No. 113

ROBERT WHEELER,
ATTORNEY AND COUNSELOR
TECUMSEH, OKLA.

My 31/11.

Hon. Frank A. Thackery,

Shawnee, Okla.

Dear Sir:

In the matter of the guardianship of Nah-wah-tahth-ka-ka et al. heirs of John
Gibson, I am enclosing blank sale bond.  I hope it will be convenient for you to fill
this bond at once so that we can make the report of sale before you leave.

I am enclosing a report of sale which you might execute as of the same date as
the execution of the bond, then return both to me.

Yours very truly,
Robert Wheeler

Have notary sign [illegible] to oath of guardin[sic] on appraisement blank, which I return herewith.

---

Ex-Judge Fifth Judicial District of Nebraska

TELEPHONE { OFFICE, No. 112 / RESIDENCE, No. 113

**ROBERT WHEELER,**
ATTORNEY AND COUNSELOR
TECUMSEH, OKLA.

In re. Ma-tahth-ka-ka et al.

June 10/11.

Hon. Frank A. Thackery,

Shawnee, Okla.

Dear Sir:

In the matter of the guardianship of Ma-tahth-ka-ka and Ke-no-che-pea-wa-se, minor heirs of Alex Gibson, deceased, I wrote you Dec. 27/10, giving an itemized statement of costs and expenses. As per the statement, there is due me in the case $35. for my services as attorney, and .70¢ for costs I advanced to close the matter up.

I suppose that as soon as the deeds are approved by the Department you will be authorized to pay me the amount due. Please look the matter up and let me know what shape it is in at this time.

Yours very truly,
Robert Wheeler

---

[The following two letters typed as given]

H. M. JARRETT
Judge

GEO. F. CLARK
Clerk

OFFICE OF

## COUNTY COURT OF LINCOLN COUNTY

June 15-1911        CHANDLER, OKLAHOMA

Mrs. S.

Please agree upon date and have Mr. Odle take all the Indians there for hearing. You have a form for restoration to competency.

Thackery

Chandler  Okla.

June 12th 1911.

Frank A. Thackery,

Shawnee, Okla.,

Dear Sir : I have your favor of the 8th inst. relative to the guardianship of certain Indians.I note what you say about the restrictions are upon the land rather that the person.The statement I made was error on my part.Be that is it may,it will be necessary for you on behalf of each of these wards,to file a verified petition stating that the ward is now competent to transact his own business.I can then fix a day for the hearing,say about 10 days off.You could come with the indians make proof that the indian is capable of taking care of himself and his property.Upon such proof beaing made,the court makes an order restoring the person to capacity.As to notice of the hearing the las is as follow:

"Upon receiving the petition the Judge must appoint a day for the hearing,and cause notice of the same to be given to ~~day~~ the guardian of the petitioner,if there be a guardian,and to his or her husband or wife,it there be one,and to his father or mother,if living in the county."This could be done by mailing or handing them a notice.As to the law see Snyder's Statute 1909, page 1212,section 5488.  You can prepare the petitions in each of these cases,send them to me and I will expedite the matter as much as possible.

Very truly,
HM Jarrett

*****************

H. M. JARRETT
Judge

GEO. F. CLARK
Clerk

OFFICE OF

## COUNTY COURT OF LINCOLN COUNTY

CHANDLER, OKLAHOMA

Chandler  Okla.

May 27th 1911.

Frank A. Thackery,

Shawnee, Okla.,

Dear Sir : I have received your final reports as guardian in certain cases,also receipt in fall from each ward, and etc.  If these incompetents have had their restrictions removed I could base an order of discharge of the guardian on that.Aside from that,there is only the regular procedure  , that is,to have them spear on a day fixed and determine if they are competent to transact their own business.  Kindly advise me.

Very truly

HM Jarrett

*******************

| H. M. JARRETT | | GEO. F. CLARK |
| Judge | | Clerk |

**OFFICE OF**

## COUNTY COURT OF LINCOLN COUNTY

CHANDLER, OKLAHOMA

Chandler  Okla.
June 20th 1911.

Frank A. Thackery,

Shawnee, Okla.,

Dear Sir :  As per your request I am sending you reports in certain guardianship matters.

Very truly,

HM Jarrett

[Copy of Original]

OKLAHOMA CITY OKLA

IN ACCOUNT WITH

## BEADLES & LAUX

GENERAL INSURANCE
SURETY BONDS
TITLE GUARANTEED

LEE BUILDING

PHONE 4659

| DATE | POLICY NO. | COMPANY | PROPERTY | TERM | RATE AMOUNT | PREMIUM |
|---|---|---|---|---|---|---|
| 6/16/11 | | | Bond Nah bah Inklla-Ka-Ka | | 100. | 1.00 |

\*\*\*\*\*\*\*\*\*\*

*Thos. M. Walker, President*

*Wm. T. Kemper, Treasurer*

*James Van Buren, Vice President*    *H. P. Fones, Ass't Secretary*
*John R. Mulvane, Vice President*    *Jo Luch Miller, III, Ass't Secretary*
*J. L. Miller, Jr., Vice President*    *E. Sanford Miller, Ass't Secretary*

### Globe Surety Company

*of Kansas City, Missouri*
*Capital $500,000.00*
*Surplus $100,000.00*

**BEADLES & LAUX**
SUITE 236 LEE BUILDING
GENERAL AGENTS
HIGHLEY & MILLS, ATTORNEYS
A. J. MCCARTHY, ASSOCIATE ATTY.
H. M. SCALES, RES. VICE PRES.
CHAS. M. BOSWORTH, RES VICE PRES.

OKLAHOMA CITY, OKLA.,    June 16th, 1911.

Mr. Frank A. Thackery,

Indian Agent, Shawnee, Okla.

Dear Sir:-

Enclose you herewith Guardian Sale Bond executed in behalf of Nah-Wah-Tahth-Ka-Ka, et al, heirs of John Gibson, deceased.

This bond in the sum of $100.00 is signed by W. H. Coyle and L. N. Beadles. Kindly send us your check for $2.00 in payment of the premium.

Yours truly,

Beadles & Laux

L-T                          General Agents.

*Thos. M. Walker, President*

*Wm. T. Kemper, Treasurer*

*James Van Buren, Vice President*    *H. P. Fones, Ass't Secretary*
*John R. Mulvane, Vice President*    *Jo Luch Miller, III, Ass't Secretary*
*J. L. Miller, Jr., Vice President*    *E. Sanford Miller, Ass't Secretary*

### Globe Surety Company

*of Kansas City, Missouri*
*Capital $500,000.00*
*Surplus $100,000.00*

**BEADLES & LAUX**
SUITE 236 LEE BUILDING
GENERAL AGENTS
HIGHLEY & MILLS, ATTORNEYS
A. J. MCCARTHY, ASSOCIATE ATTY.
H. M. SCALES, RES. VICE PRES.
CHAS. M. BOSWORTH, RES VICE PRES.

OKLAHOMA CITY, OKLA.,    June 16th, 1911.

Mr. W. A[sic]. Kohlenberg,

Indian Agent Sac & Fox Agency,

Okla.

Dear Sir:-

Enclose you herewith Guardian's bond for Lorena Manatowa in the sum of $500.00, signed by W. H. Coyle and L. N. Beadles.

Kindly send us your check for $2.00 in this matter.

Yours truly

Beadles & Laux

L-T                                                                    General Agents.

---

REFER IN REPLY TO THE FOLLOWING:

Land-
Sales.
52955-1911
J F M

Guardian's accounts
of Superintendent.

ADDRESS ONLY THE
COMMISSIONER OF INDIAN AFFAIRS

**DEPARTMENT OF THE INTERIOR,**

**OFFICE OF INDIAN AFFAIRS,**

WASHINGTON,

JUN 17 1911

Mr. John A. Buntin,

Superintendent Shawnee Indian School,

Shawnee, Oklahoma.

Sir:

Referring to your letter of May 18, 1911, relative to your accounts as guardian of certain Indian children, you are advised that a letter has been received from the Assistant Attorney General informing the Department that the United States Attorney General for the Western District of Oklahoma has been directed to assist you in the presentation and approval of these accounts.

Respectfully,

CF Hauke

6-HMS-17                                                   Second Assistant Commissioner.

Ex-City Attorney
Ex-County Attorney

## J. W. REECE
ATTORNEY-AT-LAW

Phone No. 65

Stillwater, Oklahoma, June. 22

**RECEIVED**
**JUN 24 1911**
**SAC & FOX AGENCY,**
**OKLAHOMA.**

Hon. W. C. Kohlenberg,

Stroud, Okla.

Dear Sir:

Robert Small of Perkins has filed a petition to be appointed guardian of the person and estate of Mary Small age 15 years, child of Robert Small and Angie Hot-ta-cov. He says he desires to sell the land owned by the child.

I wish you would write me just what you know about this matter and as to the description of the land and how the child became the owner of the land, and what reasons you know of that might be presented to the court that would call for the selling of the land. I was sick with the fever at the time Mr. Small was in Stillwater and had Mr. Grubbs write the petition for me, but Small did not seem able to give Mr. Grubbs any information on the matter.

In case I file the petition and commence the matter, I desire to have everything correct from the first.

Thanking you in advance, I am

Respectfully,

JW Reece

---

**COURT TERMS.**

GUTHRIE-First Monday in January.
OKLAHOMA CITY-First Monday in March.
WOODARD-First Monday in May and
    second Monday in November.
ENID-First Monday in June.
LAWTON-First Monday in October.

**Department of Justice.**

---

**Office of the United States Attorney.**
**Western District of Oklahoma.**
**Guthrie.**

July 5, 1911.

Supt. & Spl. Disb. Agt.,

Shawnee, Oklahoma.

Dear Sir:

On July 3rd, the County Judge at Norman, passed upon the final report of Frank A. Thackery as guardian of Nellie and Stella Ford, minors, and entered an order for his discharge subject to te payment of the costs in said guardianship. The final report showed no funds in the hands of the guardian, but it appears from the record that the guardianship was necessitated for the purpose of making a necessary land sale, and the court costs should be promptly paid.

The Judge was very courteous and seemed to be willing to favor us in every legitimate way in these guardianships, so I trust this matter will receive as early attention as your Department can give it.

I enclose the statement for costs.

Respectfully,

Isaac D. Taylor
Assistant U. S. Attorney.

Enclosure.
JRP.

---

**COURT TERMS.**

GUTHRIE-First Monday in January.
OKLAHOMA CITY-First Monday in March.
WOODARD-First Monday in May and
second Monday in November.
ENID-First Monday in June.
LAWTON-First Monday in October.

**Department of Justice.**

**Office of the United States Attorney.**

Western District of Oklahoma.

Guthrie.

July 11, 1911.

J. A. Buntin,
        Supt. & Spl. Disb. Agt.,
                Shawnee, Oklahoma.

Dear Sir:

Yours of the 7th instant relative to the guardianship by George L. Rose of Cooper Wilson, received. We note that in so far as you are able to report, there are no irregularities on the part of the present guardian.

As stated in our prior letter this being the guardianship of an insane person; unless the guardian voluntarily resigned, we could not procure his removal without issuing statutory ground therefor.

In the event that you discover anything which you consider amounts to wilful[sic] or gross mismanagement of the estate of the ward, we will be glad to take up the matter.

Very respectfully,

Isaac D. Taylor
Assistant U. S. Attorney.

JRP.

---

In re. John Gibson.

Tecumseh, Okla. July 11/11.

Hon J. A. Buntin,

Shawnee, Okla.

Dear Sir:

Henry Mack was to see me yesterdaylate[sic] and said you wished me to report on the three cases in which Nah-wah-tahth-ka-ka, et al are interested as minor heirs.

In respose[sic] I beg to say, that in the John Gibson allotment. NE of SW & NW of SE 33-9-2, I mailed Mr. Thackery a report of sale some days ago, and as soon as he signs and swers[sic] to the same and returns it to me I will take the necessary steps to have the sale confirmed, and then prepare the guardian's deed for him to execute. I hope he will hold the guardianship in this case until the deed is executed.

Excuse the paper I am using, as I find I must use blank paper until the printer can get some new letter heads ready.

Yours very truly,
Robert Wheeler

---

In re. Tay-la-mah,

Tecumseh, Okla. July 11/11.

Hon. J. A. Buntin,

Shawnee, Okla.

Dear Sir:

In the matter of the Tay-la-mah allotment, Lots 3 & 4 of NW. of 4-8-2, an order of sale issued on May 16/11. and I immediately mailed Mr. Thackery a blank sale bond and appraisement blank, neither of which have been returned to me.

I trust it will be convenient for Mr. Thackery to execute the sale bond in this case and to hold the guardianship until this sale is completed.

Yours very truly,
Robert Wheeler

---

In re. Ke-so-way-la-mah.

Tecumseh, Okla. July 11/11.

Hon. J. A. Buntin,

Shawnee, Okla.

Dear Sir:

In the matter of the allotment of Ke-so-way-la-mah, Lots 1 & 2 of 5-8-2, in which Nah-wah-tahth-ka-ka et al. are interested minors, as in the foregoing cases,[sic] The order of sale was issued June 5/11, and I immediately mailed Mr. Thackery a blank sale bond and appraisement blank, neither of which have been returned to me. I trust that in this case also, Mr. Thackery will execute the bond and hold the guardianship until the sale is completed. To do so in these cases will prevent delay and possible complications.

I am not surprised that there has been some dalay[sic] in these matters, as I know that the change has taken a great deal of Mr. Thackery's time.

Yours very truly,
Robert Wheeler

Ex-Judge Fifth Judicial District of Nebraska

TELEPHONE { OFFICE, No. 112
RESIDENCE, No. 113

**ROBERT WHEELER,**
ATTORNEY AND COUNSELOR
TECUMSEH, OKLA.

July 18/11.

Hon. J. A. Buntin,

Shawnee, Okla.

Dear Sir:

Your favor of the 17, inst. just received, informing me that the hearing to determine the heirs of Ma-zhe had been postponed to Sept. 12,. at which time we will have present what witnesses we have that live in this county, but it will be impossible to get the old men and women who live near Nadeau Kas. and know most about the case to come so far.

In my application to the honorable Secretary of the Interior for a hearing in this matter I requested that testimony be taken at the Indian Agency at Nadeau, Kansas, and at the Shawnee agency. The administrator of the estate of Ma-zhe and nearly all of the witnesses live near Nadeau, Kansa, and both of the heirs, Wahsahto and Ma-zhe, live there.

Do you know whether it is the intention of the Department to also take testimony at the Agency at Nadeau, Kas? If you are not informed on this point please make inquiry concerning the matter and then let me know. And if the Department has not arranged to take testimony at the agency in Kansas, I beg that you lay the facts of this letter before the proper officer, and add your request that testimony be taken at that point.

We do not want to go to the great expense of bringing any witnesses here from Kansas if it can be avoided, but will not know what to do about it until we know wheter[sic] a hearing is to be held there or not.

Please let me know about this matter as soon as you get the information.

Yours very truly,
Robert Wheeler

**COURT TERMS.**

GUTHRIE-First Monday in January.
OKLAHOMA CITY-First Monday in March.
WOODARD-First Monday in May and
    second Monday in November.
ENID-First Monday in June.
LAWTON-First Monday in October.

**Department of Justice.**

**Office of the United States Attorney.**

Western District of Oklahoma.

Guthrie.

July 11, 1911.

W. C. Kohlenberg,
   R. F. D. No. 2,
     Stroud, Oklahoma.

Dear Sir:

Yours of the 1st instant relative to the Moore guardianships, received. We will give the same consideration and write you later our views. At first blush it does not occur to me that the appointment of a guardian of Samuel L. Moore is necessary but I will give the matter careful consideration and then express my opinion on the whole proposition.

Very respectfully,

Isaac D. Taylor
Assistant U. S. Attorney.

JRP.

---

**COURT TERMS.**

GUTHRIE-First Monday in January.
OKLAHOMA CITY-First Monday in March.
WOODARD-First Monday in May and
    second Monday in November.
ENID-First Monday in June.
LAWTON-First Monday in October.

**Department of Justice.**

**Office of the United States Attorney.**

Western District of Oklahoma.

Guthrie.

July 11, 1911.

The Attorney General,
     Washington, D.C.

Copy for
Supt. Kohlenberg

Sir:

Herewith we have the honor to acknowledge receipt of your letter E.K. 152743-4 of July 3, 1911, relative to proposed action in the matter of the sale of part of the restricted allotment of Lena McCoonse.

You inquire whether suit has been instituted or if we are still unable to locate the party referred to in our letter of June 6, 1911. This party has not been located and it appears now as though we will be unable to do so. It is our intention to file the action against such parties as we have located and against those occupying the land just as soon a we can do so.

Very respectfully,

Isaac D. Taylor
Assistant U. S. Attorney.

JRP.

---

Ex-Judge Fifth Judicial District of Nebraska

Telephone { OFFICE, NO. 112
RESIDENCE, NO. 113

ROBERT WHEELER,
ATTORNEY AND COUNSELOR
TECUMSEH, OKLA.

In re.  John Gibson.

July 15/11.

Hon. J. A. Buntin,

Shawnee, Okla.

Dear Sir:

Your favor of the 14, inst. received, enclosing sale bond in the guardianship matter of Nah-wah-tahth-ka-ka et al. heirs of John Gibson, deceased. I filed the bond and it was approved this date.

I now enclose a report of sale to be signed and sworn to by Mr. Thackery and returned to me. If Mr. Thackery is not at the agency, please send thie[sic] report to him. The only other matter we will have to trouble him with in this case, will be to sign the guardian's deed after the sale has been confirmed.

Yours very truly,
Robert Wheeler

---

Ex-Judge Fifth Judicial District of Nebraska

TELEPHONE { OFFICE, No. 112
RESIDENCE, No. 113

ROBERT WHEELER,
ATTORNEY AND COUNSELOR
TECUMSEH, OKLA.

In re.  John B. Anderson.

July 29/11.

Hon. J. A. Buntin,

Shawnee, Okla.

Dear Sir:

Replying to your favor of the 28, inst. concerning the guardianship of John B. Anderson, would say:  I advanced $4. to pay for sale notice, and there will be $1. to pay for recording confirmation order as soon as the sale is confirmed.

As to my fees, Mrs. Anderson can let that part of the expense stand until the sale is confirmed.  I only mentioned it in my former letter for the reason that I thought it might be as convenient for Mrs. Anderson to pay it at this time as later.

Yours very truly,
Robert Wheeler

Ex-Judge Fifth Judicial District of Nebraska

TELEPHONE { OFFICE, No. 112
RESIDENCE, No. 113

ROBERT WHEELER,
ATTORNEY AND COUNSELOR
TECUMSEH, OKLA.

In re.  John B. Anderson.

May 5/11.

Hon. Frank A. Thackery,

Shawnee, Okla.

Dear Sir:

Replying to your favor of the 3, inst. I enclose a petition and waiver in the matter of the sale of the interest of John B. Anderson in the NE/4 of SW/4 of 27-10-3.

Have Mrs. Anderson sign the waiver as guardian, and have all the heirs, both adult and minors sign the same.

It is questionable wherether[sic] Mrs. Anderson can purchase the land of one ward for another, especially where such other is her own child. At any rate it would throw a suspicion on the title, and I would suggest that when it comes to a sale that she have one of the adult heirs buy the interest of John B. and then deed it to George.

The court will probably require a deposit of $10. in this matter at the time the petition is filed.

Yours very truly,
Robert Wheeler

COURT TERMS.

GUTHRIE-First Monday in January.
OKLAHOMA CITY-First Monday in March.
WOODARD-First Monday in May and
    second Monday in November.
ENID-First Monday in June.
LAWTON-First Monday in October.

**Department of Justice.**

**Office of the United States Attorney.**
Western District of Oklahoma.
Guthrie.

July 29, 1911.

J. A. Buntin,
    Supt. & Spl. Disb. Agt.,
        Shawnee, Oklahoma.

Dear Sir:

Herewith I return the guardianship forms transmitted a few days ago by Mrs. Seymour. I have changed some of them and noted suggestions thereon.

Soon after my return from my last trip to Shawnee, I talked over these matters with Mr. Embry, and it was his opinion that it would not be best to attempt to have the County Judge find that any of the funds in the hands of the guardian were trust funds which should be turned over to the Superintendent. I telephoned Mr. Thackery as to Mr. Embry's opinion in the matter and presume that no petitions have been filed which ask for such a finding. The forms enclosed are lettered for the purpose of the following suggestions:

"A". This form of petition and order of discharge will serve where there is a minor who has sufficient funds that is considered not best to turn the same over to him, it being necessary that a new guardian be appointed. If the minor is over the age of 14 years, you should have him sign a written statement nominating you as guardian and then add a clause to the petition for discharge at the end of the first paragraph stating that "said ward has duly nominated J. A. Buntin as his guardian." You can also insert such clause at the end of the first paragraph in the order of discharge.

"B". This is a general form which we have thought to be uses in all cases where it was desired to terminate the guardianship and have the funds decreed to be trust funds, but as above states, this is not considered best and this form is of no use. In these cases where it is still desired to hold the funds, new guardians will have to be appointed. If the ward is a minor, you can use form "A" for petition and discharge. If the ward is an adult incompetent, you could have his competency restored and have the money paid to him and then have him turn it over to the Superintendent to be held as trust funds. The form to use in terminating such guardianship would be "E".

"C". This is a form relative to Lydia E. Ring, still insane. I have changed this form by interlineation. It will be necessary to have a new guardian appointed.

"D". This form is all right for deceased wards with no funds in the hands of the guardian.

"E". This form will answer for incompetents who are being restored to capacity and receive their own money. These funds should be paid to the Indian after he is adjudged competent, and then if it is desired to hold them as trust funds, you could probably prevail upon the Indian to agree to such matter and turn them over. If you cannot get such agreement and do not want the funds turned over to the Indian, you would have to proceed to have a new guardian appointed, using a form similar to that in the Lydia E. Ring case, "C".

"F". There was only an order of discharge in this class transmitted but I presume the petition for discharge corresponds with the order and this form will answer in the cases of minor wards who have arrived at their majority to whom the balance due is paid in person. If there are any such wards whose funds it was thought best to still keep in control of the Superintendent, this would have to be effected[sic] by getting the ward to turn it over to the Superintendent or procuring the appointment of a new guardian on the ground of incompetency.

In the cases where a new guardian is appointed, a regular petition for appointment should be filed and regular notice given separate and apart from the petition of the old guardian for discharge and order of discharge. Also in cases where non-competents are restored to capacity, the special statutory notice will have to be given.

I note that some of Mr. Thackery's guardianships are set down for the 7th of August, and I will be in Tecumseh on that date. I may not arrive at Tecumseh until 1.30[sic] however, so that it will be best to have these matters not called until that hour.

Respectfully,

Isaac D. Taylor
Assistant U. S. Attorney.

Enclosures.
JRP.

---

COURT TERMS.
GUTHRIE-First Monday in January.
OKLAHOMA CITY-First Monday in March.
WOODARD-First Monday in May and
second Monday in November.
ENID-First Monday in June.
LAWTON-First Monday in October.

Department of Justice.
—
Office of the United States Attorney
Western District of Oklahoma.
Guthrie.

RECEIVED
AUG 3 1911
SAC & FOX AGENCY,
OKLAHOMA.

August 2, 1911.

W. C. Kohlenberg,
    Supt. & Spl. Disb. Agt.,
        R. F. D. No. 2,
            Stroud, Oklahoma.

Dear Sir:

Enclosed you will find the original and a copy of exceptions to the reports of Milton Bryan as guardian of Bertha Pattequa, No. 766 County Court Pottawatomie County, Oklahoma.

I wish you and William Pattequa, the father of Bertha, would sign the original and return it to me at your earliest convenience. I will then file it in the court. You can retain the copy for your own files.

Very respectfully,
Isaac D. Taylor
Assistant U. S. Attorney.

Enclosures.
JRP.

---

Ex-Judge Fifth Judicial District of Nebraska

TELEPHONE { OFFICE, No. 112
RESIDENCE, No. 113

**ROBERT WHEELER,**
ATTORNEY AND COUNSELOR
TECUMSEH, OKLA.

In re.  John Gibson est.

Aug. 7/11.

Hon. J. A. Buntin,

Shawnee, Okla.

Dear Sir:

In the matter of the guardianship of Nah-wah-tahth-ka-ka and Ma-tahth-ka-ka, as heirs of John Gibson, deceased, I am enclosing certified copy of the order confirming sale, and a guardian's deed to be executed by Mr. Thackery.

The toal[sic] costs and expense in this matter has been as follows:

| | |
|---|---|
| Court costs, | $10.00. |
| Advertising sale, | 4.00. |
| Recording conf. order, | 1.00. |
| My fees, | 30.00. |
| Total, | $45.00. |

This $45.00 was advanced by James V. Dawson the purchaser, to be repaid to him out of the purchse[sic] money, on an order from the Department, when the sale is approved.

Yours very truly,
Robert Wheeler

**********

EX-JUDGE FIFTH JUDICIAL DISTRICT OF NEBRASKA               TELEPHONE { OFFICE, NO. 112
                                                                      { RESIDENCE, NO. 113

**ROBERT WHEELER,**
ATTORNEY AND COUNSELOR
TECUMSEH, OKLA.            In re. Tay-lah-mah.

Jan. 13/12.

Hon. J. A. Buntin,

Shawnee, Okla.

Dear Sir:

In the matter of the guardianship of Nah-wah-tahth-ka-ka and Ma-tahth-ka-ka, heirs of Tay-lah-mah, I enclose a certified and recorded copy of the order confirming sale, and a guardian's deed executed by Hon. Frank A. Thackery, guardian.

The costs in this case are as follows,

| | |
|---|---|
| Court costs, | $3.00. |
| Recording order confirming sale, | 1.00. |
| Publishing notice of sale, | 4.00. |
| My fees, | 35.00. |
| Total, | $43.00. |

The money to cover these costs was advanced by Shired S. Shirey, the purchaser, to be repaid to him out of the purchase money when the sale is approved by the Department.

Also in this case, owing to the absence of Mr. Thackery and other circumstances the matter has been necessarily delayed longer than is usual in such cases.

Yours very truly,
Robert Wheeler

**********

EX-JUDGE FIFTH JUDICIAL DISTRICT OF NEBRASKA               TELEPHONE { OFFICE, NO. 112
                                                                      { RESIDENCE, NO. 113

**ROBERT WHEELER,**
ATTORNEY AND COUNSELOR
TECUMSEH, OKLA.            In re, Ke-so-way-la-mah.

Jan. 13/12.

Hon. J. A. Buntin,

Shawnee, Okla.

Dear Sir:

In the matter of the guardianship of Nah-wah-tahth-ka-ka and Ma-tahth-ka-ka, heirs of Ke-so-way-la-mah, I enclose a certified and recorded copy of the order confirming sale, and a guardian's deed executed by Hon. Frank A. Thackery, guardian.

The costs in this case are as follows,

| | | |
|---|---|---|
| Court costs, | | $3.00. |
| Recording order confirming sale, | | 1.00. |
| Publishing notice of sale, | | 4.00. |
| My fees, | | 35.00. |
| | Total, | $43.00. |

The money to cover these costs was advanced by Thomas J. Hillman, the purchaser, to be repaid to him out of the purchase money when the sale is approved by the Department.

Owing to chain of circumstances, among which was Mr. Thackery's absence, this matter has been delayed longer than is usual in such cases.

Yours very truly,
Robert Wheeler

---

August 8th, 1911

Gus Laforge,

Cushing, Oklahoma.

Copy for
Supt. Kohlenberg

Dear Sir:

Your letter of the 3rd instant to Mr. Embry relative to case No. 268 against Alex Laforge and J.N. Henderson and yourself on an Indian lease, received. We note that you ask that the matter be held off for awhile and that the Indian says he will wait till October and also that Superintendent Kohlenberg advised you to write to us.

You are advised that to-day the attorney for yourself and the other defendants with our consent, procured an extension of time of 20 days to file answer in the case. That will probably meet the situation you have in mind.

We return your enclosed stamp.

Very respectfully,

Enclosure-                              Isaac D. Taylor
CCF.                                    Assistant U.S. Attorney.

---

[Copies of the Original]

COURT TERMS.

GUTHRIE-First Monday in January.
OKLAHOMA CITY-First Monday in March.
WOODARD-First Monday in May and
  second Monday in November.
ENID-First Monday in June.
LAWTON-First Monday in October.

**Department of Justice.** **RECEIVED**

AUG 21 1911

**Office of the United States Attorney,** SAC & FOX AGENCY, OKLAHOMA.

**Western District of Oklahoma.**

**Guthrie.**

August 19, 1911.

Hon. Roy V. Hoffman,
 Atty. at Law,
  Chandler, Oklahoma.  Copy for
            Supt. Kohlenberg

Dear Sir:

  Relative to the Ruth Moore gaurdianship[sic] case in pursuance of my conversation with you at Chandler sometime ago over the telephone, I have procured authority from the Interior Department and the Department of Justice to cause the matter to be disposed of along the lines agreed upon, that is, by the sureties releasing the funds in the bank held in such guardianship and the Indian Department applying the balance necessary to make up the judgment.

  The figures as I have them are, the judgment was for $706.72; there is on hand in such guardianship in the bank at Chandler $451.49; the balance to be applied by the Indian Department out of the funds of Samuel Moore, being $255.23.

  We believe that it would be necessary to procure the appointment of a guardian for Samuel Moore relative to the payment of the above sum from his funds, and as soon as we can attend to the matter, we will procure the appointment of a guardian for him and close the matter up.

  The above disposition of the case is in accordance with our verbal agreement as I understand it. Kindly advise me in the event that your understanding does not co-incide herewith.

       Very respectfully,
       Isaac D. Taylor
JRP.       Assistant U. S. Attorney.

Ex-Judge Fifth Judicial District of Nebraska

TELEPHONE { OFFICE, No. 112
RESIDENCE, No. 113

**ROBERT WHEELER,**
ATTORNEY AND COUNSELOR
TECUMSEH, OKLA.     In re Anderson & Ah-che-tha-quah.

Aug. 24/11.

Hon. J. A. Buntin,

Shawnee, Okla.

Dear Sir:

Your favor of the 22, inst. received, enclosing reports of sale in the Anderson and Ah-che-tha-quah cases.  I have filed the reports and posted notices of the hearing, which is set for Sept. 7, at 9 A.M.

I trust it will be convenient for Mrs. Sophia Anderson to send me the remainder of $30. required to cover costs and expenses in the case in which she is interested, by that time.

Yours very truly,
Robert Wheeler

\*\*\*\*\*\*\*\*\*\*

Ex-Judge Fifth Judicial District of Nebraska

TELEPHONE { OFFICE, No. 112
RESIDENCE, No. 113

**ROBERT WHEELER,**
ATTORNEY AND COUNSELOR
TECUMSEH, OKLA.     In re. John B. Anderson &
Ah-che-tha-quah, et al.

Aug. 21/11.

Hon. J. A. Buntin,

Shawnee, Okla.

Dear Sir:

Your favor of the 18, inst. enclosing bonds and appraisements in guardianship matters of John B. Anderson and Ah-che-tha-quah received. The papers have been filed and the bonds approved, and I herewith enclose reports of sale in each case, to be signed by Sophia Anderson and James H. Odle, the respective guardians, and then returned to me.

Yours very truly,
Robert Wheeler

\*\*\*\*\*\*\*\*\*\*

Ex-Judge Fifth Judicial District of Nebraska

TELEPHONE { OFFICE, No. 112
RESIDENCE, No. 113

ROBERT WHEELER,
ATTORNEY AND COUNSELOR
TECUMSEH, OKLA.

In,[sic] re, Anderson & Ah-che-tha-quah cases.

July 6/11.

Hon. J. A. Buntin,

Shawnee, Okla.

Dear Sir:

In the matter of the guardianship of John B. Anderson the order of sale has been made, James B. Odle, John H. Seger and John Snake appointed as appraisers, and the property advertised for sale on the 27, inst.

I enclose blank appraisement, guardian's sale bond - which must be in double the amount of the appraisement, and a blank bid to be signed by the adult heir bidding on the property, and then returned to me. It will not be necessary for the bidder to be present on the day of sale.

An order of sale has also been made in the Ah-che-tha-quah et al matter, John E. Snake, John H. Seger and T. B. Alford appointed appraisers, and the property advertised for sale on the 27, inst. Either two of the appraisers can make the appraisement in any case.

In this matter I am enclosing a blank sale bond and appraisement blank. I will mail the blank bid direct to Mr. Baade, the purchaser.

Yours very truly,
Robert Wheeler

Mr. Buntin:

Please draw a check for 25¢ on the Shawnee National Bank, Authority "C 413", Account No. 235, payable to Mr. Thackery, guardian - and sign it as Supt. etc for Willie Gibson.

Another one for 25¢ on the First National Bank, "C 413", A/c No.1028, signing as Supt. for Nah wah tahth ka ka.

S.

**********

# DEPARTMENT OF THE INTERIOR

### UNITED STATES INDIAN SERVICE

Riverside, California,

September 1, 1911.

Supt. John A. Buntin,

Shawnee, Oklahoma.

Dear Mr. Buntin:

I was unable to get this acknowledged until today and an returning it, the Guardian deed of Willie Gibson et al and the two sale bonds, herein. Hope they arrive in time so that this guardianship can be closed up along with the other accounts you speak of. I had to pay 50¢ for the acknowledgement on this deed which you may send me from the funds of the minors.

Sincerely yours,

Frank A. Thackery

Supervisor.

Shawnee Natl  a/c  #235 Willie Gibson

First      "     "    1028  Nah wah tahth ka ka

---

COURT TERMS.

GUTHRIE-First Monday in January.
OKLAHOMA CITY-First Monday in March.
WOODARD-First Monday in May and
second Monday in November.
ENID-First Monday in June.
LAWTON-First Monday in October.

### Department of Justice.

### Office of the United States Attorney.

#### Western District of Oklahoma.

##### Guthrie.

September 2nd, 1911.

W.C. Kohlenberg,
Supt. & Spl. Disb. Agent,
Stroud, Oklahoma.

Dear Sir:

Your letter received relative to the settlement of the Samuel L. Moore guardianship matter. I will see you in the near future relative to this matter. Possibly by the latter part of next week or the first of the week following.

Very respectfully,

CCF.

Isaac D. Taylor
Assistant U.S. Attorney.

---

Ex-Judge Fifth Judicial District of Nebraska

**ROBERT WHEELER,**
ATTORNEY AND COUNSELOR
TECUMSEH, OKLA.

TELEPHONE ⎰ OFFICE, No. 112
          ⎱ RESIDENCE, No. 113

In re.   Rolette, &
Nah-wah-tahth-ka-ka, et al.

Sept. 5/11.

Hon. J. A. Buntin,

Shawnee, Okla.

Dear Sir:

I am just in receipt of a very pressing letter from J. W. Sturgis, the purchaser of the Jim Bolden allotment, NW4 & W2, SW4 10-9-2. The appraisement was made July 21/11, but the sale bond, which must be in the sum of $600. has not been received. I hope Mr. Odle, the guardian can get this completed right away and send it to me.

Also in two cases in which Nah-wah-tahth-ka-ka and Ma-tahth-ka-ka are the minors, neither the appraisement or bond have been received.

One is the sale of their interest in the Tay-la-mah allotment, Lots 3 & 4 in NW4 4-8-2.

The other is the sale of their interest in the Ke-so-wah-lay-mah allotment, Lots 1 & 2 of sec. 5-8-2.

In one of these cases the order of sale issued May 16/11, and in the other June 5/11.

I am enclosing some blank bonds that can be used in case the ones I mailed you some time ago have been mislaid during the rush in making the change in your office.

If anything can be done to hurry these matters please hurry them, as the purchasers are getting impatient.

Mr. Thackery is guardian of Nah-wah-tahth-ka-ka and Ma-tahth-ka-ka.

Yours very truly,
Robert Wheeler

---

COURT TERMS.

GUTHRIE-First Monday in January.
OKLAHOMA CITY-First Monday in March.
WOODARD-First Monday in May and
    second Monday in November.
ENID-First Monday in June.
LAWTON-First Monday in October.

**Department of Justice.**

**Office of the United States Attorney,**

**Western District of Oklahoma.**

**Guthrie.**

R E C E I V E D
SEP 12 1911
SAC & FOX AGENCY,
OKLAHOMA.

September 11th, 1911.

W.C. Kohlenberg,
    Supt. & Spl. Disb. Agent,
        Sac & Fox Agency,
           Stroud, Oklahoma.

Dear Sir:

    We are in receipt of yours of the 9th instant, relative to the appointment of a guradian[sic] of Samuel L. Moore.   In view of the suggestions contained in your letter, it might be well for you to have some other person appointed; but we desire that you be careful in the selection, as we would not want some one appointed who would proceed to dissipate the estate.   Select some one who will feel some concern in protecting the Indian, and have the matter attended to promptly, as this should be closed up.

Respectfully,

CCF.

John Embry
U.S. Attorney.

---

EX-JUDGE FIFTH JUDICIAL DISTRICT OF NEBRASKA

ROBERT WHEELER,
ATTORNEY AND COUNSELOR
  TECUMSEH, OKLA.

TELEPHONE { OFFICE, No. 112
            RESIDENCE, No. 113

In re. John B. Anderson

Sept. 13/11.

Hon. J. A. Buntin,

Shawnee, Okla.

Dear Sir:

In the matter of the guardianship of John B. Anderson, I am enclosing certified copy of the order confirming sale, and a guardian's deed to be executed by Sophia Anderson, guardian.

The costs in this case are as follows:

| | | |
|---|---|---|
| Court costs, | | $5.10. |
| Advertising | | 4.00. |
| Recording, | | 1.00. |
| My fees. | | 25.00. |
| | Total, | $35.10. |

Mrs. Sophia Anderson advanced $40. to cover expenses, and of this I deposited $10. with the clerk of the county court to cover costs, but it was not all consumed for costs, and there is $4.90 in the hands of the clerk to Mrs. Anderson's credit.  She can get an order of court for this money to be repaid to her, or let it stand as a credit on any future costs that may be made in the case.

Yours very truly,

Robert Wheeler

---

R. E. CORBETT, CLERK.
R. A. ISOM, DEPUTY.
EVA VANCE, STENOGRAPHER

COURT TOWNS:
NORMAN
LEXINGTON

## County Court of Cleveland County
### F. B. SWANK, JUDGE

NORMAN, OKLA., Sept. 14, 1911.

Hon. Frank A. Thackery,

Shawnee/Okla.

Dear Mr. Thackery:-

In answer to your letter of the 13th. inst., permit me to say that your final accounts have been filed, but cannot be heard till next January.  The law provides that a final account must be filed at least 20 days before a regular term of Court.  The next term of the County Court will be October 2, 1911.

The costs of the final settlement will be about as follows:

Victor Sloan---------------------$4.45.

Mark Charley------------------ $3.00.

Tom & Tewahney Mack---- $3.50.

Ge-pa-no-tha------------------ $3.00.
Total------------  13.95.

Then in the Guardianship of Nellie and Stella Ford there remains due
the sum of $8.95.  Making a grand toal[sic] in all these cases of $22.90.
Please send this amount and the accounts received this morning will be
disposed of in January 1911.

Hoping this will be satisfactory,

I am,

Very truly yours,

F.B. Swank
County Judge

# COUNTY COURT

## CLEVELAND COUNTY

### N. E. SHARP, COUNTY JUDGE
AMY NOLAN, STENOGRAPHER AND CLERK

NORMAN, OKLA.,   Nov 27th       19 09

Frank A. Thackery,
Indian Agent,
Shawnee, Okla.
Dear Sir:
Replying to your letter of the 23rd inst., requesting information in
regard to Indian Guardianships, will say that in most of these guardianships, a
full inventory has never been filed and appraised, but merely the tracts of land
desired to be sold.  Of course I could show in a statement the amount received
for these tracts where they have been sold, but in most, if not in all cases, I think
the minors own other property and especially real estate, and inventory and
appraisement of which has never been made.  It seems to me it would be well
for you to furnish an inventory and appraisement of all property now belonging
to your Indian Wards.  This would only take a few days at most and in fact is
the only correct procedure.  If you desire to proceed as I have suggested, please
forward me the names of appraisers for each guardianship and I will send you,
at once, orders appointing the persons appraisers.

Very respectfully,

___N.E. Sharp___
COUNTY JUDGE.

NES-AN

---

## THE SHAWNEE NATIONAL BANK

**OF SHAWNEE**

H.T. DOUGLAS, President
J.M. AYDELOTTE, Vice President
JNO. W. JONES, Cashier
B.B. GLASS, Asst. Cashier

**CAPITAL and SURPLUS $120,000$^{00}$**

**SHAWNEE, OKLA.**

September 21, 1911.

Hon. John A. Buntin,
Supt. and Special Disbursing Agent,
Shawnee, Oklahoma.

Dear Sir:

The parties named below on the dates named qualified as guardian for certain minor Indians and the writer became surety on their bonds.

Dec. 22, 1904    Davis Hardin--Estella & Jno. Shawneego-$2000.00
Feb. 23, 1904    S. C. Vinson--Nan-aw-she ------------------- 600.00

I write to know whether by act of Congress or a ruling made by the Commissioner of Indian Affairs whereby the agent was appointed as guardian to take care of the interests of minor Indians, the guardians appointed and named above were released from obligation, and was the writer also released from any obligation that might arise? The writer is clearing up his record in this class of business and wishes to have this information to be entered as final.

Yours very truly
President

HTD:R

REFER IN REPLY TO THE FOLLOWING:

ADDRESS ONLY THE
COMMISSIONER OF INDIAN AFFAIRS

Land-
Sales
79566-1911
E K W

Guardianship
costs.

**DEPARTMENT OF THE INTERIOR,**

OFFICE OF INDIAN AFFAIRS,

WASHINGTON,

SEP 23 1911

Mr. John A. Buntin,

    Superintendent Shawnee Indian School,

        Shawnee, Oklahoma.

Sir:

    The Office is in receipt of your request of September 6, submitted on form 5-262a, for authority to expend during the fiscal year 1912 the sum of $52.95, from the appropriation "Contingencies, Indian Department, 1911" for the settlement of final costs in guardianships of Mr. Frank A. Thackery, on behalf of certain Shawnee Indians.

    These expenses are not considered a proper charge against any appropriation now available.  If, however, the Indians interested have individual funds to their credit from which the costs may be paid, you are directed to present separate requests for authority to approve each Indian's check in the usual manner, referring at the same time, to the file number of this letter.

    Whenever it is necessary for the Clerk in Charge to sign official mail in your absence, reference should be made to the file number or date of the authority for such signature.

                    Respectfully,

                    CF Hauke

9-EBM-18             Second Assistant Commissioner.

Sac & Fox – Shawnee
1906-1914 Volume XIV

GUTHRIE-First Monday in January.
OKLAHOMA CITY-First Monday in March.
WOODARD-First Monday in May and
second Monday in November.
ENID-First Monday in June.
LAWTON-First Monday in October.

**Department of Justice.**

**Office of the United States Attorney.**

Western District of Oklahoma.

Guthrie.

September 29th, 1911.

J.A. Buntin,
Superintendent,
Shawnee, Oklahoma.

Dear Sir:

We wish you would pleaser ascertain just what guardianships connected with your agency are set for action on October 5th in the County Court at Tecumseh and notify us at once. Please be prepared to assist with the necessary records and evidence and information in any matters thus set down. I will be at Tecumseh on October 5th.

Very respectfully,

CCF.

Isaac D. Taylor
Assistant U.S. Attorney.

---

COURT TERMS.

GUTHRIE-First Monday in January.
OKLAHOMA CITY-First Monday in March.
WOODARD-First Monday in May and
second Monday in November.
ENID-First Monday in June.
LAWTON-First Monday in October.

**Department of Justice.**

**Office of the United States Attorney.**

Western District of Oklahoma.

Guthrie.

September 29th, 1911.

W. C. Kohlenberg,
Superintendent,
Stroud, Oklahoma.

Dear Sir:

As I understand it the Bryan guardianship hearing is to come up at Tecumseh on October 5th. I will be there on the morning of

146

that day to look after the same and will expect to meet you with all the necessary documents.

I wish you would advise Col. Roy V. Hoffman that while I am with you at Tecumseh we will try to take up the Moore guardianship matter at least to the extent of preparing petition for your appointment as guadian[sic] of Samuel L. Moore.

Very respectfully,

CCF.

Isaac D. Taylor
Assistant U.S. Attorney.

---

Ex-Judge Fifth Judicial District of Nebraska

Telephone { Office, No. 112
            Residence, No. 113

**Robert Wheeler,**
Attorney and Counselor
Tecumseh, Okla.

In re. Ke-so-way-lay-mah.

Oct. 14/11.

Hon. J. A. Buntin,

Shawnee, Okla.

Dear Sir:

Your favor of the 3, inst. received enclosing bonds and appraisements in the Tay-la-mah and Ke-so-way-lay-mah matters. And I herewith return the bond and appraisement in the latter matter, for the reason that I feel sure an error has been made in the appraisement.

The tract of land, Lots 1 & 2, in 5-8-2, was sold to Thomas J. Hillman for $400. and these minors would only be entitled jointly to a 5/42 part, or $47.62. This being the case I wrote the bond for $100. believing that the minors 5/42 interest would not be appraised for more the $50. But the enclosed appraisement makes it $80. and if this appraisement is to stand a new bond will have to be made, as the bond must be in double the amount of the appraisement.

I am in hopes that this appraisement was an error on the part of the appraisers, and that they will find it consistent with their dulty[sic] to reduce it to $50. or less. Return bond and appraisement to me when corrected.

Yours very truly.
Robert Wheeler

**********

Ex-Judge Fifth Judicial District of Nebraska          Telephone { Office, No. 112
                                                                    Residence, No. 113

**ROBERT WHEELER,**
Attorney and Counselor
Tecumseh, Okla.     In re. Ke-so-way-lay-mah allotment.

June 6/11.

Hon. Frank A. Thackery,

Shawnee, Okla.

Dear Sir:

In the matter of the guardianship of Nah-wah-tahth-ka-ka et al. as heirs of Ke-so-way-lay-mah, deceased, the order of sale was made on the 5, inst. and I have advertised the sale for the 26, inst.

The court appointed Charles W. Edmister, W. H. Seymour and T. B. Alford as appraisers. The sale bond must be in double the amount of the appraisement.

I enclose blank sale bond, and appraisement blank.

Yours very truly,
Robert Wheeler

**********

Ex-Judge Fifth Judicial District of Nebraska          Telephone { Office, No. 112
                                                                    Residence, No. 113

**ROBERT WHEELER,**
Attorney and Counselor
Tecumseh, Okla.     In re. Ke-so-way-lay-mah allotment.

June 20/11.

Hon. Frank A. Thackery,

Shawnee, Okla.

Dear Sir:

Replying to your favor of the 14, inst. concerning the appraisers appointed in the Ke-so-way-lay-mah allotment case, would say that at the time I had Messrs Edmister, Seymour & Alford appointed I was not aware that it would be inconvenient for either to serve. And on receipt of your letter this morning I went to see the judge immediately, in hopes I could have the order changed. But the order has been recorded, and the judge says he cannot make any change now. This being the case it will be about necessary for Mr. Seymour and Mr. Alford to make this appraisement, and I will see that parties are appointed in the future who can be more easily spared to do the work. I wish I could fix it differently, but do not see how it is possible.

Yours very truly,
Robert Wheeler

---

Ex-Judge Fifth Judicial District of Nebraska

TELEPHONE { OFFICE, No. 112
RESIDENCE, No. 113

**ROBERT WHEELER,**
ATTORNEY AND COUNSELOR
TECUMSEH, OKLA.   In re. Nah-wah-tahth-ka-ka et al.

Oct. 7/11.

Hon. J. A. Buntin,

Shawnee, Okla.

Dear Sir:

In the matter of the guardianship of Nah-wah-tahth-ka-ka et al. as heirs of Tay-la-mah and as heirs of Ka-so-way-lay-mah[sic], I am enclosing two reports of sale to be signed and sworn to by Mr. Thackery.

Please mail them to him at once, with an urgent request that he sign and swear to and return them as soon as possible, as the purchasers and Indian heirs are all getting very anxious to have the matters closed up.

Yours very truly,
Robert Wheeler

**U. S. INDIAN AGENCY**
SHAWNEE, OKLA.

Received _____ Oct. 8-1911 _____

Answered _____

\*\*\*\*\*\*\*\*\*\*

State of Oklahoma,    )
                                     )  ss.
Pottawatomie County,  )

In the County Court in and for said County and State.

In the matter of the guardianship of          )
                                                                  )
Nah-wah-tahth-ka-ka and Ma-tahth-ka-ka,   )   BID.
                                                                  )
minor heirs of Ke-so-way-lay-mah, deceased. )

I hereby bid for the above named minors' undivided five fotry[sic] seconds part of Lots One and Two of section Five, in township Eight north, range Two east of the Indian Meridian, in Pottawatomie county, state of Oklahoma, the sum of $47.62.

......Thomas J. Hillman.......

\*\*\*\*\*\*\*\*\*\*

State of Oklahoma,    )
                                     )  ss.
Pottawatomie County,  )

In the County Court in and for said County and State.

In the matter of the guardianship of          )
                                                                  )
Nah-wah-tahth-ka-ka and Ma-tahth-ka-ka,)   BID.
                                                                  )
minor heirs of Tay-la-mah, deceased.      )

I hereby bid for the above named minors' undivided 5/42 part of Lots Three and Fourt[sic] of Northwest quarter of section Four, in township Eight north, range Two east of the Indian Meridian, in Pottawatomie county, state of Oklahoma, the sum of $66.67.

.....Shired S. Shirey..........

**F. A. THACKERY,** SUPERVISOR
DISTRICT NO. 2
(ARIZONA, CALIFORNIA, NEVADA)

# DEPARTMENT OF THE INTERIOR
## UNITED STATES INDIAN SERVICE.

Riverside, California,

October 9, 1911.

Supt. John A. Buntin,

Shawnee, Oklahoma.

Dear Mr. Buntin:

With reference to the inclosed letter regarding the $52.95 from Contingencies for the guardianship costs I have written the Office asking them to re-consider the case and grant you the authority requested.

I have a letter from Mr. Grecian at Stroud wanting to know about the two deeds (quitclaim) perfecting title to the land (I think it is the SW1/4 of Sec. 29-12-2), two allotments now owned by Mathew Schueller. These deeds should have been acted upon long ago and returned. If they have not yet come back will you write and make inquiry about them. Better send all of my mail to Leupp, Arizona, instead of to Valentine as I am afraid the office at Valentine has been recently changed.

Sincerely yours,

Frank A. Thackery
Supervisor.

| | | |
|---|---|---|
| | ~~Plaintiff~~ | In the County Court in and for |
| vs. | No. 248 | Cleveland County, |
| Guardianship of | | Oklahoma |
| Arthur & Luther Rolette, | | Norman ___ Oklahoma |
| minors ~~Defendant~~ | | Oct. 19, 191 1 |

## STATEMENT OF COSTS

| Court | 17 20 |
|---|---|

| | | | | | 75 | |
|---|---|---|---|---|---|---|
| | | Sheriff, Post Notices | | | 75 | |
| | | Newspaper Costs | | | 7 | 00 |
| | | | Total | | | 24 95 |
| | | Credit by Cash | | | | 15 00 |
| | | | Balance | | | 9 95 |

STATE OF OKLAHOMA, ⎫
             ⎬ ss.
  Cleveland County,  ⎭

I,___F. B. Swank, Judge____, ~~Clerk~~ of the County Court in and for Cleveland County, Oklahoma, do hereby certify that the above and foregoing is a true and correct statement of costs taxed in the above entitled action in said County Court, and adjudged against ___said minors___

Witness my hand and official seal, this___19th___ day of_____Oct.____191_1_

                               F. B. Swank
                               Judge   ~~Clerk~~ County Court

*********

EX-JUDGE FIFTH JUDICIAL DISTRICT OF NEBRASKA          TELEPHONE { OFFICE, NO. 112 / RESIDENCE, NO. 113

**ROBERT WHEELER,**
ATTORNEY AND COUNSELOR
TECUMSEH, OKLA.    In re. Rolette.

                                         Oct. 20/11.

Hon. J. A. Buntin,

      Shawnee, Okla.

Dear Sir:

      Referring to my letter of the 14, inst. in which I was unable to give you the total costs in the Arthur and Luther Rolette matter, I now enclose a certified statement of the court costs and adverising[sic] in Cleveland county, by which you will see there is a balance of $9.95 due. I suppose this cannot be paid until the deed is approved by the Department.

                         Yours very truly,
                         Robert Wheeler

*********

EX-JUDGE FIFTH JUDICIAL DISTRICT OF NEBRASKA

TELEPHONE { OFFICE, No. 112
RESIDENCE, No. 113

**ROBERT WHEELER,**
ATTORNEY AND COUNSELOR
TECUMSEH, OKLA.

In re. Rolette.

Oct. 14/11.

Hon. J. A. Buntin,

Shawnee, Okla.

Dear Sir:

In the matter of the guardianship of Arthur and Luther Rolette, I am enclosing a certified- recorded copy of the order confirming sale, and a guardian's deed to be executed by James H. Odle, guardian.

Judge F. B. Swank of Cleveland county has not sent me a bill of the costs in the case, and I am writing him again today for this, and I will send you the bill as soon as I get it.

So far as I am able to give you the costs at this time, they are as follows:

| | | |
|---|---|---|
| Sept. 26/10  I deposited with Judge N. E. Sharp for costs, | $10. | |
| June 10/11, I paid Judge F. B. Swank, to cover advertising, | 5. | |
| Oct. 2/11.   I paid recording fees, | 1.25. | |
| My fees, | 35. | |
| Total, | $51.25. | |

This leaves me $33.75 on my fees, and I am satisfied to accept this in full for my services,

In this case J. W. Sturgis, the purchaser advanced $50. to cover costs and expenses, and this is to be repaid to him when the sale is approved by the department, out of the purchse[sic] money.

Yours very truly,
Robert Wheeler

**DAVENPORT STATE BANK, Successor to**
NO. 8668

**The First National Bank**

CAPITAL  $25,000.00

A J LANGER President
O D GROOM Cashier      **Davenport, Oklahoma**

**RECEIVED**
OCT 21 1911
SAC & FOX AGENCY,
OKLAHOMA

October 20, 1911.

W. C. Kohlenberg, Esq.

Sput.[sic] Sac & Fox Indian Agency,

Stroud, Okla.

My Dear Mr. Kohlenberg:--

Inclosed herewith you will find bond of Globe Surety Co., of Kansas City, Mo., for $3,500.00, running to you, as Guardian, substituting the one relinquished on account of consolidation of banks at Davenport.

I find this one identical in wording to that relinquished, so I presume it will meet with your approval.

Kindly acknowledge receipt, and oblige,

Respectfully,

A. J. Langer

President

---

# DEPARTMENT OF THE INTERIOR

### UNITED STATES INDIAN FIELD SERVICE
### SHAWNEE INDIAN AGENCY,

Shawnee, Oklahoma
October 27, 1911.

Mr. Mark Goode,

Shawnee, Oklahoma.

Dear Sir:

Mrs. Hannah Hardin, of Shawnee, Oklahoma, the mother of John Hardin, aged 20 years, Davis Hardin Jr., aged 17 years and Charles Hardin, aged 15 years, being children of Davis Hardin, deceased Citizen Pottawatomie Allottee No. 38, as follows: Thomas M. Hardin, aged 19 years, Mary L. Hardin, aged 17 years, Julia A. Hardin, aged 16 years, and Margaret Hardin, aged 12 years.

All of the aforesaid minor children are interested in the estate of their grandmother, Elizabeth Clinton, nee Hardin, deceased Citizen Pottawatomie Allottee No. 39, being in the nature of an allotment still held in trust and which is expected to be sold to the highest bidder on November 23, 1911. Until that time, however, nothing can be done in the way of taking this matter through the Probate Court but after that date her wish is that you have Willard Johnston appointed guardian over the above named children over their interest in the estate of Margaret Clinton.

If there is anything else you desire in the way of information it will be gladly furnished.

Very respectfully,

J. A. Buntin
Superintendent.

RS

---

**RECEIVED**
OCT 28 1911
SAC & FOX AGENCY,
OKLAHOMA.

*American Surety Company*
*of New-York.*

*H. S. Vyman,*
*President.*

LOCAL BOARD
JOHN THREADGILL, RES  VICE PRES
B  W  HOGAN                    J  L  WILKIN          BRANCH OFFICE FOR THE STATE OF OKLAHOMA
                    BD  L  DUNN                        401-2-3-4  MAJESTIC  BUILDING
            WM  F  WILSON, ATTORNEY                        TELEPHONE  1791
        ADDRESS COMMUNICATIONS TO
    HERMAN J. ROLEKE, MANAGER
HJR-B          OKLAHOMA CITY, OKLA.,  Oct. 27, 1911.

*Home Office Building*

Mr. William Kohlenberg, Agent,
    Sac & Fox Indian Agency,
        Sac & Fox, Oklahoma.

Dear Sir:--

You are, no doubt appointed guardian for Indian minor from time to time, the same as Agents located at other Agencies in this State. I have arrangements perfected whereby we wrote these bonds for the Agents expeditiously, and I should like very much to know whether you could be interested in this subject. Under an arrangement lately entered into with out Agent at Cordell, Oklahoma, such bonds as Mr. Walter F. Dickens, the Indian Agent at the Seger Agency, requires are executed for him by our Cordell representative upon request. This same arrangement could be made with a representative of the Company located near your Agency.

I would be pleased to hear from you on the subject.

Very truly yours,

Herman J. Roleke

Manager.

---

COURT TERMS.

GUTHRIE-First Monday in January.
OKLAHOMA CITY-First Monday in March.
WOODARD-First Monday in May and
second Monday in November.
ENID-First Monday in June.
LAWTON-First Monday in October.

Department of Justice.

Office of the United States Attorney.

Western District of Oklahoma.

Guthrie.

October 31, 1911.

J.A. Buntin,
Supt. & Spl. Disb. Agt,
Shawnee, Oklahoma.

Dear Sir:

I have been advised by Hon. Ross R. Lockridge, County Judge, that J. A. Steen, claiming to be guardian for Ethel Shawnee by an appointment in Seminole County, has filed a motion in the guardianship of Ethel Shawnee pending in Pottawatomie County, that the same was be transferred to Seminole County, and the matter is to be heard on the 6th of November.

Will you kindly procure me a copy of Mr. Steen's motion and forward me at once so that I can prepare on the case.

I had a similar matter up before in this guardianship about January and February, 1910. I trust you will be able to have Ethel Shawnee and Julia Shawnee present at Tecumseh on the day stated as I may need their testimony. We will also probably desire to call upon Goerge[sic] Outcelt who knows something about the matter, having prepared the original petition for appointment of guardian in Pottawatomie County, and we might ascertain whether he will be in Tecumseh on the 6th requesting him to be there if possible.

Kindly mail me the copy of Mr. Steen's motion at your very earliest convenience. I will be in Tecumseh probably about 10:30 the morning of the 6th, and trust that you will be there to assist me on the above matter and any other of your guardianships which may need attention and that you will have all necessary papers and records present.

Very respectfully,

Isaac D. Taylor
Assistant U. S. Attorney.

JRP.

---

COURT TERMS.

GUTHRIE-First Monday in January.
OKLAHOMA CITY-First Monday in March.
WOODARD-First Monday in May and
  second Monday in November.
ENID-First Monday in June.
LAWTON-First Monday in October.

Department of Justice.

Office of the United States Attorney,
Western District of Oklahoma.
Guthrie.

RECEIVED
NOV 1 1911
X AGENCY,
OMA.

October 31, 1911.

W. C. Kohlenberg,
    Supt. & Spl. Disb. Agt.,
        Stroud, Oklahoma.

Dear Sir:

Be sure and bear in mind we are to be in Tecumseh on the morning of Monday, November 6th, on the Milton Bryan guardianships.

Kindly have with you all necessary papers and records.

What were you able to accomplish toward the appointment of a guardian for Samuel L. Moore? I desire to keep in touch with that matter and get it through with as soon as possible.

Very respectfully,

Isaac D. Taylor
Assistant U. S. Attorney.

JRP.

---

Statement of funds paid to John A. Hensen, Perry, Okla.
as legal guardian of Charley Lightfoot,
Iowa Indian minor.

| | Land money | Lease money | | Total |
|---|---|---|---|---|
| Charley Lightfoot | -------- | Sept. 18, '05 | $26.67 | |
| | | Apr. 28,  06 | 13.33 | $40.00 |

---

Miss Kate Barnard
Commissioner

DR J H STOLPER
GENERAL ATTORNEY

H. Husen
Assistant

State of Oklahoma

DEPARTMENT OF CHARITIES
& CORRECTIONS.

Oklahoma City

Nov. 7, 1911.

Mr. W. C. Kohlenberg,

In Care of Hon. W. H. Wilcox, Co. Judge,

Stilwell, Okla.

Dear Sir:

I am directed by Hon. Kate Barnard, Commissioner of Charities and Corrections, State of Oklahoma, to compliment you upon the good showing made in your report of Nov. 3, 1911, in the matter of the guardianship of Rachel Hall.   Enclosed find a copy of a letter sent to the Honorable County Judge of Payne County, and we trust that you will do just as well in the future.

Yours truly,

INCLOS. 1.                                       Dr. J. H. Stolper
                        General Attorney Dept. of Char. & Cor.

Congratulations!!
W. H. Wilcox, Judge

Congratulations!
Leon M Steen
Clerk

**********

(COPY)

RECEIVED
NOV 13 1911

Nov. 7, 1911.

Hon. W. H. Wilcox,

     County Judge, Payne Co.,

       Stilwell, Okla.

Dear Judge:

     Your favor of November 3rd, 1911, with inclosed report of W. C. Kohlenberg filed Nov. 3rd, 1911, has been received.   This Department has no objection to the approval of said report, and begs to compliment the guardian upon the good showing that said report makes.

Very respectfully,

General Attorney Dept. of Charities
B/                                     and Corrections.

---

COURT TERMS.
___
GUTHRIE-First Monday in January.
OKLAHOMA CITY-First Monday in March.
WOODARD-First Monday in May and
second Monday in November.
ENID-First Monday in June.
LAWTON-First Monday in October.

**Department of Justice.**
___

**Office of the United States Attorney.**
**Western District of Oklahoma.**
**Guthrie.**

November 13, 1911.

W. C. Kohlenberg, Supt.,
 R. F. D. No. 2,
  Stroud, Oklahoma.

Dear Sir:

  Yours of the 10th instant relative to the appointment of guardian for Samuel L. Moore in Payne County, Oklahoma, received' your said letter also giving certain information as to costs.

  I will take this matter up further just as soon as I can and communicate with you.

Very respectfully,

Isaac D. Taylor

Assistant U. S. Attorney.
JRP.

---

COURT TERMS.
___
GUTHRIE-First Monday in January.
OKLAHOMA CITY-First Monday in March.
WOODARD-First Monday in May and
second Monday in November.
ENID-First Monday in June.
LAWTON-First Monday in October.

**Department of Justice.**
___

**Office of the United States Attorney.**
**Western District of Oklahoma.**
**Guthrie.**

November 15, 1911.

J. A. Buntin, Supt.,
  Shawnee, Oklahoma.

Dear Sir:

Relative to the guardianship of Pash-ko-nat by Willard Johnston, guardian, I have discussed the matter with Mr. Embry, and he agrees that the plan I outlined to you when I saw you at the Agency, seems the best one to pursue.

As soon as I can arrange my other work, I will try to come down and take the matter up in person with you and Judge Lockridge and Mr. Johnston.

Very respectfully,

Isaac D. Taylor

Assistant U. S. Attorney.

JRP.

---

**F. A. THACKERY, SUPERVISOR**
DISTRICT NO. 2
(ARIZONA, CALIFORNIA, NEVADA)

## DEPARTMENT OF THE INTERIOR

### UNITED STATES INDIAN SERVICE.

Fort Defiance, Arizona.

November 19, 1911.

Supt. John A. Buntin,

Shawnee, Okla.

Dear Mr. Buntin:

The inclosed resignation was sent to me by Mr. C. A. Outcelt of Tecumseh and thinking that I had already resigned in the papers made up my Mrs. Seymour and Mr. Embry I am sending this to you to be used only in case I have not already resigned. I think your appointment for these Shawnee children must have already been made. Unless you watch their interests very closely they are going to loose[sic] their lands in the Creek Nation.

I prefer that all of my guardian papers be made up on the forms suggested by Mr. Embry and I think that you will find that I have already signed the necessary papers in this case.

161

Please let me know how my guardianship cases are coming

on and about what time they are likely to be closed up.

Sincerely yours,

Frank A. Thackery
Supervisor.

**********

|                          | ) |     |
|--------------------------|---|-----|
| STATE OF OKLAHOMA,       | ) |     |
|                          | ) | ss. |
| POTTAWATOMIE COUNTY.     | ) |     |
|                          | ) |     |

In the County Court.

| In the matter of the        | ) |                         |
|-----------------------------|---|-------------------------|
|                             | ) |                         |
| Gouardianship[sic] of Fre-  | ) | Resignation as Guardian.|
| -donia Williams, now        | ) |                         |
| Brown, a minor.             | ) |                         |
|                             | ) |                         |

And Now comes Frank A. Thackery, guardian of the abve[sic] named minor and

hereby resigns as such guardian, and asks the Court to accept his resignation
and discharge him from said guardianship.
Dated this  :ov. 2ond.1911. [sic]

_____Frank A. Thackery_____

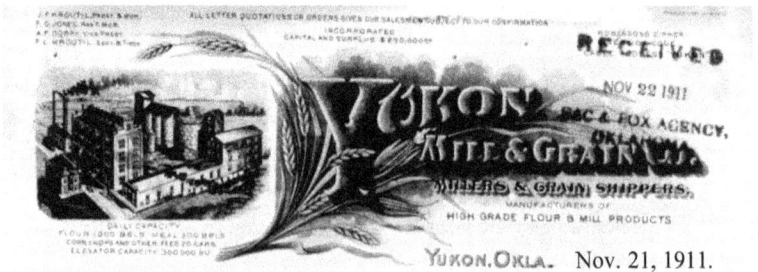

YUKON, OKLA.  Nov. 21, 1911.

Mr. W. C. Kohlenberg,

Stroud, Oklahoma.

Dear Mr. Kohlenberg:

I have your kind letter of the 18th, and am glad that Mr. Wise is satisfied with the arrangements that are made concerning Eustace and Helen. I note what you say about the rules governing the expenditure of money belonging to guardians of minors. I presume that you understand that my appointment as guardian has not been approved, for the reason that my father has never furnished a report of his expenditures of her rentals, during the time that the money has been handled by him.

He advised me that you were to furnish a statement of the amount paid over to him, and as he has receipts from the stores, and from Helen, for the expenditures, it seems that all that is necessary now is your statement. This matter should be closed up as quickly as possible, so as to avoid any trouble that Mr. Goodman may make, and if it is not asking too much, I would thank you to furnish the statement. The fund which is to be used for her expenses cannot be turned over to me until my appointment as guardian has been made.

As the matter now stands, I am powerless to do anything, according to law, and I would like to get this straight, before applying to the County Judge for appointment. I have been advancing money to her for necessary expenses, and have no authority to do this, except with the approval of her legal guardian.

I thank you very much, indeed, for the information concerning the progress that is being made in Washington with the applications for withdrawal of trust funds. I am anxious that the warrants be drawn for those whose applications are approved, before Congress convenes, in December, as there might be efforts made by the Iowa people to enjoin the Treasurer from paying the money out. I presume, however, that the matter is being handled just as quickly as possible. I am very glad indeed, to note that my name was the first on the list, and I assure you that I will be very glad to get the money.

Yours very truly,

Frank O. Jones

YUKON, OKLA., Oct. 18, 1911.

Mr. W. C. Kohlenberg,

 Stroud, Oklahoma.

Dear Mr. Kohlenberg:

 You will be interested in knowing that I went to Shawnee Sunday and too Helen and placed her in the Oklahoma Wesleyan College at Oklahoma City. She is very comfortably located, surrounded by the best influences, and I am very much pleased with the change and she is also. The cost of board, room rent, tuition, etc., up to February is $173.00, which has been paid. It was necessary to buy her a uniform and other articles for her room, amounting in all to about $30.00. I sent an itemized statement to my father and I understand he has about $60.00 of her money, leaving a balance of about $144.00 to be advanced until we can get authority from Washington to use her own funds.

 She will have $100.00 due in December, I understand, so that the balance to be used out of her own money will be very small. However I think it best to get authority from the Department to use her back money, to defray all of her expenses in the College, and let her rentals go to buy clothing and to be used for spending money. She must furnish everything, as you know it makes it quite expensive.

 My father has resigned as her guardian, and she has petitioned the Court to have me appointed so that this will be done very soon. I shall be very glad to look after her interests, carefully, and I am sure that she appreciates the opportunity she has to better her condition. I feel sure the

Department will approve our action in this matter, for it is certainly money well spent.

Kindly advise me as soon as possible when you have had information concerning funds to pay her expenses.

With very kindest personal regards, I am,

Your friend,

F.O. Jones

[Copy of Original]

First
National Conference
of the

American Indian
Association

October 12-15, 1911

on the

Campus

of the

Ohio State University

Columbus, Ohio

THE STONEMAN PRESS, COLUMBUS, OHIO

/101/

## Origin and Plans
OF THE
## American Indian Association

❦

Through a kindly interest in our race, manifested by Prof. F. A. McKenzie, of the Ohio State University, and as a result of a correspondence between him and a considerable number of the Indians carried on over a period of nearly two years, it became possible for a few Indians to meet in Columbus, Ohion, on the 3d and 4th of April past, for the purpose of organizing an Association of Indians, by Indians and for Indians. A temporary executive committee was formed, and plans started for a convention to be held at Columbus, Ohio, from the 12th to the 15th of October, 1911.

Hardly had the plans of the Executive Committee been started when the following invitation was received:

COLUMBUS, OHIO
*To the Native Americans of the United States:*

### Greeting
Word has come to our ears that you are planning to meet in national assembly for the first time in history to discuss the problems which devolve upon the Red Race, and we, therefore, hasten to invite you to light the camp-fire first in the city named for the first white man who visited these shores. Let us, if we may, forget any animosities of the past, and jointly work for those conditions and those policies which in the future will justify peace because based upon the principles of equity, intelligence and grogress. The high position which your leaders are reaching makes [illegible] to welcome the representatives of all the tribes in the name of the State University, the city of Columbus, and the civic and religious bodies of our city.

(Signed)          W. O. THOMPSON,
*President, Ohio State University.*
GEORGE S. MARSHALL,
*Mayor of Columbus.*
CHAS. J. PRETZMAN,
*President, Chamber of Commerce.*

JOSEPH TAYLOR BRITAN,
*President, Ministerial Association.*
H. M. BLAIR,
*Secretary, Y. M. C. A.*
E. O. RANDALL,
*Secretary, State Historical and Archaeological
Society.*
J. M. HENDERSON,
*President, Columbus Federation of Labor.*

✤

## April Meeting

The six people at this April meeting spent two days in canvassing the situation, and finally decided that not only had the time come for an organization of Indians, but that a call should be issued for the Conference to be held in the fall in Columbus for the purpose of perfecting a permanent organization, and of discussing the problems vital to the race.   To give meaning to the call it was further cvonsidered necessary to formulate a statement which should constitute the basis of the organization about to be formed.  The members of the Association will find in the purpose thus stated a basis not only of organization, but also a series of principles which will serve as the foundation upon which all the policies of the Association will rest.

## Provisional Platform of the American Indian Association

The Temporary Executive Committee of the American Indian Association declare that the time has come when the American Indian race should contribute in a more united way, its influence and exertion with the rest of the citizens of the United States in all lines of progress and reform, for the welfare of the Indian race in particular, and all humanity in general.

With this purpose in view this association is formed, and the purpose of this association is:

First.  To promote the good citizenship of the Indians of this country, to help in all progressive movements to this end, and to emulate the sturdy characteristics of the North American Indian, especially his honesty and patriotism.

Second.   To promote all efforts looking to the advancement of the Indian in enlightenment which leave him free, as a man, to develop according to the natural laws of social evolution.

Third.   To exercise the right to oppose any movement which appears detrimental to the race.

Fourth.   In all conferences and meetings of this association, there shall be broad, free discussion of all subjects bearing upon the welfare of the race.

Fifth.   This association will direct its energies exclusively to general principles and universal interests, and will not allow itself to be used for any personal or private interests.   The honor of the race and the god of the country will always be paramount.

Sixth.   It is the sense of this committee that every member of the association should exert his influence in every legitimate way to bring before each member of the race the necessity of promoting good citizenship.

[Illigible]mporary officers and members of this committee consisted of Charles E. Dagenett, [Illegible]; Laura M. Cornelius, Secretary; Charles A. Eastman, Carlos Montezuma, Thomas L. Sloan, and Henry Standing Bear.

It was decided that the Temporary Executive Committee should be enlarged, in order to be more truly representative and that a General Committee should also be established consisting or representatives so far as possible of every tribe or consideralbe body of Indians in the country,   Sub-Committees on Program, Finance, Publicity, and Local Affairs were also appointed.   The fact that an immense correspondence would have to be carried on let the committee to the decision that a permanent Secretary must be employed.   They were fortunate in securing the services of Mrs. Rosa B. La Flesche for that position, her experience and knowledge especially fitting her for the work.   She has been in Columbus since the 19th of May.

### Objects of the Associatioon

The American Indian Association is primarily an organization of American Indians.   It proposes to bring together all progressive Indians and friends of Indian progress for the purpose of promoting the highest interest of the Indian as a race and as an individual. It asserts that any condition of living, habit of thought, or racial characteristic that unfits the Indian for modern environment is detrimental and conducive only of individual and racial imcompetence.

While the Association and it founders most sincerely appreciate the splendid elements and achievements of the old-time Indian culture and the methods by which early conditions were met, it realizes most keenly the inefficacy [illegible] methods in meeting the conditions of modern times. It asserts that the life hope of the Indian of America depends upon the ability of the Indian to meed enlightened races upon n equal footing in all walks of life.

The Association seeks to bring about a condition whereby the white race and all races may have a better and a broader knowledge of the red race, its claims, its needs and its ability to contribute materially and spiritually to modern civilization.

The Association asserts the right of the Indian to an active voice in the rights and destiny of his race and will ever seek to defend all rights and just claims of the race. One of its high aims is to see the development of conditions whereby the Indian as an individual and as a race may take his place as a man among men, as an active member of the great commonwealth, and independent of all support not accorded to any body of people who have achieved a position equal to the most enlightened.

In stating this the Association emphatically asserts its belief that the Indian possesses natural ability and aptitude for every life mission and that under proper conditions these capacities will find a useful and successful development.

It believes that the development of individual ability and the stimulation of high ideals far better than the impressing of every man into a preconceived type. It therefore believes that Indian progress depends upon awakening the abilities of every individual Indian, the realization of individual responsibility for self and race, and the duty of responding to the call to activity. [The]

American Indian Association expects every progressive Indian to become an Active member. To its Associate membership it invites all non-Indians interested in its principles. Their kindest friends, however, will realize and insist that the Indians' first help must come from and through themselves. Let them come out of the silence, voice their common demands, and develop their strength by serious discussion in national council. Not all will agree, but allc an learn from each other, and will find many points of agreement which will lead to common action for the good of all.

Today the white man does not believe in Indian capacity—does not believe that he has either the intelligence or the dignity to hold such a conference as is here proposed. The Conference alone will by its success win great things for the race. Everyone, however, should realize that this is not an association organized for the purpose of antagonizing or opposing the efforts of the government or of other agencies in their efforts in behalf of the Indian, but to aid every move tending toward race and national advancement.

### 𝕸embership

On the 20th and 21st of June, upon the invitation of Miss Laura M. Cornelius and by vote of the members, the Exective Committee met at the Cornelius home at Seymour, Wisconsin, to make further plans for the October Conference. It was there definitely decided that the fee for Active and Associate membership in the organization should be $2.00. Voluntary contributions of larger amounts are expected from thos who can afford to do more. None but persons of Indian blood are eligible for Active membership. Membership cards will be issued upon application.

Special attention was paid to the subj[illegible] fall Conference. It was decided to issue [illegible]ers of invitation to all such persons recommended to the committee as likely to be interested to further the aims of the Association. It is hoped that the message may spread to many others equally worthy, but whose names have not as yet found their way to the rolls of the committee.

## Credentials

Those desiring to attend the Conference will receive credentials. Each tribe of the country is urged to appoint a representative. Several tribes have already practically decided to take such action.

The Executive Committee, on September 15th, will issue credentials as Delegates to all such representatives of the tribes, and to all other invited Indians *who have reported before that date* their intention to attend the Conference. At the opening of the Conference the committee will meet to consider the question of issuing additional credentials to any who may apply at that time.

Further information will be furnished to all persons applying for the same. It is especially desired that every Indian planning to attend the Conference shall keep in close touch with the Columbus office, not only by asking questions but by giving advise and help in every possible way. This is a movement in which every member has an equal right and an equal responsibility.

All communications should be addressed to

AMERICAN INDIAN ASSOCIATION,

*Ohio State University,*

Columbus, Ohio.

---

[The letter below typed as given]

**RECEIVED**

Cushing Okla

SAC & FOX AGENCY,
OKLAHOMA.

Dec. 4-1911

Mr. W.C. Kohlenberg

in Regard to that Guardineship matters I filled out that Bond and sent in some tine a go. and I will be over to Chandler this week. if there is any thing else you want me to do let me know soon for I may leave for a while.

Yours Truly

G. T. Brown

L. G. PITMAN                                                MARK GOODE

**PITMAN & GOODE**
ATTORNEYS-AT-LAW
Rooms 20 and 20 1-2, Herald Building
PHONE 283                SHAWNEE, OKLA.

Shawnee, Oklahoma
December 11, 1911

Mr. John A. Buntin

Sup't. Indian School

Shawnee, Okla.

Dear Sir:

Referring to your letter of December 7th, in the matter of the appointment of a Guardian for the minor heirs of Julia Fry, we beg to advise that we have this day called upon the successful bidder for the money necessary to make the Court deposit and our retainer fee, and as soon as the amount asked for, to-wit, $20.00, is received, we will begin proceedings to have Mr. Stelzner appointed Guardian as per your request.

Yours truly,

MG-MLK                            Pitman & Goode

---

| | |
|---|---|
| Commercial Law and | Stenographer and Notary |
| Collections a Specialty | R E C E I V E D |

Re _____

_____ vs _____

_____

No. _____ $ _____

LAW OFFICE OF   DEC 15 1911

**W. G. PARDOE**
SAC & FOX AGENCY,
OFFICE ROOMS IN    OKLAHOMA.
PARDOE BUILDING

Office Phone 87
Residence Phone 197

**STROUD, OKLA.**

12/13 – 1911

WC Kohlenberg Esq
        Sac & Fox Okla
    Dear Sir: I am herewith disclosing order obtained for allowance of fee in the matter of guardianship of Ruth and Albert Moore

Wish you would send me Ck for same.  I am enclosing Receipt herewith

Yours truly

W.G. Pardoe

---

L. G. PITMAN                                                           MARK GOODE

**PITMAN & GOODE**
ATTORNEYS-AT-LAW
Rooms 20 and 20 1-2, Herald Building
PHONE 283                        SHAWNEE, OKLA.

Shawnee, Okla.
December 14, 1911

Mr. John A. Buntin

Sup't. Indian Agency

Shawnee, Okla.

Dear Sir:

This is to acknowledge receipt of your letter of December 11, 1911, instructing us to have Mr. Robert H. Stelzner appointed Guardian for Tah-tah-pe-twa.

You also asked that Mr. Willard Johnson be appointed Guardian for Pash-ka-nat.  As he is already the Guardian of the estate of this minor we apprehend that this is unnecessary and all that will be required to be done is to have petition and so forth filed by Mr. Johnson asking for sale of land and due execution to deed when the sale is made.  We are in receipt of the necessary funds for cost deposit from Mr. Dunn and will begin proceedings forthwith.

Yours truly,

MG-MLK                          Pitman & Goode

---

L. G. PITMAN                                                           MARK GOODE

**PITMAN & GOODE**
ATTORNEYS-AT-LAW
Rooms 20 and 20 1-2, Herald Building
PHONE 283                        SHAWNEE, OKLA.

Shawnee, Oklahoma
Dec. 14, 1911

Mr. Jno. A. Buntin

Sup't. Indian Agency

Shawnee, Okla.

Dear Sir:

This is to acknowledge receipt of your letter of December 11, 1911, in re appointment of Guardian for Laura Sah-ah-pe-ah.

We have this day called upon Mr. Connor, the successful bidder, to forward us the necessary amount for the first deposit of court costs and our retainer fee and as soon as this is received we will take pleasure in starting the proceedings. In the meantime we will be pleased to have you advise us of the County in which Laura Sah-ah-pe-ah resides for the reason that under the law the proceeding must be had in the County wherein the minor is residing.

Yours very truly,

Pitman & Goode

MG-MLK

---

L. G. PITMAN                                                    MARK GOODE

**PITMAN & GOODE**
ATTORNEYS-AT-LAW
Rooms 20 and 20 1-2, Herald Building
PHONE 283                       SHAWNEE, OKLA.

Dec. 16, 19 1[sic]

John A. Buntin
Superintendent
Shawnee
Okla

Dear Sir:

Enclosed find petition for Guardian in the matter of minor heirs of Julia Fry   Kindly have Mr. S Verify etc and return at once

Very truly yours

Mark Goode

---

*Thos. M. Walker,* President          *James Van Buren,* Vice President     *H. P. Fones.* Ass't Secretary
*Wm. T. Kemper,* Treasurer           *John R. Mulvane,* Vice President      *E. Sanford Miller,* Ass't Secretary
*Jo Zach Miller,* III, Secretary     *J. L. Miller, Jr.,* Vice President    *Tom M. Murphy.* Ass't Secretary

**BEADLES & LAUX**
SUITE 236 LEE BUILDING
GENERAL AGENTS
HIGHLEY & MILLS, ATTORNEYS
A. J. McCARTHY, ASSOCIATE ATTY.
H, M. SCALES, RES. VICE PRES.
CHAS. M. BOSWORTH, RES VICE PRES.

*Globe Surety Company*
*of Kansas City, Missouri*
*Capital $500,000.00*
*Surplus $100,000.00*

OKLAHOMA CITY, OKLA.   Dec. 16, 1911.

Mr. W. K[sic]. Kohlenberg,

Sac & Fox Agency,

Okla.

Dear Sir:-

Will you please check up our Guardian bond account and send us check for those guardianships which are still alive?

Yours truly,

Beadles & Laux

LNB-T                                    General Agents.

---

L. G. PITMAN                                                    MARK GOODE

**PITMAN & GOODE**
ATTORNEYS-AT-LAW
Rooms 20 and 20 1-2, Herald Building
PHONE 283                    SHAWNEE, OKLA.

Shawnee, Oklahoma
December 21, 1911

Mr. Jno. A. Buntin

Sup't. Indian Agency

Shawnee, Okla.

Dear Sir:

Referring to your letter of December 17th in re appointment of guardian for minor heirs interested in the allotment of John Moses LaClair, I beg to advise that we have this day called upon purchasers for the funds necessary to institute these proceedings and will be pleased to take up the matter and push it to a prompt conclusion as soon as the necessary payments are in hand.

Yours very truly,

MG-MLK                                    Pitman & Goode

---

L. G. PITMAN                                                        MARK GOODE

**PITMAN & GOODE**
ATTORNEYS-AT-LAW
Rooms 20 and 20 1-2, Herald Building
PHONE 288                    SHAWNEE, OKLA.

Shawnee, Oklahoma
December 21, 1911

Mr. Jno. A. Buntin
    Sup't. Indian Agency
        Shawnee, Okla.

Dear Sir:

Referring to the case of E-ne-kohn wherein we ask for a Guardian for Alex E-ne-kohn, I beg to advise you that Mr. Wyant, the purchaser of the land in question is urging me to hurry the matter along, and we are now being delayed pending the arrival of the bond in this case. I don't know whether you experience much delay in procuring these bonds or not, but I think that we could arrange with one of the numerous bonding companies represented here in this City to get their guardianship bonds signed for the rate you are now paying and thus enable the bond to be executed any time one is needed. I merely suggest this and if it meets with your approval and you desire me to do so, and advise me of the bonding company making the bond, I am sure I can make the necessary arrangements with some of the companies doing business at Shawnee.

Yours very truly,

MG-MLK                                    Pitman & Goode

[The letter below typed as given]

Dec. 27-11
Noble, O.K.  R 1

Supt of Indian scool
       Shawnee, O.K.
Dear Sir
I recived a letter from Pitman & Good Attorneys
asking me to be appointed Guardian over Bessie O.
Roselius my daughter.
    I was appointed Guardian for Bessie O. Roselius at
Norman O.K. in the year of 1901.  we reside in
Cleveland Co O.K.
    if you want any Legal papers of the same I can send
them in.  if this is not in order pleas let me know at
once & oblige.
       C. M. Roselius  Noble, OK, R1

---

1-25163

Finance
Claims
1o8o12/1911[sic]
J.C.H.

DEPARTMENT OF THE INTERIOR

OFFICE OF INDIAN AFFAIRS

WASHINGTON

To prepare vouchers
on form 5-335a.

Dec 27 1911

Mr. John A. Buntin, Superintendent,

       Indian School, Shawnee, Oklahoma.

Sir:

    Under date of December 15, 1911, authority in the amount of $52.95 was granted
by the Secretary of the Interior for the settlement of indebtedness incurred by ex-
Superintendent Frank A. Thackery in the fiscal year 1911 as final costs in the
guardianship of the following named Indians:

| | | | |
|---|---|---|---|
| | | Pe nee she | $4^{35}$ |
| Men ah pe | $4^{35}$ | Anna Sultuska | $2^{95}$ |
| Mut twa ah quah | $3^{35}$ | Louise Sultuska | $2^{95}$ |
| Me nah quah | $4^{85}$ | Hilda Sultuska | $4^{95}$ |
| Thomas Foreman | $5^{10}$ | Jerome Sultuska | $4^{95}$ |

| | | | |
|---|---|---|---|
| Mamie Down | 4[85] | Puck ke shin no | 4[70] |
| Ma nah the quah qua ah | 4[85] | Ke ke e quah | 4[75] 52.95 |

As it is now too late for you to make payment for this indebtedness, you are directed to prepare vouchers covering the costs on form 5-335a and to submit them to this Office for payment as a claim after certification by Mr. Thackery. If his post office address is unknown to you, address him in care of this Office.

Blank form is enclosed herewith.

Respectfully,

C.F. Hauke,

Second Assistant

Wx-26. Commissioner.

(C O P Y.)

---

In the District Court of the Third Judicial District within and for Pottawatomie County, Oklahoma Territory.

Chief McKosato, plaintiff, )
)
    -vs- ) Petition in Equity.
)
Dickson Duncan and Allen G. Thurman, minors, )
)
and Milton Bryan, their guardian, defendants. )

The plaintiff, Chief McKosato, says, that one Barbara McKosato, late of Pottawatomie county and territory of Oklahoma, was a member of the Sac and Fox tribe or bank of Indians, and was in her lifetime seized of and in possession as allottee No. 102 of the following described real estate, to wit:

Northeast quarter and Lots Three and Four in Section Twenty, Township Eleven north, Range Five east of the Indian Meridian, in Pottawatomie county, Oklahoma territory.

That the defendant Dickson Duncan is a minor aged 20 years, and the defendant Allen G. Thurman is a minor aged 20 years, and that the defendant Milton Bryan is the duly appointed, qualified and acting guardian of said minors, under letters of guardianship issued by the Probate Court of Pottawatomie county, Oklahoma territory.

That said Barbara McKosato died intestate on or about the 20 day of

178

...January......A.D....1894....owning said above described real estate, and leaving surviving her as her sole heirs at law, her husband, this plaintiff, Chief McKosato, and her son, Kah-no-tah-peah, or ..David.Duncan...

That said Kan-n-tah-peah[sic], or..David.Duncan..died intestate on or about the..10....day of..April....A.D...1899...owning an undivided one half part of said above described real estate by inheritance as aforesaid, and leaving surviving him as his sole heirs at law, his two minor sons, the defendants Dickson Duncan and Allen G. Thurman.

That by the death of said Barbara McKosato, the plaintiff, Chief McKosato, became seized by descent from said Barbara McKosato of the undivided one half part of said real estate, and by the death of said Kah-no-tah-peah, or....David.Duncan......, the defendants Dickson Duncan and Allen G. Thurman, became seized by descent from said Kah-netah-peah, or..David.Duncan each of the undivided one fourth part of said real estate.

That said real estate is not subject to taxation, and no Territorial, county, school or municipal taxes have been levied upon the same, or upon any property of said estate, and all claims and debts against said estate have been fully paid.

Wherfore[sic] the plaintiff prays that a partition of the real property above described may be made by and under the direction of this court between said plaintiff, Chief McKosato, and said defendants, Dickson Duncan and Allen G. Thurman, according to their respective rights and interest herein; that his interest in said premises may be set off to him in severalty; that commissioners be appointed by the Court for the purpose of making such partition; or in case a partition of said premises can not be made without manifest injury to the value thereof, then that the said premises may be sold by and under the direction of this court, free of the rights of all the persons parties to this suit, and that the proceeds of the sale may be distributed to the parties entitled thereto in lieu of their respective parts and proportions of the estate according to their just rights therein, and plaintiff may have such other and further relief as is just and equitable.

_ _ _Chief M<sup>c</sup>Kosato _ _ _ _ _

By _ _ Robert Wheeler _ _ _ _.

His attorney.

Territory of Oklahoma )
               ) ss.
...Lincoln.....County. )
      Chief McKosato of lawful age, being first duly sworn deposes and says
that he is the plaintiff in the above entitled action, and that he knows the contents
of the above and foregoing petition, and that the facts set forth and statements and
allegations made therein are true as he verily believes.          his
Witnesses to mark                                       x
John R. S. Reeves                    _ _ _Chief M^c^Kosato_ _mark_ _
Charles Wells

      Subscribed and sworn to before me this...3....day of....Sept....A.D. 1907.

                                     _ _Charles Wells_ _ _ _ _ _ _.
                                            Notary Public
      My commission expires June 8, 1911.

---

L. G. PITMAN                                                  MARK GOODE
                          **PITMAN & GOODE**
                          ATTORNEYS-AT-LAW
               Rooms 20 and 20 1-2, Herald Building
PHONE 283                        SHAWNEE, OKLA.

                                      January 2, 1912.

John A?[sic] Buntin,

      Superintendent, Etc.,              Send to Beadles & Laux O City & say we will remit upon receipt of bill

            Shawnee,

Dear Sir:              Okla.

Please have Mr. Stenzler execute the enclosed bonds as guardian and

when so executed send to me for filing with the County Court. I presume

however that he had better go over with the first case and meet the Judge

who has expressed some desire to see that man that he is making guardian

by wholesale and he had better take the first oath of office before his

honor and thereafter we can probably arrange to have him do this before

Alford as a notary.

      There are three of these bonds, to-wit:

                Tah-peh-pe-twa's case

                Laura Sah-ah-peah's case and

                The matter of the Rock Children.

I beg to say that our friend R. Wyant, is getting "some uneasy" about the E-ne-kohn case and surely the bond should be around soon. See if you cant[sic] "jar it" lose somehow as it has been held up a very long time and besides, this is breaking into the attorneys[sic] prerogative. He should be given all the credit for <u>delay</u>. It will work better.

Very respectfully,

Pitman & Goode

---

| | |
|---|---|
| ___Guardianship of___ _____ | |
| _____ Plaintiff | In the County Court in and for |
| vs. | No. 213   Cleveland County, |
| ___Tom Mack___ | Oklahoma |
| ___Te wahn ney   Mack___ | ___Norman___ ___Oklahoma |
| Defendant | ___Jan 3___ 191 2 |

### STATEMENT OF COSTS

| Jan | 3 | To Court Costs to date | $3 | 65 |
|---|---|---|---|---|
| " | 3 | To Publication Notices to date | 1 | 00 |
| | | | $4 | 65 |

STATE OF OKLAHOMA, ⎰
     Cleveland County,    ⎱ ss.

I,___John E. Luttrell___, Clerk of the County Court in and for Cleveland County, Oklahoma, do hereby certify that the above and foregoing is a true and correct statement of costs taxed in the above entitled action in said County Court, and adjudged against ___Guardianship of Tom & Te wahn ney Mack minors___

Witness my hand and official seal, this___3rd___day of___January___1912

_____John E. Luttrell_____
Clerk County Court

**MARK GOODE**
LAWYER
SHAWNEE, OKLA.

Shawnee, Oklahoma
January 9, 1912

Mr. John A. Buntin

Shawnee, Okla.

Dear Sir:

Please find enclosed petition in the matter of the sale of the John Moses LaClair allotment. Please have this petition returned to us and we will have Guardian appointed Monday, week.

We find upon investigation that Charles A. Roselius is the Guardian for Bessie C. Roselius, and that Mr. Phillips is Guardian for the LaClair children. The Guardians aver that the children reside in Cleveland County; hence it will be necessary to carry on proceedings in that county, and unless instructed by you otherwise, we will proceed upon the theory that the present duly appointed, acting and qualified Guardians are the proper persons to consummate the sale of this land. So far as we know there can be no objections for the proceeds will never reach the Guardians but will always be under your control.

Yours very truly,

Mg-Mlk                                    Pitman & Goode

Thos. M. Walker, *President*      James Van Buren. *Vice President*   H. P. Fones. *Ass't Secretary*
Wm. T. Kemper, *Treasurer*       John R. Mulvane. *Vice President*   E. Sanford Miller, *Ass't Secretary*
Jo Zach Miller, III, *Secretary*   J. L. Miller, Jr.. *Vice President*   Tom M. Murphy. *Ass't Secretary*

**BEADLES & LAUX**
SUITE 236 LEE BUILDING
GENERAL AGENTS
HIGHLEY & MILLS, ATTORNEYS
A. J. McCARTHY, ASSOCIATE ATTY.
H, M. SCALES, RES. VICE PRES.
CHAS. M. BOSWORTH, RES VICE PRES.

**Globe Surety Company**
*of Kansas City, Missouri*
*Capital $500,000⁰⁰*
*Surplus $100,000⁰⁰*

OKLAHOMA CITY, OKLA. Jan. 19th, 1912.

RE:  Guardian bonds for Robert H. Stelzner -

Mr. J. A. Buntin,

Shawnee, Okla.

Dear Sir:-

Will you kindly advise us as to whether or not Mr. Stelzner is a bonded employe[sic]; also whether he will handle the funds of the wards himself or will they be handled through the agency, as is done at most of the agencies.  In other words, will there be any check on his actions by the Indian Service Department.

Yours truly,

Beadles & Laux

LBN-T                                    General Agents.

---

L. G. PITMAN                                         MARK GOODE

**PITMAN & GOODE**
ATTORNEYS-AT-LAW
SHAWNEE, OKLA.

PHONE 283

January 22, 1912

Mr. Jnol[sic] A. Buntin

Sup't. Indian Agency

Shawnee, Okla.

Dear Sir:

Referring to the matter of bond for the Guardian appointed in order to effect the sale of inherited Indian lands, and especially to your letter of January 3rd requesting me to submit list of rates which can now be secured for executing this bond, we beg to advise that the bonding companies have a fixed rate which is far in excess of the amount which has heretofore been paid for these bonds. It is difficult to get the bonding companies to understand that there is no liability attached when they execute such bonds, but if you would kindly advise us the rate you are paying we think we would have no difficulty in effecting an agreement with some company haveing[sic] local representative to execute bonds at the same rate. If we could say that such rates were in effect the bonding company would send a representative here to investigate and thus get a clear understanding of the situation. It is certainly not possible to get a lower rate than the one you have, but you can avoid a great deal of delay which ought to be done away with if possible; and in this connection we beg to advise that unless the bond in the case of the guardianship of En-e-kohn is forthcoming very soon, it will be necessary to file a new petition for the appointment of Guardian as the law requires the inventory to be made within a limited number of days after the appointment is made and this case has been pending so long as to be near the danger line in this respect.

Yours very truly,

MG-MLK.                                    Pitman & Goode

# DEPARTMENT OF THE INTERIOR

## UNITED STATES INDIAN SERVICE

Riverside, California,

January 25, 1912.

Mr. Isaac D. Taylor,

      Asst. U. S. Attorney,

         Guthrie, Oklahoma.

Dear Mr. Taylor:

             In harmony with our conversation of a few days ago in Guthrie I have examined the record of my Indian guardianship cases in Pottawatomie, Oklahoma, Cleveland and Lincoln counties, Oklahoma, and find the following facts in the various cases. My examination did not extend into the "jacket files" in each case for lack of time so that you will find that final reports have been made in most cases and in a few cases no doubt the cases have been closed but the records not yet brought up to date:

Pottawatomie County.

No.  1226 Ah-ko-the Incompetent.
      Shown not to be closed by record. In this same case is Wah-ne-mah-quah the wife of Ah-ko-the.

No.  1234 Ah-nah-tho-huck Incompetent.
      Shown to be closed. Would like to know from you that the orders etc. are properly made and recorded. In this same case is Wah-sha-ko-skuck, her husband.

No.  Ah-no-tho-the Incompetent.
      Shown to be closed. Please examine record and report as to its sufficiency. In this same case is Meck-ke-kah her husband. In each of these cases I am listing the names alphabetically without reference to No. of cases.

No.  1258 Paul Leon Alford, minor.
      Not closed.
No.  ---- Ah-cha-tha-to-quah  (see adv. list)

No.   274 Webster Alford, minor, age 19.
      Not closed.

No.  1063 Charles Barone, minor, age 21.
      Closed. Please examine and report.

No.   437  Jones Beaver, minor, age 22.
Not closed.

No. 1386  Andrew J. Boisclair, minor, age __
Not closed.

No. 1386  Louis Boisclair, minor, age __
Not closed.

No. 1303  Abraham Burnett, minor, age __
Not closed.  (see case No. 1640-Burnett minors.)

No. 1303  Benjamin Burnett, minor, age __
Not closed.

No. 1303  Catherine Burnett, minor, age __
Not closed.

No. 1303  Lee P. Burnett, minor, age __
Not closed.

No. 1425  Andrew Cuellar, minor, age 14.
Not closed.

No. 1425  Elle Cuellar, minor, age 15.
Not closed.

No. 1425  Leon (Leno) Cuellar, minor, age 8.
Not closed.

No. 1425  Philomen Cuellar, minor, age 11.
Not closed.

Nol. 1425  Proferio Cuellar, minor, age 13.
Not closed.

No.   952  Alex Curley, minor, age __
Not closed.

No.   952  Charley Curley, minor, age __
Not closed.

No.   952  John Curley, minor, age __
Not closed.

No.   952  Tilda Curley, minor, age __
Not closed.

No.   506  Albert Deere, minor, age 23.
Not closed.

No. 1237  Gertrude Elephant (Nay-wah-tah-pa-ma) Minor, age 22.
Not closed.

No. 1237  Henry Elephant, minor, age 24.
Not closed.

No. 1345  Jesse Ellis, minor, age 22.
Not closed.

No.   312  Eli Forman, minor, age (adult).
Not closed.

No.   312  Howard Forman, minor, age 15.
Not closed.

No.   312  Mary Forman, minor, age 21.
Not closed.

No. 1202  Minnie Forman, minor, age 12.
Not closed.

No. 1202  Thomas Forman, minor, age 17.
Not closed.

No.   955  Clarence Fox, minor, age 22.
Not closed.

No. 1414  Bernice (Berdadine[sic]) Haas, minor, age 16.
Not closed.  Publication notice gives the name as Bernadine.  Do not know which
is correct.

No. 1414  Ethel Haas, minor, age 19.
Not closed.

No. 1414  Jesse Haas, minor, age 21.
Not closed.

No. 1414  Joseph Haas, minor, age 14.
Not  closed.

No. 1414  Lucinda Haas, minor, age 6.
Not closed.

No. 1414 Paul Meritt Haas, minor (Insane) age 8.
Not closed.

No. 1414 Reuben Haas, minor, age 11.
Not closed.

No. 674 Anna Hale, minor, age 22 (Wah-pa-nah-ke-kah-qua-quah).
Not closed.

No. 674 Bessie Hale, minor, age 18.
Not closed.

No. 674 Inez Hale, minor, age 13.
Not closed.

No. 1310 Charles Hardin, minor, age age[sic] __
Not closed.

No. 1310 Davis Hardin, minor, age __
Not closed.

No. 1310 John Hardin, minor, age __
Not closed.

No. 934 Julia Hardin, minor, age __
Not closed.

No. 934 Louise (Louisa) Hardin, minor, age 19 (married)
Not closed.

No. 934 Maggie Hardin, minor, age __
Not closed.

No. 934 Thomas Hardin, minor, age 21.
Not closed.

No. 934 Zoa Belle Hardin-Haney, minor, age __ (married)
Not closed.

No. 1228 Kah-ka-nah-che-peah (Oscar Wilde) Incompetent, age 35.
Not closed.

No. 1229 Kah-ke-ne-peah, Incompetent (female) age __ dead.
Not closed.

No. 1148 Ke-ah-quah-moke (female) minor, age 23.
Not closed.

No. 1248  Ke-ke-e-quah, incompetent, age 35 (female).
Not closed. (with Wah-pah-pen-neah husband).

No. 1083  Ke-no-che-pe-wa-se (Annie Gibson) minor, age 18.
Not closed. See case No. 685 covering this same minor.

No.  823  Ke-se-to-quah (female) minor, age 10.
Not closed. Men-ah-ke-tha-quah is same case.

No. 1718  Ketch-che-quah (female) minor, age __
Not closed.

No. 1152  Ket-che-ma-qua  (John Murdock) minor, age __
Not closed.

No.  574  Etta King, minor, age 12.
Not closed.

No. 1250  Kisk-ke-ton (George), Incompetent, age 28.
Not closed. See also cases No. 661 and 672 over same man as minor.

No. 1269  Kish-ke-ton-o-quah (female) Incompetent age 23 (dead).
Not closed. See also case No. 763 over same person as minor.

No. 1244  Ki-yah-squah (Roy Kickapoo) Incompetent, age 28.
Closed. Please examine and report.

No. 1251  Ko-ke-kah-huch (female) Incompetent, age 49.
Not closed.

No.  917  Betsey Little Captain, minor, age 17.
Not closed. The notice of publication in this case does not give the number of
the case.

No.  917  Martha Little Captain, minor, age 10.
Not closed. Same remarks as above.

No. 1409  Tom Mack, Incompetent, age __
Not closed. It does not appear that I ever qualified in this case in Pottawatomie
County. Proper appointment was made in Cleveland County.

No. 1236  Mah-mah-tome-ah (male) incompetent, age 22-dead.
Not closed. See also cases No. 789 and 1315 over this same person. He was
killed by a Shawnee policeman.

No. 1298  Mah-ko-the-quah (Laura Sah-ah-peah) minor, age 18.
Not closed.

No. 1227 Mah-she-nah  (James Down) Incompetent, age 33.
Closed. Please examine and report.  This number also includes his brother-
Wah-tah-tah (Mack Down) and his sister- Mush-cho-qua-to-quah (Mamie Down)

No.   599 Mah-teck-que-not-nee (Clyde Allen) minor age 25.
Not closed.

No. 1232 Ma-ka-the-quah (female) Incompetent, age 31.
Not closed. In this same case is Sho-e-nah-quah her former husband.

No. 1233 Ma-nah-the-qua-que-ah (female) Incompetent age 49.
Not closed. In this same case is Wah-sha-ko-skuck the husband-now deceased.

No. 1083 Ma-tahth-ka-ka (Willie Gibson) Minor age 21.
Not closed.  See also case No. 685 for this same minor.  With this case is a
brother and sister—the brother having the same English name but a slightly
different Indian name.

No. 1238 Ethel Martell, minor age __
Not closed.

No. 1238 Grover Martell, minor age __ (over 21 years).
Not closed.

No. 1238 Theresa Martell, minor age __
Not closed.

No. 1231 Meck-ke-kah (Joseph Murdock) Incompetent age 37.
Closed.  In this same case is his wife Ah-nah-tho-the.

No.   823 Men-ah-ke-the-quah, minor age __ (dead). female.
Not closed. In this same case is Ke-se-to-quah her sister.

No. 1230 Men-ah-pe (female) Incompetent, age 54.
Not closed. With this case is Pe-nee-she her husband.

No. 1241 Me-nah-quah (male) Incompetent, age 34.
Not closed.

No. 1235 Me-na-mesh (Frank Reed) Incompetent, age 33.
Not closed.  His wife-Shah-kah-tah or Jennie Stevens also appears in this case.

No. 1242 Mesh-ah-quot (Harry Smith) Incompetent, age 31.
Not closed.

No.   652 John Mesh-que-ken-nock or Pa-que-shick, minor age 13.
Not closed.

No. 1239  Much-e-nen-e (male) Incompetent, age 59.
Closed.

No. 1401  Geo. C. Muller, minor, age __ (over 21).
Not closed.

No. 1169  James B. Muller, minor, age __ (over 21).
Not closed.

No. 1227  Mush-sho-qua-to-quah (mamie[sic] Down) Incompetent age 28.
Not closed. With this same case are her two brothers, Mah-she-nah or James and
Wah-tah-tah or Mack.

No. 1240  Mut-twyh-quah (female) Incompetent, age 40.
Not closed.

No.   571  Nah-she-kah-pot (John Me-nah-quah), minor age 12.
Not closed. See also case No. 218 in Oklahoma County over this same minor.

No. 1255  Nah-she-pe-eth (female)  Incompetent, age 29.
Not closed.

No. 1083  Na-wah-tahth-ca-ca (Willie Gibson) minor, age 15.
Not Closed. With this same case is a brother and a sister- the brother having the
same English name.

No. 1094  Na-ta-lo-ka, (Willie) minor age __ (over 21)
Not closed.

No. 1150  Mary Neal or Ethel Kirk or Ah-the-nah-qua-tho-quah minor age 20.
Not closed.

No. 1253  Ne-pah-hah (female) Incompetent, age 40.
Not closed.

No.   527  Joseph Nona, minor, age 22.
Not closed.

No. 1149  Pah-kah-tum-o-quah (female) minor, age 21.
Not closed.

No. 1243  Pah-ke-che-moke (female) Incompetent, age 29.
Closed. Please examine and report.

No.   571  Pe-ah-che-thot (Bert)-male, minor, age 25.
Not closed. See case No. 218 in Oklahoma County over this same person.

No.   783  Peah-puck-o-he (male) minor, age 20.
Not closed.

No.  1225  Peah-twyh-tuck (Steve Mohawk) Incompetent, age 41-dead.
Not closed.  With this same case is his former wife, We-sko-peth-o-que or Effie
Douglas.

No.   684  Pe-can (male), minor age 18.
Not closed.

No.  1274  Pe-ke-ton-o-quah (Mary Murdock) Incompetent age 27.
Not closed.  This woman is now the wife of Geo. Kishketon.

No.  1252  Pem-me-pah-hone-nah (male) Incompetent, age 49-dead.
Not closed.

No.  1230  Pe-nee-she (male) Incompetent, age 51.
Not closed.  With his wife Men-ah-pe in this same case.

No.  1254  Pen-ne-thah-ah-quah (Emma Kickapoo) Incompetent age 42.
Closed.  Investigate and report.

No.   670  Narcis Pensoneau (male) minor, age 23.
Not closed.

No.  1151  Puck-ke-shin-no (Frank) minor, age 24.
Not closed.

No.  1246  Py-ah-tho (female) Incompetent, age 26.
Not closed.

No.  1249  Quen-ne-po-thot (male) Incompetent, age 58-dead.
Not closed.

No.  --  Lydia E. Ring – Insane (see adv. list)

No.   328  James Rock, minor age 22.
Not closed.

No.  1306  Thomas Sampson, minor, age 24.
Not closed.

No.  1382  Frank Scott, minor, age __.
Not closed.  I think this person is dead.

No.  1186  David Shawnee, minor age 13.
Not closed.

No. 1186  Emiline Shawnee, minot[sic] age 22.
Not closed.

No.  575  Ethel Shawnee, minor age 15.
Not closed.

No. 1186  Fredonia Shawnee, minor age 19. (married.)
Not closed.

No. 1186  Julia Shawnee, minor age 21. (married)
Not closed.

No. 1186  Lafayette Shawnee, minor age 23.
Not closed.

No. 1186  Myrtle Shawnee, minor age 15.
Not closed.

No. 1235  Shah-kah-tah (Jennie Stevens) Incompetent, age 26.
Closed.  Investigate and report.

No.  793  Maggie Sin-bin-um, minor age __
Not closed.

No. 1256  She-pah-tho-quah (female) Incompetent, age 32.
Closed.  Investigate and report.

No. 1232  Sho-e-nah-quah (Sweeney Stevens) Incompetent age 29.
Closed.  Investigate and report.  With his wife Ma-ka-the-quah.

No.  478  Anna Skah-kah, minor age 18.
Not closed.

No.  478  Rose Skah-kah, minor age 16.
Not closed.

No.  818  Victor Sloan, minor age 22.
Not closed.  See same case in Cleveland County No. 172.

No. 1147  Frank Spybuck, minor age 24.
Not closed.

No. 1478  Anna Starr, minor age __
Not closed.

No. 1478  Gertrude Starr, minor age __
Not closed.

No. 1478  Henry Starr, minor age __
Not closed.

No. 1005  Anna Sulteeska, minor age 16.
Not closed.

No. 1005  George A. Sulteeska, minor age 9.
Not closed.

No. 1005  Hilda Sulteeska, minor age 14.
Not closed.

No. 1005  Jerome Sulteeska, minor age 13.
Not closed.

No. 1005  Louise Sulteeska, minor age 20.
Not closed.

No. 1004  Monroe Tarkington, minor age __ (minor)
Not closed.

No. 1326  Tha-ke-to, minor age __
Not closed.  I think this is a male.

No. 1004  Bertha Tierney, minor age __
Not closed.

No. 1004  Margaret Tierney, minor age __
Not closed.

No. 1004  Patrick Tierney, minor age __
Not closed.

No. 1004  Thomas Tierney, minor age __
Not closed.

No. 827  Fabien Vieux, minor age __
Not closed.

No.  827  Nicholas Vieux, minor age __
Not closed.

No.  827  Viola (Judith) Vieux, minor age __ dead.
Not closed.

No. 1259  Wah-ko-nah-ka-ka (Henry Bentley) Incompetent age 29.
Not closed.  With his former wife-Mish-ke-ton-o-quah (dead)

No. 1248  Wah-pah-pen-neah (Henry Murdock) Incompetent age 33.
Closed.  Investigate and report.  With his wife Ko-ke-o-quah.

No. 1226  Wah-ne-mah-quah (female) Incompetent age 51.
Not closed.  With her husband Ah-ko-the.

No. 1256  Wah-pe-pah (John Garland) Incompetent age 42.
Not closed.  With his wife She-pah-tho-quah.

No. 1249  Wah-que-tah-no-quah (female) Incompetent age 49.
Not closed.  With her husband Quen-ne-po-thot now dead.

No. 1234  Wah-sha-ko-skuck (male) Incompetent age 47-dead.
Closed.  Investigate and report.  With his wife Ah-nah-tho-huck.

No. 1227  Wah-tah-tah or Mack Down, Incompetent age 26.
Closed.  Investigate and report.  With his brother James (Mah-she-nah) and his sister Mamie (Mush-sho-qua-to-quah).

No. 1174  Wah-we-ah (male) minor age 25.
Not closed.

No. 1245  Waw-nah-ke-tha (old) Incompetent age 82.
Not closed.

No. 1225  We-sko-peth-o-que (Effie Douglas) Incompetent age 27.
Not closed.  With her former husband Peah-twyh-tuck now dead.

No. 1427  Charles Whipple, minor age __
Not closed.

No. 1427  Nathan (Nathaniel C.) Whipple, minor age __
Not closed.

No. 1427  Viola Whipple, minor age __
Not closed.

Cleveland County.

No. 223  Mark Charley, minor age 21.  (Ah-e-tah-com-ska-ka)
Closed.  Investigate and report.

No. 228  Nellie Ford, minor age __
Closed.  Investigate and report.

No. 228  Stella Ford, minor age __
Closed.  Investigate and report.

No. 186  Co-pa-no-tha (Co-ba-ne) Incompetent age 55.
Closed. Investigate and report.

No. 213  Tom Mack, (Quah-ka-la) Incompetent age 58.
Closed. Investigate and report.

No. 213  To-wahn-ney Mack, Incompetent age 57.
Closed. Investigate and report.

No. 164  John Myers, minor age __
Closed. Investigate and report.

No. 225  Pa-ma-kim-se et al (3 children of Charley Bob) minors.
Closed. Investigate and report. Ages not known. The names are:
Pa-ma-kim-se, Pay-mah-com-se and Wi-pi-pea-ski-ki.

No. 188  Alex Pambogo, minor age __
Closed. Investigate and report.

No. 188  Alice Pambogo, minor age __
Closed. Investigate and report.

No. 188  George Pambogo, minor age __
Closed. Investigate and report.

No. John Pambogo (jr) minor age __
Closed. Investigate and report.

No. 106  Lydia Ring, insane, age 55.
Not closed. This was formerly Lydia [?]. Riordan.

No. 172  Victor Sloan, minor age 22.
Closed. See Pottawatomie County. Investigate and report.


Lincoln County.

No. 779  Ah-kah-tah-she-mah (Judge Boles) Incompetent age 41.
Not closed. I am not sure of age but he is an adult.

No. 779  Pen-ne-ah-kah-quah, Incompetent (adult)-male.
Not closed.

No. 840  Ah-sko-pah-kah-the-ah, minor age about 20.-male.
Not closed. See also case No. 632 over this same minor.

No. 778  Ke-ma-si-quah, Incompetent (adult)
Closed. Investigate and report. With her husband Mi-o-nah.

No. 778  Mi-o-nah, Incompetent (adult)
Closed. Investigate and report. With his wife Ke-ma-si-quah.

No. Mah-teck-que-net-noe, minor age __ (adult) Clyde Allen.
Not closed.

No. Ma-ko-the-quah, Incompetent (adult) deceased.
Not closed. Formerly wife of a Sac & Fox Indian.

No. ___ John Mesh-que-ken-nock (Pa-que-shick) minor age 14.
Not closed.

No. 862  Much-e-no-ne, Incompetent (adult)-male.
Not closed. Same case in Pottawatomie County.

No. 774  Pah-mah-ka-quah, Incompetent-female- adult.
Closed. Investigate and report.

No. 774  Tah-pah-she (Charley Moshashe) Incompetent adult.
Closed. Investigate and report.

No. 775  Peah-maw-ske (male) Incompetent (adult)
Not closed.

No. 775  Wah-pah-nah-pe-quah (female) Incompetent (Adult)
Not closed.

No. 777  Pem-ma-ho-ke-quah (Axie Lunt)-adult.
Not closed. I do not know whether I was appointed in this case over a minor or incompetent.


Oklahoma County.

No. 687  Ah-che-ko (male) Incompetent age 44.
Not closed.

No. 687  Way-lah-com-se, (female) Incompetent age 35.
Not closed.

No. 619  Ah-seno-he-ah (male) minor 22.
Not closed. Case No. 653 Pottawatomie County.

No. 688  I-nesh-kin (female) Incompetent age 28 now dead.
Not closed.

No. 615  Kesh-ko (Cleveland) minor age 19.
Am not sure that I was appointed in this and case No. 619.

No. 615  Pah-ka-no-quah (Na-mah-pe-quah)[sic] minor age 19-female.
Same remarks as above.

No. 218  Mah-she-kah-pot, minor-male (John Me-nah-quah) age 11.
Not closed. With Pe-ah-che-thot. No. 571 in Pottawatomie County.

No. 615 Pem-mah-ho ke (Axie Lunt) Minor age__ (adult)
Same remarks as No. 615.

No. 218  Peah-che-thot (Bert) minor age 22.
Not closed. See case No. 571 in Pottawatomie County.

No. 688  Tah-nah-ke (female)  Incompetent-adult.
Not closed.

I would like to have you go over each of these cases and report to me each case as fast as it is closed up. Those cases that were closed a few days ago are shown on this list not closed because the records have not yet been completed. I have checked each of these cases so that you can tell them from the rest. I am sending Mr. Buntin a copy of this letter and in your correspondence about these cases I wish you would both send me copies of your correspondence so that I can keep in touch with the work and assist wherever possible. I am very anxious to know that they are finally out of the way. Thanking you for many favors in the past, I am sincerely yours,

Supervisor.

Some of the cases were advertised in Tecumseh as minors whereas they were incompetents.

L. G. PITMAN                                                                MARK GOODE

PITMAN & GOODE
ATTORNEYS-AT-LAW
SHAWNEE, OKLA.

PHONE 283

Mr. John A. Buntin, Supt. Etc.

Shawnee, Okla.

Dear Sir:-

Please find enclosed inventory and appraisal blank in the cases of Wah-pe-puck-e and Pash-ko-nat.

Kindly have the appraisal made and return as soon as convenient.  The hearing in these two cases is set for the 29th so that we will have ample time.

Yours very truly,

MG-PC                                          Pitman & Goode

---

COURT TERMS.

GUTHRIE-First Monday in January.
OKLAHOMA CITY-First Monday in March.
WOODARD-First Monday in May and
    second Monday in November.
ENID-First Monday in June.
LAWTON-First Monday in October.

**Department of Justice**

RECEIVED
FEB 8 1912
SAC & FOX AGENCY,
OKLAHOMA.

**Office of the United States Attorney.**
**Western District of Oklahoma,**
Guthrie.

February 3, 1912.

W. C. Kohlenberg,
    Supt. & Spl. Disb. Agt.,
        R. F. D. No. 2,
            Stroud, Oklahoma.

Dear Sir:

Herewith I enclose an application and form of order in the Samuel L. Moore guardianship, A. B. Collins, guardian, pending in Payne County, Oklahoma, for the payment of the costs mentioned in your letter of December 12th last, incurred in the court proceedings in Lincoln Count.

Have Mr. Collins sign and file the application as soon as possible.  You should be present when the same is heard and see that a guardian ad litem is appointed, who I think should be an attorney at law.  The form of order, you will notice, omits the items.  I have left space so that you can fill the same in.  I enclose three extra copies of the order, as I think the guardian might want one, and yourself, and the Department, also.

I also enclose a form of denial for the guardian ad litem to file before or at the time of the hearing on the application, which

199

general denial the law requires guardians ad litem to make in all matters involving applications where the interests of the ward are concerned.

We trust that you will get this matter disposed of as soon as possible and advise us.  I will not be able to be at Stillwater with you as we are busier if possible, than usual, and will be for some months.

You will note that the application has also been left blank for you to fill in the character and amounts of the items for which authority for payment is desired.  I do not think any regular form of notice of the application for the hearing, is necessary.  You can submit that question however, to the Judge.

Very respectfully,

Isaac D. Taylor
Assistant U. S. Attorney.

Enclosures.
JRP.

[Illegible]
We filled in the data.  Please rush this matter & advise us when done.

Taylor

---

Complete Report of Accounts of Lee Bass and Ione Bass,

from Nov. 4th, 1907, to Feb. 13, 1912.

### R E C E I P T S

LEE BASS.

*Settled*

1909
July    20    Received from John Foster, former Guardian.................$250.73
1911
Mar.   31    "    " 1st National Bank, Davenport, Okla.,
                    interest on open a/c from Feb. 24, 1910,
                    to March 1, 1911, @ 5%........................    1.25

1912        Received from Davenport State Bank, interest on
Feb.   12        open a/c from April 1, 1911, to date.        .60

Total.................................................................$252.58


IONE C. BASS.

1909
July    20    Received from John Foster, former Guardian................ $261.88
1911
Mar.    31    "       "   1st Nat'l Bank, Davenport, Okla.,
                          interest on open a/c from
                          Feb. 24, 1910, to Mar. 1, 1911, @ 5%.        12.75

Apr.    10    "       "   1st. National Bank, Davenport, Okla.
                          interest on open a/c from
                          Mar. 1, 1911, to April 1, 1911, @ 5%          1.10
1912
Feb.    12    "       "   Davenport State Bank, interest on
                          open a/c from April 1, 1911, to date,        11.25
                                                                      _____

Total.................................................................$286.98


D I S B U R S E M E N T S

1907.                                                          Vou.
May     3    Paid Lee Bass for clothing, etc.                   1.    $10.00

Aug.    1    "    "         "  Inc. Exp.                         2.     5.00
1909
Aug.    28   "    Beadles & Son, premium on bond                3.     2.62

Nov.    30   "    "    "    "   "    "    "    "                 4.      .88
1910
Feb.    5    "    O. B. Harvey as part payment for team
                 for Lee Bass, balance of cost price (325.00)   5.    205.00

| Jan. | 22 | " | County Court Costs | | 2.10 |
|------|----|----|---------------------|----|------|
| Feb. | 6 | " | Register of Deeds, Lincoln County, for filing bills of sale for team and other articles | | .50 |
| Dec. 1911 | 30 | " | L. N. Beadles, premium on bond | 6. | .87 |
| July 1912 | 25 | " | Lee Bass, for clothing, etc. | 9. | 10.00 |
| Feb. | 7 | " | L. N. Beadles, premium on bond | 12. | .00 |
| " | 13 | " | Paid Court Costs | | 2.88 |
| " | 13 | " | Lee Bass | | 11.85 |

*Settled*

Total......................................................................$ 252.58

Total amount received a/c Lee Bass          $252.58

"        "    paid out a/c   "      "              252.58

\*\*\*\*\*\*\*\*\*\*

## D I S B U R S E M E N T S

IONE C. BASS

| | | | | Vou. | |
|------|----|----|---------------------|----|------|
| 1909.<br>Aug. | 28 | | Paid Beadles & Son, premium on bond | 7 | $ 2.63 |
| Nov. | 30 | " | "     "     "     "     "     "     " | 4 | .87 |
| 1910<br>Jan. | 22 | " | County Court costs- 1/2 | | 2.10 |
| Dec. | 15 | " | Ione C. Bass, Christmas money | 8. | 2.00 |
| " | 30 | " | L. N. Beadles, premium on bond | 6. | .88 |
| 1911<br>June | 17 | " | Coffman Optical Co., eye glasses | | 3.50 |
| " | 17 | " | Dr. T. C. Nichols, Dental work | | 1.00 |

| | | | | | |
|---|---|---|---|---|---|
| Dec. | 23 | " Ione Bass, Christmas expense | 10. | 7.00 |
| 1912 | | | | |
| Jan. | 20 | "    "    "  shoes & clothing | 11. | 11.20 |
| Feb. | 7 | " L. N. Beadles, premium on bond | 12. | .87 |
| " | 13 | " Court costs | | 1.87 |

Total amount paid a/c Ione C. Bass.............................$ 33.92

Total amount received a/c Ione C. Bass.........................$286.98

"        "     paid,     a/c   "   "   "  ........................ 33.92

Balance due Ione C. Bass....................................... 253.06

R E C A P I T U L A T I O N

Total amount received.............................................$539.56

"        "     paid out............................................ 286.50

Balance due...................................................... 253.06

(Due Ione C. Bass)

---

H. M. JARRETT
JUDGE

CLAUDE McLAUGHLIN
STENOGRAPHER AND DEPUTY CLERK

GEO. F. CLARK
CLERK

OFFICE OF

**COUNTY COURT LINCOLN COUNTY**

CHANDLER, OKLA.

Feby 19 – 1912

W. C. Kohlenberg

Stroud, Okla.

Dear Sir-

Complying with your request of the 16th Inst. am enclosing certified copy of Order appointing Guardian Letters of Guardianship and Bond of Gdn. In the matter of the guardianship of Stephen Harrison Insane

Very Sincerely

Geo. F. Clark

A.C. CUMMINGS, Clerk

County Court of Pottawatomie County

ROSS F. LOCKRIDGE, Judge

JUVENILE
PROBATE
MISDEMEANOR
CIVIL

Tecumseh, Okla.,   February 19, 1912.

RECEIVED

FEB 20 1912

Superintendent W C Kohlenberg,

Sac and Fox Indian Agency,

SAC & FOX AGENCY,
OKLAHOMA.

Stroud, Oklahoma.

Dear Sir:- IN RE GUARDIANSHIP OF THOMAS BROWN, ET AL.

Your final report in the above guardianship has just been received.   The Clerk advises me that the accrued costs, including final settlement, amounts to $16.75.   Kindly remit at once.

Yours very truly,

__Ross F Lockridge__

County Judge.

RFL/RG

---

COURT TERMS.

GUTHRIE-First Monday in January.
OKLAHOMA CITY-First Monday in March.
WOODARD-First Monday in May and
 second Monday in November.
ENID-First Monday in June.
LAWTON-First Monday in October.

Department of Justice.

Office of the United States Attorney.

Western District of Oklahoma.

Guthrie.

February 20, 1912.

J.A. Buntin,
 Supt. & Spcl. Disb. Agent,
 Shawnee, Oklahoma.

Dear Sir:

The four guardianships of Mr. Thackery which were set for final hearing on Monday, February 12th, last, were continued to Thursday, April 4th, next.

Kindly have Mrs. Seymour investigate Mr. Thackery's guardianships and have the Judge set down all the other cases of Mr.

Thackery's on the same date, that are in such shape that they can soon be set down. This will have to be attended to at once as publication has to be made for about twenty days or possibly longer than that, prior to the commencement of a regular term of the County Court.

I received a letter from Mr. Thackery under date of January 25, 1912, which lists his guardianships in Pottawatomie, Oklahoma, Cleveland and Lincoln Counties. He states that he sent a duplicate of this letter to your office. I wish you would have the guardianships set forth in said list, checked up, showing those closed and those not closed so that when I come down I can note such matters on my list, also.

You should also take steps to have all of Mr. Thackery's guardianships in Oklahoma, Cleveland and Lincoln Counties set down for final hearing as rapidly as possible, keeping me advised. We will have to depend on your office almost entirely in preparing these guardianships for final hearing, but we will try to be present whenever any of them come up on such hearing.

Very respectfully,

Isaac D. Taylor

CCF.                                    Assistant U.S. Attorney.

---

COURT TERMS.

GUTHRIE-First Monday in January.
OKLAHOMA CITY-First Monday in March.
WOODARD-First Monday in May and
    second Monday in November.
ENID-First Monday in June.
LAWTON-First Monday in October.

Department of Justice.

—

Office of the United States Attorney.
Western District of Oklahoma.
Guthrie.

November 13, 1911.

J. A. Buntin,
        Supt. & Spl. Disb. Agt:,
            Shawnee, Oklahoma.

Dear Sir:

Replying to your letter of the 11th instant, and referring to my letter of the 9th instant, relative to certain Mexican Kickapoo guardianships, you are advised that the files which I herewith return in case No. 1225, County Court, guardianship of Peah-twyh-tuck, et al, Frank A. Thackery, guardian, is not what I desired.

I understand that in some of these guardianships, contests were had between Mr. Thackery and Mr. Johnson, and appeals were taken to the District Court and you may be able to find the missing files in the District Court.

You state that the bond cannot be located in case No. 662, L. C. Grimes, guardian of Wah-pe-com-e, but that the record in Book D, Page 165 shows that a bond for $500.00 was approved by the Judge on June 30, 1902. Was the bond recorded verbatim? If so, please furnish me a certified copy; if not, please give me copies of all record entries relative to the bond. We must get sufficient information upon which to base our action against the American Surety Company, which I am advised is the surety in this case.

Trusting that I may receive the information asked for in this and my previous letter as soon as convenient, I am,

Yours very respectfully,

Isaac D. Taylor
Assistant U. S. Attorney.

Enclosures.
JRP.

---

COURT TERMS.

GUTHRIE-First Monday in January.
OKLAHOMA CITY-First Monday in March.
WOODARD-First Monday in May and
    second Monday in November.
ENID-First Monday in June.
LAWTON-First Monday in October.

Department of Justice.

RECEIVED
FEB 26 1912
SAC & FOX AGENCY,
OKLAHOMA.

Office of the United States Attorney

Western District of Oklahoma.

Guthrie.

February 24, 1912.

W.C. Kohlenberg,
    Supt. & Spcl. Disb. Agent,
        Stroud, Oklahoma.

Dear Sir:

Herewith we are pleased to acknowledge receipt of your letter of Feb. 22, 1912 stating that all matters in the Moore guardianships are disposed of except yourself being discharged as guardian. I assume that you will file your final reports and have yourself discharged in these cases.

It might be well to let Mr. Collins remain as guardian for Samuel L. Moore.

Very respectfully,

Isaac D. Taylor
Assistant U.S. Attorney.

CCF.

---

STATE
TERRITORY OF OKLAHOMA,                COUNTY
                                   ss.  To The Judge Of The Probate Court Of Said County
COUNTY OF LINCOLN.

The undersigned, guardian of_____Fryor Franklin Brown_____

minor child_____of_____Kah-ah-sen-we_____deceased, would respectfully submit to the Court the following reports of his acts and doings as such Guardian from____October, 1906____to____Feb. 20____A.D. 1912 ;_____He_____charges _____himself_____with the following to-wit:

| DATE | | ITEMS OF RECEIPTS | AMOUNT | | TOTAL AMOUNT |
|---|---|---|---|---|---|
| **1906** | | | | | |
| Dec. | 21 | Received from P. S. Hoffman former Gdn | 106 | 65 | |
| **1907** | | | | | |
| Jan. | 21 | "    interest on Hoffman note | 96 | 00 | |
| Nov. | 18 | "    "    "    "    " | 96 | 00 | |
| **1908** | | | | | |
| Feb. | 29 | "    "    " open acct. Jan.&Feb. '08 | | 52 | |
| April | 6 | "    "    "    "    "    March | | 27 | |
| " | 20 | "    " from 1st. Nat'l Bank, Chandler | | | |
| | | Okla., $160.00 at 5% C.D. | 8 | 00 | |
| **1909** | | | | | |
| Jan. | 1 | Received interest on open acct. from 1st. | | | |
| | | National Bank, Chandler, Okla. | 5 | 75 | |

| | | | | |
|---|---|---|---|---|
| Mar. | 3 | Received from interest on Hoffman note | 96 | 00 |
| " | 11 | " " " " " " to date | 32 | 00 |
| " | 11 | " Principal on Hoffman note | 1200 | 00 |
| 1910 | | | | |
| Mar. | 15 | " interest from 1st. National Bank, Chandler, Okla., on C.D. at 5%. | 78 | 60 |
| 1911 | | | | |
| Mar. | 28 | Received interest from 1st. Nat'l. Bank, Okla., C.D. $1600. at 5%..................... | 80 | 00 |

| | | |
|---|---|---|
| TOTAL AMOUNT OF MONEY RECEIVED OR COLLECTED | 1799 | 79 |

# CONTRA.

..........He..........asks to be credited with the following sums, paid out as per receipts exhibited:

| DATE | | ITEMS PAID OUT | AMOUNT | TOTAL AMOUNT |
|---|---|---|---|---|
| 1906 | | | | |
| Dec. | 27 | Paid Court Costs | 17. 00 | |
| " | 31 | " Beadles & Son premium on bond | 6. 00 | |
| 1907 | | | | |
| June | 14 | " Register of Deeds recording assn. of Mort | 1. 00 | |
| Dec. | 3 | " W.C. Leonard expenses returning Fryor | 3. 40 | |
| | | Franklin Brown to school after deserting | | |
| " | 3 | Paid Charles Carter for apprehending said Ward..................................... | 1. 00 | |
| " | 14 | Paid Fryor Franklin Brown Xmas spend money | 1. 00 | |
| " | 24 | " " " " " " " | 1. 00 | |
| 1908 | | | | |
| Mar. | 7 | " " " " Spending money. | 1. 00 | |
| Apr. | 11 | " " " " Spending money | 1. 00 | |
| June | 20 | " Sam Brown Board for July, 1908. | 10. 00 | |
| July | 1 | " Fryer Franklin Brown 4th. July exp. etc. | 5. 00 | |
| Aug. | 12 | " Court Costs | .40 | |
| Dec. | 5 | " Fryor Franklin Brown spending money | 1. 00 | |
| " | 22 | " " " " " " | 1. 00 | |
| 1909 | | | | |
| Feb. | 20 | " " " " " " | 1. 00 | |
| June | 15 | " " " " 4th. July exp. money. | 5. 00 | |
| Aug. | 28 | " Beadles & Son premium on bond 2 yrs. | 6. 00 | |

| Oct. | 9 | " Fryor Franklin Brown spending money | 1. 00 |
| | 30 | "    "    "    " entertainment tckt. etc | 2. 00 |
| Nov. | 20 | "    "    "    " spending money | 1. 00 |
| Dec. | 1 | " Beadles & Son premium on bond | 3. 00 |
| " | 15 | " Fryor Franklin Brown for clthg. etc., | 5. 00 |
| 1910 | | | |
| Mar. | 26 | "    "    "    "    " spending money | 1. 00 |
| Apr. | 9 | "    "    "    "    "    "    " | 1. 00 |
| May | 28 | "    "    "    "    "    "    " | 1. 00 |
| July | 2 | "    "    "    "    " clothing, etc. | 10. 00 |
| " | 18 | "    "    "    "    "    "    " | 6. 00 |
| Oct. | 29 | "    "    "    "    " Base ball &Mitt | 2. 00 |
| Dec. | 15 | "    "    "    "    " Xmas Spending | 4. 00 |
| " | 30 | " L. N. Beadles Premium on bond | 3.00 |
| 1911 | | | |
| Mar. | 3 | " Claud Chandler expenses in returning Fryor Franklin Brown to school after deserting | 5. 50 |
| May | 6 | " Fryor Franklin Brown for gloves, &c. | 2. 00 |
| " | 30 | "    "    "    "    " Expense Money | 1. 00 |
| June | 17 | "    "    "    "    "    "    " | 1. 00 |
| July | 6 | "    "    "    "    "    "    " | 5. 00 |
| "" | 11 | " Froug & Smulian, clothing for Ward | 20. 00 |
| Aug. | 9 | " Fryor Franklin Brown for provisions | 8. 00 |
| Oct. | 2 | " Rhode Bros. for shoes | 2. 75 |
| " | 26 | " Fryor Franklin Brown, Expense Money | 1. 00 |
| Dec. | 16 | "    "    "    " Xmas Money | 5. 00 |
| 1912 | | | |
| Feb. | 7 | "    "    "    " Misc. purposes | 10. 00 |
| " | 7 | " L. N. Beadles premium on bond | 3. 00 |
| " | 20 | " Paid Court Costs. | 3. 85 |

TOTAL AMOUNT PAID OUT                    169 90

## RECAPITULATION

| | DOLLARS | CENTS | DOLLARS | CENTS |
|---|---|---|---|---|
| TOTAL AMOUNT RECEIVED. | 1799 | 79 | | |
| TOTAL AMOUNT PAID OUT. | 169 | 90 | | |
| BALANCE DUE. | 1629 | 89 | | |

The following is an itemized account of all notes, bonds, accounts and evidences of indebtedness, which are herewith presented for inspection, composing the personal estate of my said wards.

## DESCRIPTION

| Kind of Instrument | DATE | PAYOR | SECURITIES | Rate of Interest | AMOUNT | REMARKS |
|---|---|---|---|---|---|---|
| | | The above consists of all funds in hands of Guardian. All other property is held in trust by the United States. | | | | |
| Cert. of 3/28/11. Deposit. | | First National Bank, Chandler, Okla. | None | | 1600  00 | Due 3/27/11 |

I hereby tender my resignation as Guardian of the within named ward.

All of which is respectfully submitted.

_____
Guardian.

STATE ~~TERRITORY~~ OF OKLAHOMA ⎱ ss.    _____W. C. Kohlenberg_____ Guardian of
COUNTY OF LINCOLN ⎰
_____Fryor Franklin Brown_____

minor child____of____Kah-ah-sen-we____deceased, being duly sworn, says that the foregoing is a full and perfect account of all his dealings and transactions, and of all moneys and effects received and paid out by him on account of said minor ___from_____

___Oct. 1906___to the __20__ day of___Feb.____A.D. 1912__, and of all moneys, notes, bonds, accounts and evidences of indebtedness, composing the personal estate of said minor___, on hand the __20"__ day of___Feb.____1912

_____W.C.K._____
Guardian.

Subscribed and sworn to before me this__20_ day of_____Feb._____, A. D. 1912.

_____
Probate Judge.

\*\*\*\*\*\*\*\*\*\*

No._____

# Guardian's Reports
### Of the Account of

_____ W. C. Kohlenberg _____

---

### Guardian of

_____ Fryor Franklin Brown _____

---

### Minor Child \_\_\_\_ of

_____ Kah-ah-sen-wa.[sic] _____
Deceased.

Filed the \_\_20\_\_ day of \_\_\_Feb._____
A.D. 19**12**\_\_

_____
Probate Judge.

Approved by me this_____day of
_____190\_\_\_\_.

_____
Probate Judge.

*In the County Court of the State of Oklahoma, in and for Pottawatomie County.*

I, _____ A. C. Cummings _____ ,*Clerk of the County Curt in and for the County and State*

*aforesaid, do hereby certify the above and foregoing to be a full, true and complete copy of the* _____

_____ Order Confirming Sale of real estate _____

*as the same appears on file and of record in my office.*

*Witness my hand and the seal of said Court this* 8th *day of* March _____ 191 2

_____ A.C. Cummings _____
*Clerk of the County Court.*

\*\*\*\*\*\*\*\*\*\*

State of Oklahoma,  )
                  ) ss.
Pottawatomie County.  )

IN THE COUNTY COURT IN AND FOR SAID COUNTY AND STATE.

In the Matter of the Guardianship of    )
George Anderson, Lizzie Anderson, Ben- )
jamin Anderson, and John B. Anderson,  )   ORDER CONFIRMING SALE
                   Minors.  )      OF REAL ESTATE.

An order having been made by this Court on the 8th day of January, 1912, authorizing Sophie Anderson, as the Guardian of the estate of George Anderson, Lizzie Anderson, Benjamin Anderson, and John B. Anderson, Minors, to sell certain real estate belonging to said minors, and afterwards to-wit on the 5th day of February, 1912, said Sophie Anderson having made to this Court and filed in the office thereof, a return of her proceedings under the said order of sale, and duly returned to this Court an account of sale verified by affidavit of said Sophie Anderson, this Court having examined the said return, and having in open Court also having examined the said Sophie Anderson, and it appearing to the satisfaction of this Court; that in pursuance of said order of sale, Sophie Anderson, as such Guardian, caused notices of the time and place of making said sale, to be posted up in thee[sic] of the most public places in said County of Pottawatomie, in which the land to be sold is situated, and to be published in the Shawnee Dispatch, a News Paper printed and published in said County, for two weeks successively, next before such sale, in which notice the lands and tenements to be sold were described with common certainty.

That at the time and place of holding such sale specified in said notices, said Sophie Anderson caused to be sold at private sale to the highest bidder for cash in hand, and subject to confirmation by this Court, the following real estate described in said order of sale in said notice, to-wit:

The undivided Four Fourteen hundred eighty fifths (4-1485) of the South East Quarter of Section Seven (7) in Township ten North of Range Three (3) East of the Indian Meridian in Pottawatomie County, State of Oklahoma, belonging to each of said minors, George Anderson, Lizzie Anderson, and Benjamin Anderson, for the sum of $21.53, for each of said interests of each of said minors, and the undivided Two One hundred sixty fifths (2-165) of said tract of land, belonging to said minor, John B. Anderson, for the sum of $96.96.

That at such sale A. B. Jones, and S. D. Heal, became the purchasers of said real estate for the said sums above mentioned, they being the highest and best bidders, and said sums being the highest and best sums bid.

That said sale was legally made and fairly conducted, that the sum bid was not dis-proportionate of the value of the property, sold and that a sum exceeding such bid at least Ten per cent (10%) exclusive of the expenses of a new sale cannot be obtained.

And that the said Sophie Anderson as such Guardian in all things proceeded and conducted and managed such sale as by the Statute in such case made and provided, and by said order of sale as directed and required;

And no objections to the confirmation of said sale being made and the Court being fully advised.

It is therefore ordered adjudged and decreed by the Court that the said sale be and is hereby confirmed and approved and declared valid; and the the[sic] proper and legal conveyance to said real estate are hereby directed to be executed to said purchasers, A. B. Jones, and S. D. Heal, by said Guardian, Sophie Anderson.

Witness my hand and seal of said Court, this the _19th_ day of February, 1912.

(Seal)

_____Ross F. Lockridge_____
County Judge.

---

Olathe, Kan.

RECEIVED
MAR 12 1912
SAC & FOX AGENCY
OKLAHOMA

Dear Mr. Kohlenberg,

Replying to your kind letter advising me' of the arrival of [Illegible]'s warrant, I had advice a few days ago from [Illegible] attorneys that the certified copies of Letters of Guardianship would be sent to me at once. However, immediately [illegible] them to forward same to you if not already sent to me at Pittsburg.

I took this action so as to get the matter sealed up before you leave. If the letters have been mailed to me I should be able to return them to you early this week.

Thanking you very much for your information. I am,

Yours truly,
Frank O. Jones

Pittsburg, Kan.

\*\*\*\*\*\*\*\*\*\*

RECEIVED
MAR 16 1912

THE GOODLANDER
HOTEL
W. D. WITWER, Prop.

Fort Scott, Kans. 3/ 14    1912

Mr. W.C. Kohlenberg
Sac & Fox, Okla.

Dear Sir

On receipt of the cert. copy of Letters of Guardianship please forward to me at Pittsburg, Kan. care Stilwell Hotel the warrant for Helen and oblige.

Yours truly

F.O. Jones

**********

RECEIVED

PITTSBURG, KANS.          3/3/12

Dear Mr Kohlenberg,

I wrote Mr. Johnson a few days that I had been appointed legal guardian for Helen but since received a letter from you enclosing my voucher for $23$^{20}$ and thought perhaps you have not been relieved. If his [illegible] annuity has come you may mail the warrant to me here. If should be in the office by this time and I hope to receive it soon as I have been advancing my own funds for her expenses in school.

Thanking you in dvance[sic] for your usual prompt attention to the matter, I am,

Yours truly

F.O.Jones

---

Appointment of
guardian of
Pearl Conger.

Sac and Fox Indian School,
Stroud, Okla., May 26, 1913.

Hon. H. M. Jarrett,
   Judge of the County Court,
      Chandler, Oklahoma.

Sir:-

I hand you herewith a petition for appointment as guardian of Pearl Conger, a Sac and Fox Indian under my jurisdiction.

When Mr. Kohlenberg was Superintendent at this Agency, he was the legal guardian. He has, however, I believe filed his resignation as such and the approval thereof by the court over which you preside is being withheld until the appointment of a new guardian.

I think no further explanation is necessary as I believe you fully understand the situation.

Very respectfully,

Supt. & S. D. A.

HJJ/AM
Enc. petition.

**********

Sac and Fox Indian School,
Stroud, Okla., July 14, 1913.

Thomas J DeLashmutt,
      Washington, D. C.

Sir:

Referring to former correspondence on the subject of Guardianship bonds, I am enclosing herewith for execution a bond in the sum of $2600.00 to cover my actions as Guardian of Pearl Conger.

A copy of the appointment is enclosed herewith. Please return it with the executed bond.

Very Respectfully,

Supt. & S. D. A.

Encl. Bond and Appointment.

**********

Guardian's
Bonds.

Sac and Fox Indian School,
Stroud, Okla., July 23, 1913.

Hon. H. M. Jarrett,
   Judge of the County Court,
      Chandler, Oklahoma.

Sir:-

Referring to guardian's bonds in the cases of Fryor Franklin Brown, Stephen Harrison, and Edward L. Norris I have to advise that the Illinois Surety Company cannot do business in Oklahoma, and I am filling in their stead bonds executed by Southern Surety Company. Please advise me when these bonds are approved. Also please return the Illinois Surety Company bonds.

I am also enclosing for approval a guardian's bond in the sum of $2500.00 on account of Pearl Conger executed by Southern Surety Company.

Very respectfully,

Horace J Johnson
Supt. & S. D. A.

HJJ/AM
Enc. guardian's bond

\*\*\*\*\*\*\*\*\*\*

H. M. JARRETT
JUDGE

CLAUDE McLAUGHLIN
STENOGRAPHER AND DEPUTY CLERK

GEO. F. CLARK
CLERK

OFFICE OF
COUNTY COURT LINCOLN COUNTY
CHANDLER, OKLA.

July 26" 1913

Mr. Horace J Johnson
Stroud, Okla.
Dear Sir

Surety Bonds in Guardian cases received and approved and I herewith return to you the original Bonds given in these cases, also enclosed please find Letters of Guardianship in case of Pearl Conger in which case you will take the oath of office (as appears on back) and return same to this office for filing & record.

Very Rincerely[sic]
Geo. F. Clark

\*\*\*\*\*\*\*\*\*\*

Oath of
Guardian.

Sac and Fox Indian School,
Stroud, Okla., July 28, 1913.

Hon. H. M. Jarrett,
Chandler, Oklahoma.

Sir:

I enclose herewith Oath of Guardian properly executed in the matter of the Pearl Conger guardianship case.  Please file the same.

Very respectfully.

Supt. & S. D. A.

HJJ/AM
Enc. oath of guardian.

---

EDWIN WARFIELD,
PRESIDENT

## Fidelity and Deposit Company of Maryland
### CASUALTY INSURANCE  SURETY BONDS.

#### HOME OFFICE BALTIMORE

COMPANY'S BUILDING

HAMILTON  YERKES & HAMILTON.
COUNSEL.
DOUGLAS  BAKER, RUFFIN & O'BEAR
COUNSEL

WASHINGTON  D. C.  OFFICE
SUITE 209 RIGGS BUILDING.

THOS. J. DE LASHMUTT.
MANAGER
J. SPRIGG POOLE,
RESIDENT VICE-PRESIDENT

TELEPHONES { MAIN 1140
{       1787

WASHINGTON. D. C.

July 31, 1913

Mr. Horace J. Johnson,

Sac & Fox Agency,

Strouf[sic],

Okla.

Dear Sir:

Your favor enclosing applications received.  Enclosed find voucher for premiums amounting to $31 paid on the first three bonds.

We enclose bill for the last bond, amounting to $10.40.  We have arranged with a Company to issue you these bonds at once, so when your bond is forwarded to me, I will return it to you the same day.

Yours very truly,

Thos. J. DeLashmutt

JMR

---

**DEPARTMENT OF THE INTERIOR** RECEIVED

UNITED STATES INDIAN SERVICE

AUG 12 1913

SAC & FOX AGENCY,
OKLAHOMA.

Crow Creek Indian Agency,

Crow Creek, S. D., Aug. 9, 1913.

Mr. H. J. Johnson,

Supt. Indian Agency,

Stroud, Okla.

Dear Mr. Johnson:

I have your letter of the 28th ultimo and in reply will say that as soon as I receive statements from the bank with interest credits up to date I will forward you checks for the amount due each of the wards you mention.

Very respectfully,

W.C. Kohlenberg

WCK                              Supt. & Spl. Disb. Agent.

[Copy of Original]

KANSAS CITY, MO.   Aug. 10th   191 2

Mr. Jno. H. Buntin,   U. S. Indian Agency,

Shawnee, Oklahoma.

IN ACCOUNT WITH

# GLOBE SURETY COMPANY
### OF KANSAS CITY, MISSOURI
### CAPITAL $500,000.00
### SURPLUS $100,000.00

WE ISSUE
SURETY BONDS
FIDELITY
JUDICIAL
CONTRACT
OFFICIAL

COMMERCE BUILDING

TO PREMIUM ON BONDS AS FOLLOWS

| | | | | |
|---|---|---|---|---|
| Mch.11th | #25040 | Robt. Stelzner | | 5 00 |
| " | 25041 | " " | | 5 00 |
| " | 25042 | " " | | 5 00 |
| " | 25043 | " " | | 5 00 |
| May 16th | 25145 | " " | | 12 00 |
| " | 25144 | " " | | 12 00 |
| " 21st | 25131 | Jas. Odle | | 10 00 |
| " " | 25130 | John Buntin | | 5 00 |
| " " | 25129 | " " | | 10 00 |
| " " | 25128 | " " | | 10 00 |
| " " | 25127 | " " | | 5 00 |
| June 3rd | 25166 | Gilbert Nadeau | | 5 00 |
| " " | 25164 | Robert Stelzner | | 5 00 |
| July 8th | 25198 | " " | | 5 00 |
| | | | | 99 00 |
| | | CREDIT | | |
| June 17th | | Check | | 40 00 |
| | | | Balance | 59 00 |

**********

*Thos. M. Walker, President*     *James Van Buren, Vice President*   *H. P. Fones, Ass't Secretary*
*Wm. T. Kemper, Treasurer*       *John R. Mulvane, Vice President*   *E. Sanford Miller, Ass't Secretary*
*Jo Zach Miller, III, Secretary* *J. L. Miller, Jr., Vice President* *Tom M. Murphy, Ass't Secretary*

## Globe Surety Company

### of Kansas City, Missouri

Capital $500,000.00
Surplus $100,000.00

**Kansas City, Mo.**   Mch. 10, 1913.

Mr. Robert H. Stelzner,

      Shawnee, Oklahoma

Dear Sir:

      Referring to the guardian bonds issued in your behalf in the following estates, viz:

      Mary Henry and Florina Rock
      Alex En-e-kohn, or Pam-e-kah-of
      Tah-tah-pe-twa

we would make inquiry as to whether or not you have filed annual settlements.  If so, please send us copies of same.

      Yours very truly,

            James Van Buren

JVB  T           Vice-president

**********

Thos. M. Walker, President     James Van Buren, Vice President    H. P. Fones, Ass't Secretary
Wm. T. Kemper, Treasurer      John R. Mulvane, Vice President    E. Sanford Miller, Ass't Secretary
Jo Zach Miller, III, Secretary     J. L. Miller, Jr., Vice President     Tom M. Murphy, Ass't Secretary

**Globe Surety Company**

*of Kansas City, Missouri*

Capital $500,000.00
Surplus $100,000.00

*Kansas City, Mo.* Mch. 13, 1913.

Mr. J. A. Buntin, Superintendent,

Shawnee Indian Agency,

Shawnee, Oklahoma

Dear Sir:-- Re:  Robert H. Stelzner

We are in receipt of your letter of the 11th inst., in which you state Mr. Stelzner has resigned as guardian, in some of the cases in which we have made bonds for him.

Of course, it will be necessary for Mr. Stelzner to make final settlement in these matters and a certificate furnished us, showing his discharge and release as guardian.

We trust this can be arranged very shortly as the subsequent premiums in these cases are about due.

Yours very truly,

J VanBuren

SECRETARY[sic]

[Copy of Original Deposit Slip]

DEPOSITED BY

*Edward L. Morris*

WITH

FIRST NATIONAL BANK

Chandler, Okla., Sep 30 191

PLEASE LIST EACH CHECK SEPARATELY

| | | |
|---|---|---|
| Currency | | |
| Silver | | |
| Gold | *Less Ck* | 95 43 |
| CHECKS AS FOLLOWS: | | 945 43 |
| *Duplicate* | | |
| *Roy Dam* | | |
| 9/2 | | |

Total $

SEE THAT ALL CHECKS AND DRAFTS ARE ENDORSED

**********

No. 5354.

THE FIRST National Bank
OF CHANDLER.
CAPITAL $ 50,000.00

CHANDLER, OKLA.   Sept. 30-1913

Mr. Horace J. Johnson, Supt.,
    Sac & Fox Agency,
        Stroud, Okla.

Dear Sir

As requested we enclose you herewith the following Certificates of Deposits:

| | |
|---|---|
| #1358 | $1820.97 |
| #1359 | 1155.31 |
| #1360 | 920.68 |

These being the amounts of the Gaurdianship[sic] accounts transferred.

The balance of interest in the Edward L. Morris account is $4.78; and the Pearl Conger account $6.04; and the Fryor Franklin Brown, $9.60.

Yours very truly,

E C Love

Cashier

W

**********

Sac and Fox Indian School,
Stroud, Okla., Oct. 1, 1913.

W. C. Kohlenberg,
    Supt. Crow Creek Indian School,
        Crow Creek, South Dakota.

Dear Mr. Kohlenberg:
        After so long a time I am enclosing receipts for Guardianship moneys received from you in the cases of

| | |
|---|---|
| | Edward L Morris |
| | Pearl Conger |
| and | Fryor Franklin Brown. |

I deposited the checks yesterday and had Certificates of Deposit issued in lieu thereof. There was a small amount of interest in each case and I have made out receipts for this in triplicate. I am sending you two copies of each and shall be obliged if you will send me checks covering same. These checks will close out the three accounts and lose no interest thereon.

I paid the premium on the bonds in these cases as you requested in your letter of August 15th.

Hoping that this will get these three cases off your hands, I am,

Very Respectfully,

Supt. & S. D. A.

Enclose Receipts in Triplicate
6 sets.

**********

Sac and Fox Agency,

Stroud, Okla., ~~Aug.~~ Sept. 30 1913.

Received of W. C. Kohlenberg, former guardian of Pearl Conger, the sum of Eleven hundred, fifty-five and 31-100 ($1155.31) Dollars in full of all demands against him account of his guardianship of said Pearl Conger a minor.

Said Amount of $1155.31 includes the following:

Balance per Final Report Filed February 20, 1912,    $1024.86
Interest Credited April 1, 1912,.........................    50.00
Interest credited to date (Aug. 11, 1913),.............    80.45
                                                          $1155.31

(Said amount is on deposit with the First National Bank Chandler, Okla., on open account, and the interest credits could not be included in final report filed Feb. 20, 1912.)

_____ Horace J Johnson ___
Legal    Guardian of Pearl Conger, a minor.

**********

Sac and Fox Agency,

Stroud, Oklahoma, ~~August~~ Sept. 30 1913.

Received of W. C. Kohlenberg, former Guardian of Edward L. Morris, the sum of Nine Hundred Twenty and 68/100 ($920.68) Dollars, in full of all demands against him account of his guardianship of said Edward L. Morris, a minor.

Said Amount of $920.68 includes the following sums:

Balance per final Report filed Feb. 20, 1912,        $812.44
Interest Credited April 1, 1912,.................       37.50
Interest credited to date (Aug. 11, 1913),.......      _70.74_
                                                      $920.68

Deposited with First National Bank, Chandler, Okla., on open account.

_____Horace J Johnson___
Legal  Guardian of Edward L. Morris, a
minor.

**********

Sac and Fox Agency,

Stroud, Okla., ~~August~~ Sept. 30 1913.

Received of W. C. Kohlenberg, former guardian of Fryor Franklin Brown, the sum of Eighteen Hundred Twenty and 97/100 ($1820.97) in full of all demands against him account of his guardianship of said Fryor Franklin Brown, a minor.

Said amount of $1820.97 includes:

Balance per final Report filed Feb. 20, 1912,..... $1629.98
Interest Credited April 1, 1912,.....................     80.00
Interest credited to date (Aug. 11, 1913),..........    _111.08_
                                                      $1820.97

Deposited with First National Bank, Chandler, Okla., on open account.

_____Horace J Johnson___
Legal  Guardian of Fryor Franklin Brown,
a minor.

**********

Sac and Fox Agency, Oklahoma,
Sept. 30, 1913.

Received from W. C. Kohlenberg, former Guardian of Fryor Franklin Brown the sum of nine dollars and sixty cents ($9.60), the same being interest accruing on seventeen hundred nine dollars and eighty nine cent ($1709.89) from August 11, 1913 to Sept. 30, 1913, the former date being the date on which interest was last added to the account, the latter being the date on which check drawing it out was cashed, this being the amount of interest credited by the First National Bank of Chandler, Chandler, Oklahoma, in which institution the funds in question were deposited.

Horace J Johnson
Legal Guardian of Fryor Franklin Brown,
a minor.

\*\*\*\*\*\*\*\*\*\*

Sac and Fox Agency, Oklahoma,
Sept. 30, 1913.

Received from W. C. Kohlenberg, former Guardian of Pearl Conger, the sum of six dollars and four cents ($6.04), the same being interest accruing on ten hundred seventy four dollars and eighty six cents ($1074.86) from August 11, 1913 to Sept. 30, 1913, the former date being the date on which interest was last added to the account, the latter being the date on which the check drawing it out was cashed, this being the amount of interest credited by the First National Bank of Chandler, Chandler, Oklahoma, in which institution the funds in question were deposited.

Horace J Johnson
Legal Guardian of Pearl Conger,
a minor.

\*\*\*\*\*\*\*\*\*\*

Sac and Fox Agency,
Stroud, Oklahoma, Sept. 30, 1913.

Received from W. C. Kohlenberg, former Guardian of Edward L Morris the sum of four dollars and and[sic] seventy eight cents ($4.78), the same being interest accruing on eight hundred forty nine dollars and ninety four cents ($849.94) from August 11, 1913 to Sept. 30, 1913, the former date being the date in which the interest was last added to the principal, the latter being the date on which check drawing it out was cashed, this being the amount of interest credited by the First National Bank of Chandler, Chandler, Oklahoma, in which institution the funds in question were deposited.

Horace J Johnson

Legal Guardian of Edward L Morris,                                          a
Minor.

\*\*\*\*\*\*\*\*\*\*

Guardianship
Bonds.

Sac and Fox Indian School,
Stroud, Okla., Sept. 29, 1913.

L. N. Beadles,
Oklahoma City, Okla.

Sir:

I enclose herewith check for $9.00 to pay premium on Guardianship bond of W. C. Kohlenberg for;

|       | Fryor Franklin Brown | $3.00 |
|-------|----------------------|-------|
|       | Edward L. Morris     | 1.75  |
| and   | Pearl Conger         | 4.25  |

Mr. Kohlenberg has been relieved of these Guardianships and I have been appointed. On this account the bonds of Mr. Kohlenberg should be cancelled.

Very respectfully,

Supt. & S. D. A.

HJJ/AM

Carbon for W. C. Kohlenberg,

Enc. check

Rel. to the
holding of
papers.

Sac and Fox Indian School,
Stroud, Okla., Aug. 19, 1913.

W. C. Kohlenberg,
Supt. & S. D. A.
Crow Creek, S. Dak.

Dear Sir:

This is to acknowledge receipt of your communication of the 15th. inst., to Mr. Johnson and to advise that he is away on a little vacation, but expecting to return about the first of September.  As the time necessary in reaching him with these papers would probably equal the balance of the time he expects to be gone, I will hold same and call his attention to them immediately upon his return.

We are experiencing another disastrous drouth[sic], with the mercury climbing up to the century mark every day.

Very respectfully,

TMP/LG

Clerk in Charge.

## DEPARTMENT OF THE INTERIOR

### UNITED STATES INDIAN SERVICE

RECEIVED
AUG 19 1913
SAC & FOX AGENCY,
OKLAHOMA.

Crow Creek Indian Agency,

Crow Creek, S. D., Aug. 15, 1913.

Mr. Horace J. Johnson,
Supt. Indian Agency,
Stroud, Okla.

Dear Mr. Johnson:

In further reference to your letter of the 28th ultimo, I have to advise you that I have a statement of account from the First National Bank, Chandler, Okla., crediting interest on Indian funds, to Aug. 11, 1913.

I have not yet filed my final report in the case of Stephen Harrison, incompetent, but will do so and forward check for balance as soon as I can.

I inclose herewith checks covering all balances due the following:

| | | |
|---|---:|---:|
| Fryor Franklin Brown,....................$1820.97 | | |
| Edward L. Morris,......................... 920.68 | | |
| Pearl Conger,.............................. 1155.31 | $3896.96 |

In connection herewith I have to say that since I filed my final report in these cases Feb. 20, 1912, I have no right to pay out any funds on behalf of the minors. I have, however received interest in each case from and after the date of filing my final report and I trust that the same may be satisfactory to the honorable court.

I am inclosing receipts in triplicate for your signature. One you may retain, one is for the court and one is for my use.

In connection I may say that there is due my bondsman, for furnishing guardianship bonds, the following amounts:

Fryor Franklin Brown,..................$3.00
Edward L. Morris,......................... 1.75
Pearl Conger,.............................. 4.25

This should be paid before Oct. 1, in order to avoid another years premium. This payment should be made to L. N. Beadles, 709 Herskowitz Bldg., Oklahoma City, Okla. I trust that you will make settlement since under the arrangements made by John Embry with Beadles premiums are payable until date of guardians discharge. Under the circumstances it is impossible for me to pay the same myself, as explained, since I have filed my final accounts and you have been appointed.

This leaves only myself as guardian in the cases of Ione C. Bass in Stillwater, and Stephen Harrison and Wm. H. Jefferson at Chandler.

Very respectfully,

W.C. Kohlenberg
Supt. & Spl. Disb. Agent.

WCK

**********

Sac and Fox Indian School,
Stroud, Okla., Dec. 12, 1913.

W. C. Kohlenberg, Supt.
Crow Creek Indian School,
Crow Creek, S. Dakota.

Dear Mr. Kohlenberg:-

Referring to your letter of December 6th., I think my receipts to you for the funds inclosed were dated September 30th. Shall I take up these funds in my Guardianship Accounts s of September 30th or December 6th, the date when the checks were drawn?

Very respectfully,

Supt. & S. D. A.

HJJ/AM

**********

## DEPARTMENT OF THE INTERIOR

### UNITED STATES INDIAN SERVICE
Crow Creek Indian Agency,

Crow Creek, S. D., Dec. 6. 1913.

Mr. H. J. Johnson,

Supt. Indian School,

Stroud, Okla.

Dear Mr. Johnson:

In reply to your letter of the 1st of October, 1913, I am enclosing you herewith checks as follows:

For Fryor Franklin Brown, ..............$9.60
For Pearl Conger,........................ 6.04
For Edward L. Morris,................... 4.78

You have already furnished me rec3ipts[sic] in these cases and I am now forwarding same to the court for final settlement.

The balance of the guardianship cases will receive early attention.

Very respectfully,

W.C. Kohlenberg

WCK                                         Supt. & Spl. Disb. Agent.

**********

Copy

Oklahoma City, Okla.,
Dec. 15th. 1913.

Mr. Horace J. Johnson,

Sac & Fox Agency, Okla.

Dear Sir:-

I beg to acknowledge the receipt of your favor of September 29th. 1913, in which was enclosed check for $9.00 in payment of premiums on bonds executed on behalf of W. C. Kohlenberg, Guardian as listed below.

| | |
|---|---|
| Fryor Franklin Brown | $3.00 |
| Edward L Morris | 1.75 |
| Pearl Conger | 4.25 |

I very much regret the fact that a receipt was not furnished you at the time but the writer was ill for two months and most every thing went wrong in the office.

Yours very truly

(S) L. N. Beadles

General Agent.

**********

[The above letter given again]

**********

Sac and Fox Indian School,
Stroud, Okla., Mar. 30, 1914.

First National Bank,
          Chandler, Oklahoma.

Gentlemen:-

          I hand you herewith three certificates of deposit Nos., 1358, 1359, and 1360 drawn payable to my order as guardian of Fryor Franklin Brown, Pearl Conger and Edward L. Morris, respectively. These certificates mature today. Please issue new certificates if even date herewith adding to the principal on the Fryor Franklin Brown certificate $31.37, on the Pearl Conger certificate $17.38 and on the Edward L. Morris certificate $13.74. Send me drafts for the balance of the interest due on each certificate, which is, I believe, $9.40, $8.61 and $6.97 respectively.

                    Very respectfully,


                              Supt. & S. D. A.

HJJ/AM
Enc. certificates.
                    **********

Guardianship
     bonds.

                    Sac and Fox Indian School,
                    Stroud, Okla., Aug. 5, 1914.

J. L. Fletcher,
     Washington, D. C.

Sir:-

          I enclose herewith check for $30.66 to pay premium on guardianship bonds as follows:

|  |  |
|---|---|
| Edward L. Morris, | $10.00 |
| Pearl Conger, | 10.00 |
| Fryor F. Brown, | 10.66 |

The Conger statement does not agree with the card.   I have remitted as per the card.

Relative to the Stephen Harrison case, I have to say that I have not yet received any funds belonging to Stephen Harrison, consequently it does not appear to me that a premium should be charged on this bond. I do not know why the funds have not been turned over, but it is a fact that they have not.

Very respectfully,

Supt. & S. D. A.

HJJ/AM
Encl. check.

---

SOUTHERN SURETY COMPANY

RECEIVED AUG 17 1914 ...L, OKLA.

C. S. COBB, President
J.H. HUCKLEBERRY, Vice Pres.-General Counsel
E.G. DAVIS, Sec'y and Treas.
E. J. CROCKETT, Asst. Secretary
H. M. CAMMON, Vice President

J. F. HOLDEN, Vice President
F. A. UNGLES, Vice President
OSCAR A. WELLS, Vice President
WILBER, Vice President
O.D. SMITH, Vice President
W.L. TAYLOR, Vice President

GENERAL OFFICES NEW NATIONAL BANK OF COMMERCE BLDG. ST. LOUIS

JOHN L. FLETCHER
GENERAL AGENT
605 F STREET N-W

WASHINGTON, D. C.   August 12, 1914.

Mr. Horace J. Johnson,
         Supt & Special Disbursing Agent,
         Sac and Fox Indian School,
                  Stroud, Oklahoma.          RE:  Guardianship Bonds.

Dear Sir:-

Your esteemed favor of the 5th instant enclosing check for $30.66, duly received, and I have credited the same as follows:

| | |
|---|---|
| Second annual premium on bond Edward L. Morris | $10.00 |
| "        "        "     "     " Fryor F. Brown | 10.66 |
| On a/c 2d  "     "     "     " Pearl Conger | 10.00 |

Enclosed herewith find receipts.  In connection with the Pearl Conger bond, would state that the premium thereon is $10.40, the figures on the card being wrong, and I have therefore credited your account with $10.00 and would thank you to forward the balance, $.40.

With reference to the Stephen Harrison case, would state that the liability on the bond runs on just the same, even though you have not yet received any funds belonging to this minor, the liability having commenced on the date of execution of the bond, namely July 19, 1913. The second annual premium therefore, was due on the 18th ultimo, and I would be pleased to have you remit at your earliest convenience.

Thanking you for your prompt attention to above, I am

Very truly yours,

John L. Fletcher
General Agent.

Re guardian
bonds.

Sac and Fox Indian School,
Stroud, Okla., July 28, 1913.

W. C. Kohlenberg, Supt.,
Crow Creek Indian School,
Crow Creek, So. Dakota.

Dear Mr. Kohlenberg:

Bonds have been approved for me as Guardian of Edward L. Morris, Stephen Harrison, Fryor Franklin Brown and Pearl Conger. I am now ready to receipt you for their funds when you turn them over to me.

Very respectfully,

Supt. & S. D. A.

HJJ/AM

Guardian-
ship bond.

Sac and Fox Indian School,
Stroud, Okla., Dec. 12, 1913.

L. N. Beadles,
Oklahoma City, Oklahoma.

Sir:-

Under date of September 29th 1913 I forwarded you a check in the sum of $9.00 to pay premium on Guardianship bond of W. C. Kohlenberg for:

|  | Fryor Franklin Brown | $3.00 |
|--|--|--|
|  | Edward L. Morris | 1.75 |
| and | Pearl Conger | 4.25 |

To date no receipt has been received showing that the above mentioned was received by you.

I shall be obliged if you will furnish me a receipt for same.

Very respectfully,

Supt. & S. D. A.

AM

---

*Capital and Surplus over $6,000,000*

**American Surety Company**

of New York.

F. W. Lafonl,
President

| LOCAL BOARD | | BRANCH OFFICE FOR THE STATE OF OKLAHOMA |
|--|--|--|
| D. W. HOGAN | J. L. WILKIN | 401-406 MAJESTIC BUILDING |
| | ED. L. DUNN | TELEPHONE WALNUT 176 |
| | W. F. WILSON, ATTORNEY | |
| HERMAN J. ROLEKE, MANAGER | | |
| | W. H. LEWIS, ASS'T MANAGER | OKLAHOMA CITY, OKLA. |

Home Office Building

HJR-GR.                          June 7, 1913.

Mr. Horace J. Johnson,
c/o Sac & Fox Indian School,
Stroud, Oklahoma.

Dear Sir:

I have your favor of the 5th inst., asking for the return of the applications you filed with us in the Brown and Morris guardianship cases. I take pleasure in returning them herewith.

You asked me to return the order of the court in the Brown case. I returned that order, together with the one in the Morris case, in my letter of the 29th.

Please make a search for it and I believe you will find it.

Very truly yours,

Herman J. Roleke
M a n a g e r.

Enc.

\*\*\*\*\*\*\*\*\*\*

Sac and Fox Indian School,
Stroud, Okla., May 31, 1913.

Herman J. Roleke,
Agt. American Surety Co.,
Oklahoma City, Oklahoma.

Sir:

Referring to your letter of the 29th inst., I am enclosing herewith application for bonds as Guardian of Fryor Franklin Brown and Edward L. Morris. I think you have a copy of the bond in each case and the copy of the order of the Court in the Morris case is enclosed. Please expedite this matter as much as possible.

The funds belonging to the estate will be deposited in the bank to my credit as Guardian. They will not be covered by my bond as Superintendent. There will be no great amount accrue to the present funds as all funds exclusive of those which this bond is to cover, belonging to the wards are at this time handled by me as Guardian ex-officio and are covered by the bond which I give as Superintendent.

Very respectfully,

HJJ/AM                    Supt. & S. D. A.

**********

*Capital and Surplus over $ 6,000,000*

**American Surety Company**

*F. W. Lafronh* *of New York.*
*President*

| LOCAL BOARD | BRANCH OFFICE FOR THE STATE OF OKLAHOMA |
| D. W. HOGAN    J. L. WILKIN | 401-406 MAJESTIC BUILDING |
| ED. L. DUNN | TELEPHONE WALNUT 1791 |
| W. F. WILSON, ATTORNEY | |
| HERMAN J. ROLEKE, MANAGER | |
| W. H. LEWIS. ASS'T MANAGER | OKLAHOMA CITY, OKLA. |

*Home Office Building*

HJR-GR.                         May 29, 1913.

Re:   Application Horace J. Johnson, Gdn. Edward L. Morris, a minor,
      Guardian's Bond $1800.00.
Re:   Application Same, Gdn. Fryor F. Brown, a minor,
      Guardian's bond $4,000.00.

Mr. Horace J. Johnson,

    c/o Sac & Fox Indian School,

        Stroud, Oklahoma.

Dear Sir:

    With reference to your applications for the two above bonds, will you kindly inform me whether the assets belonging to the estates of these minors will be held by the Department of the Interior and disbursed under the rules and regulations of the Department or will they be held by you, individually, as guardian of the minors?

    I desire to be informed upon this point in view of the fact that you expect to require quite a number of bonds of this character, which may have to run for long periods and aggregate a very large liability. We should be pleased to handle this business for you and upon being informed as to the conditions surrounding this business, we shall be able to handle your applications with alacrity.

    We have your application for the bond of Fryor F. Brown. We have none as to Edward L. Morris and I am enclosing a blank for your attention. It will not be necessary to complete the entire application, the second page may be left incomplete, the other parts of the application, however, should be properly prepared. The application should be signed by you at the foot of page six and acknowledged on page seven.

    The premium charges for this business are $4.00 per thousand per annum, minimum $10.00 unless the bond is for less than $1000.00, when it will be one per cent., with a minimum of $5.00. The annual renewal premium is two-thirds of the first year's premium, unless the first year's premium is $10.00 or less, in which case the renewal premium will be the same as the first year's premium.  Should it be desired to pay the premium for the term for which the bond is likely to run in advance, the premiums for the second and subsequent years are two-thirds of the first year's premium, irrespective of the amount of the first Year's premium.  If the premiums are paid in advance and the bond is cancelled before the term for which they have been paid has expired, we will make a pro rata refund of the unearned premiums except the first year's.

The amount of the premium should be inserted in the proper blank spaced on page five of the application and the second paragraph of the application indemnity agreement as I have inserted it in your application for the bond of Fryor F. Brown, which is, herewith, returned in order that you may properly sign and acknowledge it.

Very truly yours,

Herman J. Roleke
M a n a g e r.

\*\*\*\*\*\*\*\*\*\*

Sac and Fox Indian School,
Stroud, Okla., May 31, 1913.

Herman J. Roleke,
    Agt. American Surety Co.,
        Oklahoma City, Oklahoma.

Sir:

Referring to your letter of the 29th inst., I am enclosing herewith application for bonds as Guardian of Fryor Franklin Brown and Edward L. Morris.  I think you have a copy of the bond in each case and the copy of the order of the Court in the Morris case is enclosed.  Please expedite this matter as much as possible.

The funds belonging to the estate will be deposited in the bank to my credit as Guardian.  They will not be covered by my bond as Superintendent.  There will be no great amount accrue to the present funds as all funds exclusive of those which this bond is to cover, belonging to the wards are at this time handled by me as Guardian ex-officio and are covered by the bond which I give as Superintendent.

Very respectfully,

HJJ/AM                                          Supt. & S. D. A.

Enc. application,
copy, order of Court

\*\*\*\*\*\*\*\*\*\*

Bonds.

Sac & Fox Indian School,
Stroud, Okla., Aug. 2, 1913.

Thomas J. De Lashmutt, Manager,
    Fidelity & Deposit Company,
        Suite 209 Riggs Bldg.,
            Washington, D. C.
Sir:-

Referring to former correspondence concerning guardianship
bonds, I have to advise that I have recalled and destroyed those given by the
Illinois Surety Company in the cases of Edward L. Morris, Fryor Franklin
Brown, and Stephen Harrison.

Very respectfully,

Horace J Johnson

HJJ/WMH.                                      Supt. & S. D. A.

EDWIN WARFIELD,
PRESIDENT.

**Fidelity and Deposit Company of Maryland**
CASUALTY INSURANCE SURETY BONDS.
HOME OFFICE BALTIMORE

HAMILTON JUKES & HAMACTER
OCTOBER BAKER RUFFIN 1914 AR
Sac & Fox
RECEIVED
JUL 17 1914
FOX AGENCY,
OKLAHOMA.

WASHINGTON, D. C. OFFICE
SUITE 209 RIGGS BUILDING.
TELEPHONES { MAIN 1140
                    1787

WASHINGTON, D. C.

THOS. J. DE LASHMUTT,
MANAGER
J. SPRIGG POOLE,
RESIDENT VICE-PRESIDENT

July 8, 1914

Mr. Horace J. Johnson,

Stroud, Oklahoma

Dear Sir:

Enclosed please find bills for premiums due on your bonds as guardian. The Southern Surety ask that you kindly fill in on back of each card the statutes of the case.

Will you kindly remit through this office and i will see that you get proper receipts for same.

With kind regards from the office and hoping you are well, we remain,

Yours very truly,

Thos. J. De Lashmutt

TJD/JMR

**********

*Capital and Surplus over $5,000,000*

*American Surety Company*

*of New-York.*

*F. W. Lafferty*

*President*

| LOCAL BOARD | BRANCH OFFICE FOR THE STATE OF OKLAHOMA |
|---|---|
| D. W. HOGAN    J. L. WILKIN | 401-406 MAJESTIC BUILDING |
| ED. L. DUNN | TELEPHONE WALNUT 177 |
| W. F. WILSON ATTORNEY | |
| HERMAN J. ROLEKE, MANAGER | |
| W. H. LEWIS ASS'T MANAGER | OKLAHOMA CITY, OKLA. |

*Home Office Building*

HJR-GR.                        June 4, 1913.

Re: Application Horace J. Johnson, Gdn. Edward L. Morris, minor.
Re: Application Same, Gdn. Fryor F. Brown, minor.

Mr. Horace J. Johnson,

c/o Sac & Fox Indian School,

Stroud, Oklahoma.

Dear Sir:

I have yours of the 31st ult., wherein you inform me that your appointment as guardian of the above minors will be a private matter, in no way connected with your official duties as Superintendent & S. D. A.

This Company, some years ago, established a rule not to write any Indian guardianship business and I shall, therefore, be unable to execute these bonds for you. I hoped to be able to handle this business, in case it should develop that you were appointed guardian merely for the purpose of complying with local laws, leaving the management of the minors' estates, including the care and distribution of moneys, under the control of the Department.

As this does not seem to be the case, I regret to have to return the papers to you.

Very truly yours,

Herman J. Roleke
M a n a g e r.

\*\*\*\*\*\*\*\*\*\*

Applications.

Sac and Fox Indian School,
Stroud, Okla., June 5, 1913.

Herman J. Roleke,
Oklahoma City, Oklahoma.

Sir:-

I have your letter of the 4th inst.  Please return to me the applications which I made for Guardianship bonds in the Fryor Franklin Brown and Edward L. Morris cases.  Also return the order of the Court in the Fryor Franklin Brown case.

I shall be obliged if you will do this at the earlist[sic] possible date.

Very respectfully,

Supt. & S. D. A.

HJJ/AM

Applications
for Guardianship
bonds.

Sac and Fox Indian School,
Stroud, Okla., July 23, 1913.

Thomas J. DeLashmutt, Manager,
        Fidelity and Deposit Co., of Maryland,
                Washington, D. C.

Sir:

I return herewith applications for guardianship bonds to Southern Surety Company. I have recalled the Illinois Surety bonds and forwarded for approval the Southern Surety bond instead.

Very respectfully,

Supt. & S. D. A.

HJJ/AM
Enc. Applications.

**********

EDWIN WARFIELD
PRESIDENT

# Fidelity and Deposit Company of Maryland

## CASUALTY INSURANCE  SURETY BONDS.

### HOME OFFICE BALTIMORE

HAMILTON  YERKES & HAMILTON
COUNSEL
DOUGLAS  BAKER  RUFFIN & O BEAR
COUNSEL

COMPANY'S BUILDING

THOS. J. DE LASHMUTT
MANAGER
J. SPRIGG POOLE
RESIDENT VICE-PRESIDENT

WASHINGTON, D. C.  OFFICE
SUITE 209 RIGGS BUILDING
TELEPHONES MAIN 1140
1797

WASHINGTON, D. C.  July 18, 1913.

Mr. Horace J. Johnson,

Stroud,

Okla.

Dear Sir:

The Illinois Surety Company have just wired you, at our suggestion, that they were not represented in Okla., and that their bonds could not stand. This we regret so much, as we, of course thought it was all right. We have a Company here, who are in Okla., and if you will send us new bonds, we will have executed and returned to you at once.

We were just forwarding the bond for $2600 to-day, but will have it copies and signed by another Company. We will use checks sent for the signing of new bonds.

Regretting this delay, which was no fault of ours, we remain

Yours very truly,

Thos. J. De Lashmutt

**********

Sac and Fox Indian School,
Stroud, Oklahoma, July 9, 1913.

Thos J DeLashmutt
Washington, D. C.
Sir:

Under date of June 10, last, I submitted to you applications for three guardianship bonds together with the bonds for execution asking that you would expedite the matter their preparation as much as possible. So far I have heard nothing from you and I shall be obliged if you will advise me what is their status.

Very Respectfully,

Supt. & S. D. A.

**********

Sac and Fox Indian School,
Stroud, Oklahoma, June 10, 1913.

Thos J DeLashmutt
Washington, D. C.

Sir:

Referring to your letter of May 27, 1913, concerning Guardianship Bonds, I am enclosing herewith three applications for bonds in three separate cases.

I also enclose the bonds in each case.   I have signed them but have not inserted the date of execution.

I shall be obliged if you will expedite the matter of the execution of these bonds as much as possible.

Very Respectfully,

Supt. & S. D. A.

Fryor Brown
Edward L Morris
Stephen Harrison

**********

EDWIN WARFIELD,
PRESIDENT

# Fidelity and Deposit Company of Maryland

## CASUALTY INSURANCE. SURETY BONDS.

### HOME OFFICE BALTIMORE

HAMILTON  YERKES  &  HAMILTON
COUNSEL
DOUGLAS  BAKER  RUFFIN  &  O BEAR
COUNSEL

WASHINGTON, D. C.  OFFICE
SUITE 309 RIGGS BUILDING
TELEPHONES | MAIN 1140
           |      1797

COMPANY'S BUILDING

THOS. J DE LASHMUTT
MANAGER
J. SPRIGG POOLE,
RESIDENT VICE-PRESIDENT

WASHINGTON, D. C.   May 27, 1913.

Mr. Horace J. Johnson,

Supt., Sac and Fox Indian School,

Stroud,

Okla

Dear Sir:

Your favor of the 23 received.  In reply have to say we have an agency at Chandler, Okla, where we presume your bond would be filed.

Enclosed please find applications, which if you will fill up and send to this office, we will then instruct our Agent at Chandler to sign bonds for you.

You will note from the enclosed card that the American Bonding Company and the Fidelity & Deposit Co., have merged, and hereafter the American Bonding Company will be known as the Fidelity & Deposit Company. I am Manager, the same as heretofore and we still have our same office force, and are in the same position to render you prompt service when needed.

Our rate on Guardian bond is $4 per thousand up to $10,000 and 2/3 of first premium for second year. Minimum premium is $10 on a $1000 bond, under $1000 is $5.00.

We shall be glad to hear from you and render such service as you may require.

Yours very truly,
Thos J De Lashmutt
P. S. Our agent at Chandler is J. W. Green.

**********

Sac and Fox Indian School,
Stroud, Okla., Dec. 3, 1913.

Southern Surety Co.,
St. Louison, Mo.

Gentlemen:

Referring to your letter of the 21st ult., concerning Guardianship matters covered by bonds given by your company, #53901/4, I have to advise that the Wards are Indians under my jurisdiction as Supt. & S. D. A. of the Sac and Fox Indian School, Oklahoma. All funds coming to their credit now except those that are derived from the investment of the funds mentioned in my application for these bonds are handled by me under Government supervision.

I received from W. C. Kohlenberg former Guardian for

| | |
|---|---|
| Edward L Morris | $920.68 |
| Fryor F Brown | 1820.97 |
| Pearl Conger | 1155.31 |

These funds are all deposited in The First National Bank of Chandler on Certificates of Deposit drawing 4 1/2% (6 or 12 Month Certificates). I expect to keep them in Certificates of Deposit until the ward becomes of age. The Wards are all full Blood Indians. One of them Stephen Harrison is insane and is confined in the Insane Asylum at Canton, South Dakota. He is the only one of age. However, no funds have as yet been turned over to me by his former Guardian for him.

No money is being distributed to them at this time and none will be except upon an order from the Court.

Very Respectfully,
Horace J Johnson
Supt. & S. D. A.

\*\*\*\*\*\*\*\*\*\*

GENERAL OFFICES NEW NATIONAL BANK OF COMMERCE BLDG ST LOUIS

November twenty-first,
Nineteen hundred thirteen.

Horace J. Johnson, Supt.,
Sac & Fox Agency,
Stroud, Okla.

Dear Mr. Johnson:

RE:  GUARDIAN BONDS IN YOUR BEHALF
#53901, $1800, Edward L. Morris, minor.
#53902, $375.00. Stephen Harrison, ward.
#53903, $4000, Fryor F. Brown, minor.
#53904, $2600, Pearl Conger, minor.

Along in July of this year our agent, Mr. John L. Fletcher, Washington, D. C., executed in your behalf the above four guardian bonds.

Mr. Fletcher being located in Washington was not familiar with our requirement on this class of bonds in the State of Oklahoma.  It is our uniform rule to require joint control agreement covering deposit of funds or securities belonging to individual estates on Oklahoma.  I wrote Mr. Fletcher at the time these bonds were made to see if he could not secure our regular provisions in this regard from you, but have no affirmative answer from him.

Apparently the funds that were not in your hands at the time the papers came in to us were to come from cash at that time in the hands of a previous guardian who had not been discharged.  We would like to know just what funds have been received by you up to this date in each case, and also whether the money received is deposited and in what bank, or if it has already been invested in form of mortgages we would like to know about them.

According to the dates given in some of these cases we notice that the wards are more than twenty-one years of ager.  Are these wards full blood Indians that you are guardian for?  If that is the case we would like to know just what method is being followed in the distribution of the money to them.

We are writing to you direct so that we may get the actual situation in these cases.  I trust you will advise us.

Yours very truly,

E.G. Davis
S E C R E T A R Y.

D-D

**********

RECEIVED
DEC 22 1913
SAC & FOX AGENCY,
OKLAHOMA.

**DEPARTMENT OF THE INTERIOR**

**UNITED STATES INDIAN SERVICE**

Crow Creek Indian Agency,
Crow Creek, S. D.
December 18, 1913.

Mr. Horace J. Johnson,
        Supt. & Spl. Disb. Agent,
                Stroud, Oklahoma.

Dear Mr. Johnson:

I have your letter of the 12th inst., relative to taking up guardianship funds and in reply, have to state that they should probably be taken up the date you receive the checks.

Very respectfully,

W. C. Kohlenberg
WCK/D                              Supt. & Spl. Disb. Agent.

**********

## DEPARTMENT OF THE INTERIOR

### UNITED STATES INDIAN SERVICE

Crow Creek Indian Agency,
Crow Creek, So. Dak., Dec. 21, 1912.

Mr. Horace J. Johnson,
    Supt. Indian School,
        Stroud, Okla.

Dear Mr. Johnson:

Inclosed please find copies of my final reports filed in guardianship cases just before you arrived at Sac & Fox, as follows:

Fryor Franklin Brown, Balance $1629.89, First National Bank, Chandler.
Pearl Conger,          "    2024.86,  "    "    "    "
Edward L. Morris,     "     812.44  "    "    "    "

The guardianship is in the County Court of Lincoln Co., in above cases.

Ione C. Bass, Balance, $253.06, Davenport State Bank, Davenport.
   In the Ione C. Bass case the guardianship is in Payne Co.

I am also the guardian of Stephen Harrison, insane, in St. Elizabeth's, Washington, D. C. and have a balance of $148.62, balance of an amount transferred from St. Elizabeth's March 8, 1912.

I am also the guardian of Wm. H. Jefferson, and have a balance of $1.44. I did not resign in this last case for the reason that the Sarah Hall or Harris land sale was pending and thought it probable that some other papers would be required before another guardian might be appointed. The funds in both cases last mentioned are in the First National Bank, Chandler, Okla.

You will therefore see that I am still in on six cases which I want to get rid of very much. If Pearl Conger and Edward L. Morris are nearly of age, I would thank you to advise me so that i may know what to do in their cases. or, if you will, kindly advise if you expect to take these guardianships over.

The reports herewith are copies of my final reports on file in the courts mentioned. They cover all my acts as guardian in each case. As it now is, the money is drawing only three per cent, because I cannot make arrangements for time deposits, for the reason that I have tendered my resignation and may be called on for the funds at any time.

Very respectfully
W.C. Kohlenberg
SUPT. & SPL. DISB. AGENT.

\*\*\*\*\*\*\*\*\*\*

Sac and Fox Indian School,
Stroud, Okla., May 23, 1913.

American Bonding Co.,
  Washington, D. C.

Gentlemen:

I am bonded in your company for $60000 in my present position of Superintendent of Indian School, Sac and Fox Agency Oklahoma and desire to get some more bonds to cover some Indian Guardianships which I am taking over from my predecessor, perhaps $10000 in all.   I should like to have you have your agent in Oklahoma furnish me with a rate and the necessary papers to make application therefor at as early a date as practicable.   I have triesd[sic] to find your agent in this locality but so far have been unsuccessful.

Very Respectfully,

Horace J. Johnson
Supt. & S. D. A.

www.ingramcontent.com/pod-product-compliance
Lightning Source LLC
Chambersburg PA
CBHW020248030426
42336CB00010B/670